OCCUPYING THE ACADEMY

OCCUPYING THE ACADEMY

Just How Important Is Diversity Work in Higher Education?

Edited by Christine Clark, Kenneth J. Fasching-Varner, and Mark Brimhall-Vargas

ROWMAN & LITTLEFIELD PUBLISHERS, INC.

Lanham • Boulder • New York • Toronto • Plymouth, UK

Published by Rowman & Littlefield Publishers, Inc.
A wholly owned subsidiary of The Rowman & Littlefield Publishing Group, Inc.
4501 Forbes Boulevard, Suite 200, Lanham, Maryland 20706
www.rowman.com

10 Thornbury Road, Plymouth PL6 7PP, United Kingdom

British Library Cataloguing in Publication Information Available

Library of Congress Cataloging-in-Publication Data
Occupying the academy : just how important is diversity work in higher education? /
Edited by Christine Clark, Kenneth J. Fasching-Varner, and Mark Brimhall-Vargas.
    pages cm
  In English with two chapters in Spanish.
  Includes bibliographical references and index.
  ISBN 978-1-4422-1272-5 (cloth : alk. paper) — ISBN 978-1-4422-1274-9 (electronic)
  1. Minorities—Education (Higher)—United States—Case studies. 2. Educational equalization—United States—Case studies. 3. Universities and colleges—United States—Case studies. I. Clark, Christine, 1962- II. Fasching-Varner, Kenneth J., 1979- III. Brimhall-Vargas, Mark.
  LC3727.O33 2012
  378.1'982—dc23

                                                                              2012010580

∞™ The paper used in this publication meets the minimum requirements of American National Standard for Information Sciences—Permanence of Paper for Printed Library Materials, ANSI/NISO Z39.48-1992.

Printed in the United States of America

For the Equity and Diversity
Workers of the World . . .
Unite!

Contents

Acknowledgments

THERE ARE SEVERAL PEOPLE WE WOULD LIKE TO THANK for their help in pulling this volume together. Most important are our significant others, Tyrone Robinson, Joe Kaufman, and DB. Your support of, and patience with, us while we worked on this project is what ultimately made it possible. Other family members also made invaluable contributions: A. Rocio Brimhall-Vargas did the lion's share of the work on the Spanish translations of opening and closing sections of this volume, and Dwight and Lisa Brimhall provided logistical support during this translation process.

We would also like to thank Sonia Nieto, Bailey W. Jackson, and Damon A. Williams for their thoughtful contribution of the foreword, section introductions, and afterword, respectively. We also appreciate the contributions of the book cover blurb authors: Thandeka K. Chapman, Adrienne Dixson, Kimberly L. King-Jupiter, and Francisco A. Rios. Your collective willingness to lend your professional stature to this project has meant the world to us.

Of course, the volume would not be what it is without the heartfelt contributions of the case chapter and case-response chapter authors: Katrice A. Albert, Allison Daniel Anders, A. Leslie Anderson, Marco J. Barker, Roderick L. Carey, Leah K. Cox, James M. DeVita, Vanessa Dodo Seriki, S. Kiersten Ferguson, Eugene Oropeza Fujimoto, Shaunna Payne Gold, Bryant Griffith, Cleveland Hayes, Michael E. Jennings, Glenda Jones, Brenda G. Juárez, Virginia Lea, Douglas J. Loveless, Shirley Mthethwa-Sommers, Steven Thurston Oliver, Sherri L. Sanders, Margaret-Mary Sulentic Dowell, Hollace Anne Teuber, Gregory J. Vincent, Susan Wolfgram, and Laura S. Yee.

Thanks as well to Desiree Cho, Aura Escobar, Cat Maiorca, Maria Marinch, and Martha Murray for their help organizing and copyediting various pieces of the volume.

Also of note are the attendees to our sessions about this volume given at the 2010 National Conference on Race and Ethnicity (NCORE), the 2011 American Educational Research Association (AERA) Annual Meeting, and the 2011 Annual International Conference of the National Association for Multicultural Education (NAME). Your thoughtful engagement with, and feedback on, our emergent thinking related to this volume was invaluable.

Finally, we want to thank Rowman & Littlefield editor Patti Davis and assistant editor Jin Yu for their commitment to this volume from its inception to its publication.

Foreword

Sonia Nieto

THE INTRIGUING QUESTION THAT IS AT THE CENTER of this volume, *Just how important is diversity work in higher education?*, is a rhetorical one, and yet not easily answered. Those who work in higher education—whether administrators, professors, professional or support staff, students, or consultants—face challenges related to diversity that are unique to the academy. Yet, few books exist on what these challenges are or how to address them. Providing both sound theoretical perspectives and tested practical strategies concerning the centrality of diversity in higher education, this volume is a welcome addition to the limited literature on the topic.

U.S. colleges and universities are now more diverse than at any time in history. At the same time, the notion of 'diversity' has also changed. Whereas a decade or two ago diversity focused almost exclusively on race and ethnicity, today the term also includes, in most institutions, sexual orientation, social class, ability, native language, national origin, and religion, among other differences. Each of these differences is embedded in particular contexts, making a 'one-size-fits-all' model for addressing diversity not only problematic but, in the end, ineffectual. That is a major reason why the editors of this volume have chosen to focus on race and racism. Given its unique history in our nation, and the brutal consequences of slavery and exclusion, the editors make a good argument for addressing race, while at the same time not downplaying the significance of the many other manifestations of diversity. The book's case studies of institutions across the nation make it clear that context matters, not only the context of race, but also the particular region and state where an institution is located. These case studies illuminate that no particular region or state has a single solution to the many problems associated with making the academy a civil, accepting, and respectful venue for diversity; in fact, the case studies reinforce that there is no magic template to remedy the intractable matter of racism.

It has never been easy to negotiate differences on campuses; and today, given the growing diversity in our nation and our institutions of higher learning, it has become in some ways harder than ever. Incidents of hate-filled speech, not to mention atrocious acts of violence, still take place in higher education, a contradiction that should not be lost on anyone. After all, colleges and universities are supposed to be places where tolerance and respect are held in the highest regard, and students are taught the virtues of civil discourse and critical thinking. Yet, as the case studies in this book illustrate, in too many places that is far from the reality.

Using a Critical Race Theory framework and embedded in the Obama-era reality, the book, beginning with its preface, rejects the facile 'postracial era' argument by illustrating the many ways in which difference is not "post" anything but rather that race and racism are very current indeed. Whether having to do with admissions criteria, hiring and tenure and promotion policies, or an examination of the curriculum, and whether focused on the implications of such policies and practices for students, staff, professors, or administrators, the editors and authors help debunk the myth that discussions of diversity are a relic of the past, no longer needed in this more "enlightened" era. In regional state colleges or prestigious flagship campuses, the problems are uncannily similar: lack of awareness of diversity, 'let's all get along' rhetoric, an inability to be inclusive of all differences, a 'blame-the-victim' mentality, or alleged support for diversity while all manner of efforts to dismantle it simultaneously take place.

The stories captured in the case studies are instructive, maddening, heartbreaking, and sometimes even humorous, but they all speak to a bitter reality: Support for diversity on campuses across the nation is frequently flimsy, superficial, and at times Machiavellian. It becomes, in too many situations, a means to assuage demands for dignity, respect, and representation on the part of those who are excluded or invisible on campus. Even in those instances where well-meaning and knowledgeable people make honest attempts to support the visibility and access of everyone on campus, these efforts may fail because of institutional indifference or active resistance. The issue of power, of course, is central in all of these case studies. *Who has power? How it is used? On behalf of whom?* These are all questions posed by Paulo Freire (1970) decades ago. Because those in positions of power are largely White, middle-class, English-speaking, able-bodied, heterosexual, and male, they reflect and reify the status quo in the institutions they manage. It is no surprise then, that tinkering with the edges of the system yield few positive results. It is only when the very center of power is disrupted by including those whose voices have been silenced that we see change begin to happen. Here we are reminded of the famous quote by Frederick Douglass (1857):

> Power concedes nothing without a demand. It never did and it never will. Find out just what any people will quietly submit to and you have found out the exact measure of injustice and wrong which will be imposed upon them, and these will continue till they are resisted with either words or blows, or with both. (p. 22)

Thus, injustice will continue until those most affected by it demand change. This is one of the important lessons highlighted by the book's editors and authors.

To answer the question posed by the title of the book: Diversity is indeed crucial in higher education. The authors of the case chapters make it clear that without serious and honest attempts to honor diversity in academia in both words and deeds, the system will continue to fail people of color, the LGBT (lesbian, gay, bisexual, and transgender) community, the poor and disenfranchised, and others whose experiences do not necessarily reflect the majority population. This volume's courageous editors and authors urge us to remember these truths; if not, all our efforts to honor diversity will fall by the wayside.

The Permanence of Diversity

Mark Brimhall-Vargas, Christine Clark, and Kenneth J. Fasching-Varner

"The whole point of this protest [Occupy Wall Street] is that it doesn't go away—that's the tactical point . . . its tactics are about physical presence, continued physical presence."

—Rachel Maddow (TRMS, 2011a)

We Thought It Would Get Better

WE (COEDITORS) RECALL WATCHING THE TELEVISED INAUGURATION of President Obama with his campaign slogan running like a marquis in our heads: *Change we can believe in.* We were filled with a sense of possibility that, previously, we imagined as adults we might never again experience in relationship to our leadership: a real sense of hope for the future not immediately tinged with cynicism. The United States of America had *actually* elected its first Black president, and we were alive to experience it. People, including one of this volume's editors, braved *freezing* weather for *hours* just to witness this event. It really happened.

It was not by accident that we and many of our colleagues who do equity/ diversity work in higher education dared to believe that the difficult work of advocating for social justice would become more respected following this momentous event. Our initial logic went something like this: If a majority of American voters elected Obama, clearly this means: (a) that attitudes about race, and presumably other dimensions of diversity, are improving; and (b) equity/diversity workers will find it easier to engage those attitudes with less concern about being reproached or ignored. Colleagues will now more willingly come to us and ask how academic and cocurricular programs can be constructed to take advantage of this extraordinary moment in history. There was a spirit of celebration that brought with it a renewed sense of commitment to 'the work.' We, as a nation, had entered the Obama era. But as it turns out, it is not the era we had imagined.

Defining the Obama Era

Literally, the Obama era *so far*, marks the campaign, election, and first presidential term of President Barack Obama. In actuality what demarcates this era is far less clear and far more complicated, particularly as it relates to diversity in general and race more specifically.

While we (coeditors) continued to celebrate what we envisioned might be a new age of American enlightenment and virtue, half of the country was seething with anger at the reality that somehow, against all the machinations of a political system designed to unfairly favor the southern, wealthy White male electorate, a Black man from humble beginnings, born and raised outside the *contiguous* United States, won the election. Another, smaller segment of the population was erroneously heralding Obama's victory as evidence that racism was now a thing of the past, that we had, indeed, entered a wholly "postracial" era.

The vitriol expressed by those disappointed by Obama's election, coupled with the desperately shrill accusations leveled at him personally (e.g., a closeted Muslim in league with al-Qaeda, a socialist bent on destroying American capitalism, a Kenyan citizen without a real Hawaiian birth certificate, a naïve and inexperienced politician who would weaken America's military defenses) were disconcerting. Also disconcerting was the superficiality of those claiming that Obama's African name, brown skin, biracial heritage, multiracial family, and international upbringing meant race and racism were no more. In these contradictory, but equally concerning, reactions the Obama era was revealed as but another flashpoint in the continuing struggle for social justice, especially for the most perpetually and permanently disenfranchised among the 99 percent.

Here to Stay

In *Faces at the Bottom of the Well: The Permanence of Racism*, Bell (1992) focuses attention on the intractability of racism. He discusses the many strategies, approaches, and methods that civil rights activists, broadly defined, have employed over several hundred years to try and bring about the demise of racism, ultimately to little avail. He highlights the ability of racism to mutate and adapt within the human psyche as well as in human-made superstructure in response to each and every effort launched against. As insidious as HIV, racism repeatedly recovers. But in describing the persistence of racism, Bell also describes the persistence of antiracist struggle—indeed, he cannot talk about one without talking about the other.

Likewise, we (equity and diversity workers) cannot tell our stories of ongoing struggles to institutionalize diversity in the academy, without also telling the story of the persistence and permanence of diversity in public higher education. And this is the reality even in the Obama era. So while we thought, perhaps naïvely and perhaps simply hopefully, it would get better and it hasn't, we are still here to stay: Equity and diversity workers will continue to occupy public colleges and universities *no matter what*. Toward that end this book is directed.

La Permanencia de la Diversidad

Mark Brimhall-Vargas, Christine Clark,
y Kenneth J. Fasching-Varner

"El punto de esta protesta [Occupy Wall Street] es que no se desaparezca, y ese es el punto táctico . . . sus tácticas son sobre la presencia física, la presencia física continua."

—Rachel Maddow (TRMS, 2011a)

Pensamos que iba a mejorar

NOSOTROS (LOS CO-EDITORES) RECORDAMOS HABER VISTO POR TELEVISIÓN la toma de posesión del Presidente Obama con su lema de campaña, corriendo como cintillas televisivas por nuestra mente: *Un cambio en el que nosotros podemos creer.* Estábamos llenos de un sentimiento de lo que podría ser posible, algo que anteriormente no nos imaginábamos que nosotros, los adultos, podríamos creer sobre nuestro liderazgo: un verdadero sentido de esperanza para el futuro inmediato y que no estaba teñido de cinismo. Los Estados Unidos había elegido *en realidad* a su primer presidente afro-americano, y estábamos vivos para poder presenciar este suceso. Muchas personas, incluyendo a uno de los editores de esta obra, desafiaron temperaturas *bajo cero durante horas* solo para presenciar este magno y apoteósico evento. Sí, realmente sucedió.

No fue por casualidad que nosotros y muchos de nuestros colegas que trabajan en equidad y diversidad en la educación universitaria nos atreviéramos a creer que el trabajo difícil de abogar por la justicia social sería más respetado después de este acto tan trascendental. La lógica inicial detrás de este pensamiento asemejaba algo como lo siguiente: Si la mayoría de los votantes estadounidenses eligieron a Obama, claramente, esto significaba: 1) que las actitudes sobre la raza y sobre las otras dimensiones de diversidad, estában mejorando; y 2) que las personas que trabajan en equidad/diversidad encontrarían que sería más fácil trabajar con esa actitud sin tener que preocuparse tanto por ser ignorados o recibir reproches. Nuestros colegas, ahora con más gusto, podían venir a preguntarnos cómo los programas académicos y los planes de estudios (co-curriculares) podrían formarse para aprovechar este momento extraordinario de la historia. Había un espíritu de fiesta que trajo consigo un renovado sentido de compromiso con 'el trabajo.' Nosotros, como nación, habíamos entrado en la época de Obama. Pero, resulta que no es la época que nos habíamos imaginado.

Definiendo la época de Obama

Literalmente, la época de Obama *hasta ahora*, representa la campaña, la elección y el primer periodo de gobierno del Presidente Barack Obama. En realidad, lo que demarca esta época no es tan claro y es mucho más complicado, sobretodo con respecto a la diversidad en general y más específicamente sobre el tema del racismo.

Mientras que nosotros (los co-editores) continuamos celebrando lo que imaginábamos podría ser una nueva época de iluminación y virtud de los norteamericanos, la mitad del país fue plagada por la ira debido a la realidad que de alguna manera, y en contra de todas las maquinaciones de un sistema político diseñado para favorecer injustamente al electorado masculino, rico y blanco del Sur, un Afro-Americano de origen humilde, nacido y criado fuera de los Estados Unidos *contiguos,* en Hawái, fue quien ganó las elecciones presidenciales. Otro segmento más pequeño de la población fue erróneamente anunciando la victoria de Obama como evidencia de que el racismo ya era cosa del pasado. De hecho, que ya habíamos entrado en una época totalmente "postracial."

La virulencia feroz expresada por los que se decepcionaron con la elección de Obama, en adición a las acusaciones desesperadas y estridentes dirigidas a él personalmente (por ejemplo, que él, en secreto, era un Musulmán aliado con al-Qaeda, un socialista con intención de destruir el capitalismo estadounidense, un ciudadano de Kenia sin un certificado verdadero de nacimiento de Hawái, un político ingenuo y sin experiencia que debilitaría las defensas militares de los Estados Unidos) fue algo desconcertante. También fue desconcertante la superficialidad de los que dijeron que el nombre Africano de Obama, un hombre de piel morena, de herencia bi-racial y de una familia multirracial, con una educación e infancia internacional, significaba que la raza y el racismo ya no existían, y que todo era cosa del pasado. En estas reacciones contradictorias, pero igualmente preocupantes, la época de Obama se dio a conocer como otro punto de ignición en el que se sigue la lucha por la justicia social, especialmente para los que permanentemente están marginados y que se encuentran entre el 99 por ciento.

Llegó para quedarse

En *Faces at the Bottom of the Well: The Permanance of Racism*, Bell (1992) centra la atención lo inextricable del racismo. El autor analiza las múltiples estrategias, los enfoques y las metodologías que han utilizado los activistas de los derechos civiles, en líneas generales, por más de varios cientos de años para tratar de lograr la desaparición del racismo, en última instancia, con muy poco éxito. Bell destaca la capacidad del racismo de poder mutar y adaptarse dentro de la psique o mente humana, así como en la superestructura hecha por el hombre en respuesta a todos y cada uno de los esfuerzos en su contra. Tan insidioso como el VIH, el racismo se recupera repetidamente. Sin embargo, al descubrir la *persistencia del racismo*, Bell también describe la persistencia de la lucha en contra del racismo, más conocida como la lucha anti-racista. De hecho, no se puede hablar de una, sin hablar de la otra.

Del mismo modo, nosotros (los trabajadores de equidad y diversidad) no podemos contar nuestras historias sobre nuestras continuas batallas para institucionalizar la diversidad en las universidades o la academia, sin también relatar la historia de la perseverancia y la permanencia de la diversidad en la educación superior pública. Y esta es la realidad, incluso en la época de Obama. Por lo que aunque pensamos, quizás con algo de ingenuidad y con esperanza sencilla, que las cosas se mejorarían, y aunque esto no ha sucedido, nosotros seguimos aquí para quedarnos: las personas que trabajan por la equidad y la diversidad seguiremos ocupando las universidades públicas *sin importar lo que nos tome*. Hacia ese fin está dirigido este libro.

Occupying Academia, Reaffirming Diversity

Christine Clark, Kenneth J. Fasching-Varner, and
Mark Brimhall-Vargas

Obama-Era Context Setting

THIS WORK IS ORGANIZED AS AN EDITED VOLUME of institutional case studies written by public higher-education equity/diversity workers across levels and institutional locations. The cases are situated in the Obama era—the period of time spanning President Obama's presidential campaign, election, and first term of office. The cases broadly describe what these workers face in relationship to the presence or absence of an institutional Chief Diversity Officer (CDO) and corresponding institutional equity/diversity structure during this era. More specifically, these cases document the experiences of equity/diversity workers in public higher education across the United States in their efforts to negotiate, survive, and thrive in 'the work.'

In the wake of the election of President Obama in 2008, many equity/diversity workers imagined that renewed national and institutional commitments to educational equity and diversity, moreover to social justice, were 'just around the corner.' In several instances, however, the opposite has become our Obama-era reality. Across the country, many equity/diversity workers find themselves personally, academically, and/or professionally under assault. This volume asks the questions: *Is this assault a result of a premeditated and carefully calculated conservative political agenda? Or, is this assault simply the unfortunate consequence of how largely White conservative fundamentalists, and the power bases they represent and/or control, express their anger about the changing racial landscape in the United States?* This work explores and deconstructs these questions by examining manifestations of the assault across the variety of public higher-educational contexts the case studies represent.

In the process of this exploration and deconstruction, we contend that the assault on diversity is connected to the assault on all things public, especially public higher education, that predates but has become more visible and vitriolic in the Obama era (Arnsdorf, 2011; Bloom, 1987; Bork, 2003; Democracy Now!, 2010; D'Souza, 1998; Editorial, 2011; Exec. Order, 2011; Glazer, 1998; Guiner, 1994; King & Smith, 2011; Paglia, 1991; Patterson, 2009; Stefancic & Delgado, 1996; Tapia, 2009; Will, 1992).

Akin to how the 9/11 attacks were manipulated by the Right and the economic resources they control to further proliferate their politics of *militarization for profit* (Giroux, 2011a), this work argues that Obama's presidency is likewise being manipulated to revitalize White supremacy under the guise of *free market enterprise*. Against this backdrop, it is ironic to consider that while expenditures on diversity work in higher education are treated as socialist entitlement programs, they are driven by the "hegemonic alliances of the New Right" (Apple, 2001, p. 8). The alliances promote a very conservative, workforce-focused set of market-driven imperatives, and are jointly supported by neoliberals, neoconservatives, authoritarian populists (religious fundamentalists and conservative evangelicals), and members of the professional/managerial class. It is important to note that the many *Fortune 500* companies that signed the amicus brief in support of the University of Michigan's recent bid to protect affirmative action practices in admissions (*Gratz v. Bollinger*, 2003; *Grutter v. Bollinger*, 2003) have driven the emergence of the CDO position in the private sector and public higher education alike, evidence of the increasing corporatization and market alignment of public education. Business and industry did not support Michigan in this bid because of their commitment to progressive social justice. Rather, their support draws from business interests' need to have an available workforce that is both highly diverse in composition *and* culturally competent so that the United States can continue to not merely compete in, but control, the world economy (Giroux, 2011a; Jaschik, 2011).

President Obama has been derided by the Right, while the vast majority of his policies have been undergirding their hegemonic alliances (in this instance with neoliberalism). This should make even the implicit calls to Whiteness embedded in this derision at once obvious and reprehensible to all Americans. It is perhaps of most compelling interest that as this volume was being compiled, President Obama signed Executive Order 13583 (2011) "Establishing a Coordinated Government-Wide Initiative to Promote Diversity and Inclusion in the Federal Workforce" aimed at increasing the representation of historically underrepresented groups in federal employment (para. 1). Common responses to the Order range from a prudent analysis of it in a *Wash-*

ington Post article (Arnsdorf, 2011), to a highly hyperbolic, conspiratorially racist *Washington Times* editorial entitled, "Whites need not apply" (2011). While the Order does not expressly create a CDO position or a federal equity/ diversity office per se, there is wide positive and negative perception that such a position or office has effectively been established.

For senior leaders, particularly from nondominant identity groups who show support for, or formally lead, diversity efforts (e.g., CDOs), the pull to 'join the group' at the senior leadership table is coupled with the push to 'represent the people' (Guiner, 1994; King & Smith, 2011; Patterson, 2009; Tapia, 2009). This work amply considers this push–pull dynamic in blending discussion of personality-related, personal, institutional, and political dimensions of equity/diversity work/workers in public higher education.

Methodological Approach

Voice

What counts as a scholarly source? Are peer-reviewed academic journals of a certain caliber/stature the only sources that pass muster as scholarly? Of course qualitative work that engages discrete cases and draws heavily on personal narrative must be grounded in relevant, related research from myriad methodological points of entry, as well as contextualized historically and sociopolitically. The integration of the personal/institutional with the academic/ superstructural is paramount, and supports Peshkin's (1988) value of the *subjective I* in scholarly work. That said, it is also important to note that even traditionally conceived scholarly work has been less warmly received if it challenges status quo perspectives. While work that challenges the status quo may be just as rigorous as work that supports the status quo, it typically does not find its way into the most elite publishing venues. Further, there are *ways of knowing* (Belenky, Clinchy, Goldberger, & Tarule, 1997), especially by members of nondominant groups, that the academy has been even slower to accept as legitimate. Voice is clearly a consideration in how we conceptualized this volume, and in turn, how volume contributors crafted their case chapters. In academia, a dispassionate voice is taken as objective and, therefore, more valid. This work asserts that the dispassionate voice can be used to erroneously persuade readers toward a particular perspective in exactly the same way that an intentionally passionate and subjective voice is assumed to persuade them. Accordingly, the focus of this work is on the care with which any voice reasons, rather than assuming there is 'a voice of reason.' Despite our posture here, there is still an element of dispassionate voice in many of the case chapters. We attribute this in part to our academic training to speak 'credibly,' and in part to our conditioning as equity/diversity workers to speak 'cautiously,' both of which ultimately serve neoliberal and right-leaning interests. We encourage readers to trouble this dispassion in their consideration of the chapters.

Timeliness is also a concern in scholarship. This work wants to engage in discourse about the current Obama-era political climate as it is unfolding. As a result of this delimitation, we acknowledge that the available body of scholarly research on this climate is simply far more scant today than it will be five years from now.

In sum, this work labors to ensure that personal narrative is punctuated with rigorous analysis in a manner that lends the greatest degree of credibility to it, without sacrificing its authenticity. And this work seeks to accomplish all this while grounded in the current historical moment.

Critical Theory

The term Critical Theory (CT), which derives from sociology, was first used by Horkheimer in 1937 to describe a theory of society specifically designed to critique society and, based on that critique, change society at the institutional or systemic level. CT draws from what today is called neo-Marxism, a dialectical and historically located, interdisciplinary and liberatory form of Marxism. Accordingly, CT was developed in response to the so-called logical positivism promoted in scientific method that typically engages Traditional Theory to simply explain or understand, but not critique or change, societal and other phenomenon (Horkheimer, 1972).

This work uses a Critical Theory (CT) framework generally, but more specifically, a Critical Race Theory framework, at the same time that it flexibly and reflexively accepts additional theoretical scaffolds. Precisely because this work focuses on the personal and institutional experiences of equity/diversity workers broadly conceived, a single theoretical lens is unlikely to meet every individual/institutional need. This is especially true when these workers' experiences focus on a dimension of equity/diversity work or are related to an institutional context that is highly unique. Accordingly, this work is grounded in Critical Race Theory, informed by additional existing theories, and open to the construction of new (grounded) theories that emerge through the case study development process.

Critical Race Theory

Critical Race Theory (CRT) emerged at the intersection of radical jurisprudence, the practice of especially Civil Rights law, and legal activism in the middle 1970s (Delgado & Stefancic, 2001, 2005). Recognizing that progressive social change predicated on legislative victories was not only not continuing to progress, but regress, legal scholars, practitioners, and activists sought out new mechanisms for combatting racism and other forms of discrimination, especially in their more insidious, stealthy, furtive, and surreptitious forms (Banks, 2004; Bell, 1987, 1992, 1995a; Dixson & Rousseau, 2006; Orfield, 2001).

CRT examines the intersections of race, racism, and institutional power from a radical point of entry into debate and related praxis (Berry, 1994; Harris, 1993; Ladson-Billings & Tate, 1995; Lawrence & Matsuda, 1997). Rather than employing these examinations toward bringing about social change in the same manner that typically suits the societal status quo, CRT questions the capacity of this manner of change to bring about real, structural change at all (Bell, 1995a; Guiner, 1994; Perea, Delgado, Harris, & Wildman, 2007). In so doing, CRT cultivates a highly academically grounded and strategic, but unapologetically resolute and impatient, dispositional cadence in pursuing social change.

CRT, perhaps not surprisingly, made its way from law into other fields of study, including education, in the 1990s (Delgado & Stefancic, 2001, 2005; Dixson & Rousseau, 2006; Ladson-Billings & Tate, 1995). One tool of CRT—the use of counterstorytelling—has, unfortunately, been overused and largely uncritically employed in applying CRT to the educational arena (Dixson & Rousseau, 2006; Ladson-Billings, 2006; Popkewitz & Fendler, 1999; Taylor, Gillborn, & Ladson-Billings, 2009).

The goal of counterstorytelling is to reveal deficit thinking embedded in so-called objective research located within dominant narratives, with an explicit focus on nondominant groups. Further, counterstories aim to reveal the deficiency of law and policy that derives from, and favors, dominant groups. By challenging dominant narratives, while locating research in the experience and knowledge bases of nondominant groups instead, counterstorytelling challenges the embedded biases of researchers from historically overrepresented groups at the same time that it produces research findings that testify to the resiliency and ability of nondominant groups, even in the face of sustaining systemic discrimination.

In educational research, however, the use of counterstorytelling has often been watered down to the point where the counterstories lack the critical consciousness to challenge dominant paradigms; hence, they become simply alternative stories. Alternative stories, although often framed as counterstories, simply present a different perspective on dominant narratives without revealing their absurdity or the real-life perils of the hegemony they promote. Because alternative stories claim to be counterstories, they create confusion as to what actually counts as counterstory in CRT. Typically, alternative stories can be distinguished from counterstories because they embody neoliberal perspectives that lack the critical consciousness necessary to effectively trouble dominant ideologies (Dixson & Rousseau, 2006; Popkewitz & Fendler, 1999; Taylor, Gillborn, & Ladson-Billings, 2009).

In the effort to guard against this trend emerging in the invocation of CRT in this book, chapter authors who used counterstorytelling as a part of their case presentation were asked to couple its use with at least one other foundational CRT tenet: (a) a critique of liberalism (and, in this historical moment, also neoliberalism); (b) a discussion of the centrality/centering of Whiteness, the exchange value or currency of Whiteness, and/or the concept of Whiteness as property; (c) an examination of interest convergence in undermining and/or leveraging equity/diversity work; (d) an analysis of the permanence and pervasiveness of racism; and (e) an assessment of the roles of restrictive views of equality (which focus on discriminatory *intent* in the long-term process of bringing about equality) versus expansive views of equity (which prioritize the *impact* of discrimination in seeking more immediate and concrete redress from it) (Bell, 1987, 1992, 1995a; Berry, 1994; Collins, 1998; Delgado, 1995a; Delgado & Stefancic, 1997a, 2001, 2005; Dixson & Rousseau, 2006; Haney-López, 2006; Harris, 1993; Lawrence, 2005; Lawrence & Matsuda, 1997; Matsuda, Lawrence, Delgado, & Crenshaw, 1993; Perea, Delgado, Harris, & Wildman, 2007; Popkewitz & Fendler, 1999; Stefancic & Delgado, 1996; Taylor, Gillborn, & Ladson-Billings, 2009). We acknowledge that in case chapters where the notion of counterstory is discussed in passing or evoked as a substantive part of the delineation of the case (chapters 2–3, 5–7, and 10–15), that the conceptualization of counterstory may not match with this editorial perspective. Accordingly, we encourage readers to think through and, again, trouble these tensions as they engage these chapters. As educational scholars have wrestled with these tensions for at least the past 10 years, it is fitting that others do so as well.

Case Study

Creswell (2007) describes Case Study Method (CSM) as the study of a bounded system—the case—or a critical issue within the system. Further, CSM involves inquiry into a system or systems, during a specific time period, using data collection from several sources. The goal of CSM is to paint a picture of the system or systems, including of the themes that typify the system and/or that all the systems share ("cross-case themes," p. 79). Yin (2009) describes CSM as investigation of current phenomena within their natural milieus in which the bounds between the phenomenon and milieu are not immediately obvious, consequently warranting elucidation, and in which there is more than one source of data in play. Precisely because these descriptions of CSM are at least somewhat paradoxical, the chapters in this volume draw from both of them in bounding their institutional cases, as does the volume as a whole in bounding its system of institutional cases.

Several case-study methodologists (Creswell, 2007, 2009; Merriam, 1998; Stake, 1995; Yin, 2003) delineate forms of CSM: single or instrumental, collective or multiple, holistic or entirety, intrinsic, exploratory, explanatory or embedded, and descriptive. In the single or instrumental, a single issue within one bounded case is examined in order to develop insight into an issue within a case context. With the collective or multiple, a single issue is explored through various bounded cases. In the holistic or entirety, a comprehensive examination of bounded systems is undertaken. The study is of the case itself (reflexively) in the intrinsic. With the exploratory, the goal is less explicit, and often there is no clear outcome or outcomes. An answer or answers to one or more complex questions are sought, and/or a specific element is engaged to unpack a system complexity in the explanatory or embedded. Finally, in the descriptive, the focus is on the study of, and in, a specific real-world context. Each case in this volume, as well as the cases in aggregate, represent all of these forms of CSM; some do this discretely and others do it intersectionally.

The mosaic engagement of CSM herein may appear to confound our research. But all forms of CSM seek to develop a clear or clearer depiction of the case or cases. Thus, whether dovetailed or divergent in their case positioning herein, these forms contribute to the development of greater theoretical and conceptual knowledge. Accordingly, this volume *employs CSM to build (on) theories and concepts* related to diversity in higher education, especially to its fruitful proliferation. Accordingly, each case study gives brief, yet appropriate, formal attention to the particulars of CSM that pertain to the development of the case (Creswell, 2007, 2009; Merriam, 1998; Stake, 1995; Yin, 2003, 2009). In so doing, each case *also employs CSM as an analytical tool* through which areas of convergence and divergence across all of the cases can be culled. For this reason, a version of the same institutional pseudonym is used in all of the cases.

The Use of "ACME"

In the spirit of the case study approach, and also to provide a bit of 'political cover' to those who may need it to be able to write as honest a chapter as is possible, we decided that all of the institutions referenced in all of the case chapters should be configured in relation to the pseudoacronym "ACME" (short for Academy). To use this pseudoacronym most effectively, we established the following use convention *examples* to ensure that institutional type is still conveyed:

- *University of Rhode Island* would become *University of ACME* (the only campus in a state; sometimes these campuses are also considered flagships)
- *University of Nebraska, Lincoln* would become *University of ACME, Flagship* (the founding campus in a multicampus university system)
- *University of New Hampshire, Manchester* would become *University of ACME, Local Area* (the nonflagship campus in a two-campus university system)
- *University of South Carolina, Aiken* would become *University of ACME, Regional* (a nonflagship campus in a multicampus university system)
- *University of Northern Colorado* would become *University of Regional ACME* (a regional institution)
- *University of Baltimore* would become *University of ACME City* (a city-, not state-, named university)
- *Alabama State University* would become *ACME State University* (the only campus in a state)
- *California State University, San Marcos* would become *ACME State University, Regional* (a campus in a multicampus university system)

Each case chapter employs this naming convention to discuss the institution(s) at focus in it. The full or formal convention is used at the outset of each chapter; thereafter, more institution-specific versions of the convention are used. For example, if University of California, Berkeley is familiarly called UC, Berkeley, the corresponding naming convention would be UA, Flagship.

For all case chapter author bylines, the actual name of each author's current institutional affiliation is used; author institutional affiliations may or may not have any correspondence to the institution(s) discussed in the corresponding case chapter. In the same vein, unless otherwise specified, all people names used in the case chapters are pseudonyms.

In sum, the ACME use convention is designed to encourage readers' attention to focus on the ideas/issues that emerge across in the case chapters, rather than on specific institutions or people within those institutions. We are not seeking to praise or indict any institution/person. Rather, we seek to identify themes that live across institutions and/or institution types, as well as the people that comprise them. In so doing, both the case study foundation of each and all the case chapters is simultaneously buttressed.

Additional Case Delimitations

As mentioned above, in addition to the volume's overarching engagement of CRT and CSM, each case study also interweaves CRT with CSM as a theoretical or conceptual framework. Interwoven as a theoretical framework, the chapter briefly recounts the original source of theory, the prior application of theory, and the manner in which the theory informs the institutional case. Interwoven as a conceptual framework, the chapter briefly describes the relevant concept(s), where the concept(s) derives from, the prior use of the concept(s), and the manner in which the concept(s) informs the institutional case.

Further, each case: (a) is expressly situated in the Obama-era context, (b) is focused on a public state college or university, and (c) employs a contextual frame of reference for examining equity/diversity in the institution (e.g., a teaching/learning context, a tenure and promotion context, a hiring context, a policy context, a rhetorical context, a student context, a faculty context, a staff context, an administrator context, or a context that mixes elements of several contexts and/or that crosses several contexts). Each case study concludes, in some way, with a discussion of strategies employed for responding to the assault on equity/diversity workers and work and an assessment of their efficacy.

Thus, each case is structured to be presented in a productive manner, though this does necessarily mean that any or all of the cases present generally positive institutional pictures, nor that they "balance" negative institutional features with positive ones. This work seeks realism. For this reason, the tone in which the cases are presented is not scripted.

It is important to point out the paradox that equity/diversity workers experience great pressure to be 'nice' while doing work that often makes them witness to appalling cruelty. Concomitantly, scholarship on equity/diversity work experiences coercion to be also 'positive' or, at least, 'not so negative' when it seeks simply to tell harsh truths. For this reason, a lot of the extant scholarship about equity/diversity work and workers—especially the CDO—focuses almost exclusively on so-called best practices. Yet, this scholarship rarely experiences critique for its lack of substantive attention to the challenges that equity/diversity workers face. It does not even engage the notion of 'best practices for CDOs to overcome hostile work environments.' Accordingly, this book purposely uses a tone of urgency because even when the overall environment for diversity on campus appears healthiest *on the surface*, it is actually so structurally flawed *underneath the surface* that failure over time can often be predetermined.

In fact, this book rejects a best-practices approach (Maguire, 2007). While this book acknowledges that there are basic things that minimally need to be in place on all campuses for equity/diversity work to have fundamental success, meaningful equity/diversity work must emerge in a more organic fashion from campus-wide, democratically engaged processes that cannot be codified into universal *best* practices. Instead *good* practices, especially local ones, are identified that may be robust enough to be adapted across institutional contexts. We wish also to be clear, however, that it would still be a mistake to assume that any of these strategies or principles of action can be employed without myriad institution-specific adaptations. In sum, for each case study there are lessons learned that this volume as a whole presents as potential resources for equity/diversity workers. These potential resources are presented to assist equity/diversity workers to sustain themselves and their work in ways that offer hope for improving the progress of diversity in higher education in manners that are more open, frank, fair, authentic, and effective.

Further Critical Considerations

While equity/diversity workers at all levels in the academic hierarchy have found ways to be highly effective, regardless of the structural and political challenges they face, we feel it is important to ask the following questions:

- *How are these successes being measured? By whom? Toward what ends?*
- *What is the campus model for diversity and how was it established?*
- *If there is a CDO, how is the CDO role defined?*
- *What, if any, is the relationship between the campus model for diversity and the CDO role?*
- *And does bringing in a CDO necessarily mean a serious engagement with diversity and equity on campus?*

The last question is particularly important if the CDO does not possess specific skill sets, resources, staffing, lines of authority, and *oversight for equity functions as well as diversity ones.*

To the extent that equity/diversity workers have been meaningfully successful, they have had to work exceedingly hard because of, and in spite of, structural and political challenges that few other senior leaders/professionals in other fields face. The diversity component of equity/diversity work is perceived to be 'hospitality work' (though not perceived to be undertaken in exceedingly inhospitable climates), as well as work in which the opinions/experiences of everyone in the community *are equally valid and as valid as* the academic and professional expertise of the equity/diversity worker—even at the CDO level. These perceptions marginalize equity/diversity workers, their expertise, and all equity/diversity work.

To provide some perspective on this, imagine if the experiences of a philosophy professor and the opinion of a volleyball coach about a campus engineering project were granted equal status to those of the project engineers. Further, imagine that the engineers had to work really collaboratively with this professor and this coach to integrate their concerns into the approach developed to execute the project. While every discipline has its uniqueness and related challenges, those in the diversity arena often require practitioners/ scholars to be 'super nice' and 'super team-oriented' to engender the smallest accomplishments and/or recognition for good work. The complex nature of these dynamics requires a point of reference that interrogates the double standard, not one that suggests that such a standard does not exist and/or that the standard merely needs to be skillfully negotiated as opposed to eliminated. This book does not shy away from the fact that diversity work is often left unaccompanied by the systemic support and authority afforded other functions; instead, it proactively confronts these double standards.

Here again, our point of entry in this book is not intended to be negative or positive, but realist; with the good, the bad, the neither good nor bad, and so forth as a part of the mix. Most of what has already been presented in the literature about the CDO and the related nature of equity/diversity work in higher education has been focused on helping the CDO to 'get a foot in the door,' codifying the CDO role as a senior leadership role, strategically and otherwise carefully negotiating the politics of diversity to garner its greater acceptance, and selling diversity in a business-like manner (Williams & Wade-Golden, 2007, 2008a, 2008b, 2011, 2012a, 2012b). This volume speaks more freely, not seeking to promote an optimistic view of equity/diversity work/workers, and not trying to protect the work/its workers from reprisal by framing it/them in the most palatable way to potential critics. Rather, this volume creates a context for workers to tell their equity/diversity work stories as candidly as possible. Resultantly, this work not only welcomes the notion of an 'outlaw spirit' in equity/diversity workers, it argues that possessing, if not always enacting, such spirit is necessary for the work to be done efficaciously, particularly on behalf of those whose success in higher education is most tenuous.

In sum, this volume is not a gripe piece, nor a cheerleading tableau. It does not beg for diversity workers to be "let into" the game or to be "given" a seat at the table. It does question the value of playing the game, and of sitting at the table, when no matter how well one plays or politely one sits, the results of the work are almost equally as fragile when viewed over time. While skillful play and strategic engagement can, and do, lead to "multicultural moments," extending these moments to effect sustaining systemic level structural change proves largely elusive. That is, hard work, good work, righteous work will not necessarily produce the desired wholly transformative results we—equity and diversity workers—seek. In the interim, we have to work as best we can with the tools we have, understanding that they are imperfect, often messy, and ultimately limited.

This volume seeks to elucidate and deconstruct mechanisms of power that initiate and/or enable assaults on equity/diversity workers and their work. From there, the volume seeks to analyze efforts to resist and counter these assaults, highlighting those efforts that have been the most effective in sustaining and growing equity/diversity efforts in the face of adversity. In so doing, this volume reveals *glocal* pattern matching across the cases—the common, but different, local pieces of equity/diversity work that appear to have the greatest efficacy and resiliency (Brooks & Normore, 2010). While the *master's tools* may not dismantle his house, they can begin to remodel it, to ready it for new/different occupiers/occupants who are also in the process of crafting new and better tools (Lorde, 1984).

One new and better tool that we challenge ourselves and our colleagues to craft through consideration of this work is the capacity for radical self-critique, as well as openness to radical critique from others (Enck-Wanzer, 2010). As equity/diversity workers, we sometimes avoid acknowledging reasoned critique of our performance and collegiality by proclaiming that all critique is only and always about the politics of the work we do. While it is absolutely true that equity/diversity workers are almost always scrutinized more harshly, it is also true that we, like everyone else, have performance and collegiality challenges that at times warrant radical self-reflection. The fact that these challenges may be complexly linked with the nature of the work we do in equity/diversity makes this self-critique more complex and, therefore, more vital. We have to be willing to be fiercely honest with ourselves and each other about what behaviors we might need to 'check' in order to make the equity/diversity message clearer and, hopefully, reduce resistance to it more ably. The work cannot only, or always, be about us as the equity/diversity workers. We have to be able to 'get out of the way' for our efforts to progress.

As equity/diversity workers we have been disparaged in part for the issues we raise and the passion with which we raise them. But, we also have to look at ourselves and say, "*What, if any, part of the scrutiny I am experiencing is a function of my personality, my approach, my impatience, my anger, etc.?*" Of course, it is exceedingly difficult to tease out where personality and approach, for example, may not dovetail with race, gender, class background, and other dimensions of our identities and the experiences that flow therefrom. But to argue that *all* the negative feedback that we have received as equity/diversity workers is only a function of other people's issues with the work, and not ever about what we do/don't do in the course of undertaking that work, is anticritical on our parts. With brutally honest self-critique, we can get better in doing the work. And while getting better does not guarantee that the work will still not be vehemently resisted, it does mean that we will have fewer detractors, more supporters, and that the work will go further. To enter into the work with the expectation that we will be treated fairly in doing it suggests that we have one foot in two opposing camps simultaneously. On the one hand, we are suggesting that our presence is needed because of the lack of fairness. Yet on the other hand, we are expecting that we will not experience the lack of fairness we were hired to help eradicate. While this expectation may be ideal(istic), it is not realistic; taking postures in doing the work that are unrealistic undermines the work.

We recognize that our positionalities as editors, and the positionalities of the case chapter authors as well, can lend to this work being dismissed in a number of ways, especially from a number of academic and political points of entry into debate and analysis. For this reason, we question whether or not political solutions can be achieved through research, including this current body of it. With that in mind, we want to affirm our belief that the most significant avenue for equity/diversity-related change in higher education comes from engagement with students and the broad communities they represent. At least for the moment, the spaces we occupy with students are the most diverse and the least surveilled in the public arena—spaces we owe to the tenets of academic freedom.

Institutional Diversity Structure Configurations

While this work ultimately places special emphasis on the challenges faced by CDOs in public higher education, it is important to note that what constitutes a CDO in many institutions is hard to assess (Clark, 2010; Williams & Wade-Golden, 2008a, 2011). This is because in many institutions:

1. The president claims the CDO designation, either in an attempt to empower or limit institutional diversity efforts;
2. The role of the CDO is ill-defined and/or poorly supported;
3. There is no bona fide CDO or even a person at a senior administrative level with explicit oversight for diversity;
4. The CDO, or the senior person with explicit responsibility for diversity, has no academic and/or professional experience in a field/role related to diversity;
5. The CDO is someone who places overt emphasis on business approaches to diversity (i.e., "managing" diversity for particular political/economic outcomes);
6. The diversity structure is decentralized such that more than one person has an aspect of coordinating responsibility for diversity, and these aspects are operationalized in manners that are largely or completely separate and

distinct from one another; further the CDO is often expected to 'fix' the negative outcomes of this structure without the resources or authority to do so, or to simply 'PR' them;

7. There is little or no diversity infrastructure in existence; and/or,

8. The CDO is disconnected from the equity function, thus from the legally tethered power base in the work; in short the CDO is not the CDEO—Chief Diversity and Equity Officer.

On this last point, this book argues that the power of the diversity function in the academy comes from its tethering to the equity function. In contrast, the dominant discourse in equity/diversity work is that equity/diversity functions should be separate because equity work: (a) makes especially White people suspicious as to the diversity motive (that "reverse" discrimination or punishment is the goal), and/or (b) eats up time as well as human and capital resources leaving little for proactive diversity efforts (though ample resourcing renders this point moot) (Bowen & Bok, 1998; Chang, Witt, Jones, & Hakuta, 2003; Cokorinos, 2003; Gurin, Lehman, & Lewis, 2007; Orfield, 2001). But diversity work is the work we do because we *choose* to value its efficacy. Whereas we do equity work because we are *compelled* to do it by policy and law. If all the things we do in the diversity arena fail, the equity arena is still there to either prevent discrimination from occurring, or to provide avenues for redress after the fact. Further, trends in equity transgressions also offer valuable insight into where diversity education efforts need to be concentrated. In the discussion of the cases that ensue, we believe the basis for the legitimacy of our argument here is amply made.

In considering the various manifestations of these institutional diversity structure configurations operating across public higher education, it becomes clear that no one configuration alone can accurately describe what is happening with regard to diversity in any institution. Further, we have only codified eight configurations drawn from our review of the literature and the experiences delineated in the case chapters. Undoubtedly, more configurations exist and/or will emerge in time. In many institutions, elements of all eight configurations are at play at once, and likely a host of others that, again, we have yet to clearly identify.

Overview of the Cases and Response Chapter

There are 15 discrete cases presented in this work, organized by their loosely shared "institutional perspective" as: (a) CDO-focused cases, (b) Mid-Level Administrator (MLA)-focused cases, and (c) faculty-focused cases. At the same time, our CRT orientation herein works against neatly packaging human experiences into discrete categories; thus, these three institutional perspectives are not meant to lock the voice(s) in any of the chapters into a singular perspective. For that reason, we also characterize these perspectives as "stories from the frontlines," to emphasize their unscripted and unscriptable nature.

Still, our organization of the case chapters into the three institutional perspectives has emerged organically over the past year based in part on how authors situated their work, and in part, how we understood it. We offer the three institutional perspectives as a conceptual tool for readers, recognizing that no case chapter fits neatly into the perspective we assigned it. This is particularly true for case chapter 5, which speaks from both MLA as well as CDO voice. We assigned this case chapter the last slot in the CDO perspective as a way of transitioning to the MLA one, but we could have just as easily assigned it the first slot in the MLA one. Similarly, as case chapter 10 speaks simultaneously from a MLA and faculty voice, we situate it at the end of the MLA perspective as bridge to the faculty one. But in truth, all the case chapters within the MLA perspective serve as bridge to the faculty one. This is because all of these case chapters are either authored or coauthored by MLAs that are also faculty or that also perform faculty functions, or they are coauthored by MLAs and faculty. These case chapters also bridge work in administrative affairs, academic affairs, and student affairs through the lens of the work of diversity offices and/or diversity committees (writ large). Of the chapters in the faculty perspective, four examine the dynamics of racism in teacher education. Accordingly we chose to break up the common focus of these chapters by placing the other chapter in this perspective in the third slot. And while this other chapter examines resistance to diversifying the faculty ranks across higher education, because it is written from the perspective of an Affirmative Action officer we could have chosen to include it in the MLA perspective as well.

From the CDO frontlines, Case 1: "Extra, Extra, Read All About It! Diversity Soul-ed Out (and Sold/Out) Here," by Christine Clark, focuses on the historical evolution of the CDO role at an institution within a contentiously led university system in which conservative legislators, donors, and media have undue influence. Case 2: "Balancing Act: A Contextual Case Analysis on Recentering Diversity in the Midst of Social and Economic Fluctuations," by Katrice A. Albert and Marco J. Barker, describes the diversity trajectory of a southern institution as a result of a federal desegregation consent decree. Case 3: "Deconstructing Hope: A Chief Diversity Officer's Dilemma in the Obama Era," by A. Leslie Anderson, provides an in-depth theoretical analysis of the process by which a CDO position was developed, focusing on the challenges posed by leadership colorblindness. Case 4: "Transforming Lives and Communities: Case Study of a Diversity and Community Engagement Portfolio at a Flagship Institution," by Gregory J. Vincent, Sherri L. Sanders, and S. Kiersten Ferguson, recounts an unlikely, sustaining, diversity success story in which the robust portfolio of the CDO, and broad leadership support from across campus, figure prominently. And, Case 5: "Southern Predominantly White Institutions, Targeted Students, and the Intersectionality of Identity: Two Case Studies," by Allison Daniel Anders, James M. DeVita, and Steven Thurston Oliver, offers a comparison of the lived experiences of three campus diversity workers, including one CDO, on two campuses using the intersection of LGBT (lesbian, gay, bisexual, and transgender) and other dimensions of identity, including race, as points of comparison.

From the MLA frontlines, Case 6: "The Myth of Institutionalizing Diversity: Structures and the Covert Decisions They Make," by Mark Brimhall-Vargas, takes up the struggle to institutionalize campus-wide diversity efforts in manners that are expansive and broadly participatory. Case 7: "Swimming up Mainstream: Facing the Challenges to Equity, Diversity, and Inclusion on a University of ACME, Regional Campus in Obama's Era," by Virginia Lea, Hollace Anne Teuber, Glenda Jones, and Susan Wolfgram, directly illustrates the way national political rhetoric influences state and local, as well as system and campus, resource allocations and related support for diversity. Case 8: "The Search for Questions and Tellings of Silenced Students," by Douglas J. Loveless and Bryant Griffith, details how privilege-normal and diverse-strange stereotypes operate in the everyday borderlands that individuals and groups traverse while pursuing higher education. Case 9: "The Evolution of a Campus: From the Seat of the Civil War to a Seat on the Freedom Rides," by Shaunna Payne Gold and Leah K. Cox, describes the important role that sincere support from senior leadership can play in moving a prestigious university with a challenging history of desegregation from a climate of exclusion to one of affirmation. Case 10: "The Unmet Promise: A Critical Race Theory Analysis of the Rise of an African American Studies Program," by Michael E. Jennings, lays out an administrative history of an African American Studies minor from initial establishment, to neglect, through adversity, into decline, and toward revitalization.

From the faculty frontlines, Case 11: "'Just (Don't) Do It!' Tensions between Articulated Commitments and Action at The ACME State University," by Kenneth J. Fasching-Varner and Vanessa Dodo Seriki, explores the complex role of race within a university's teacher education program in exposing the unfair burden scholars of color face. Case 12: "Déjà Vu: Dynamism of Racism in Policies and Practices Aimed at Alleviating Discrimination," by Shirley Mthethwa-Sommers, examines the radically different experiences of two faculty of color in two departments within the same institution in which the presence or absence of racial consciousness in the departments' leaders is central. Case 13: "'Isn't Affirmative Action Illegal?,'" by Eugene Oropeza Fujimoto, exposes how, in many instances, hiring a White woman masquerades as diversity progress, despite persistent underrepresentation and isolation of faculty of color and the resultant lack of in-group role models for students of color. Case 14: "Equity at the Fringes: The Continuing Peripheral Enactment of Equity and Diversity in the Preparation of PK–12 Teachers," by Roderick L. Carey and Laura S. Yee, considers a university's struggle to recruit and retain students of color in a historically and predominantly White teacher-education program and the role of dialogic pedagogy. Finally, Case 15: "On the Battlefield for Social Justice in the Education of Teachers: The Dangers and Dangerousness of Challenging Whiteness in Predominantly White Institutions and Teacher Preparation Programs," by Brenda G. Juárez and Cleveland Hayes, surveys the challenges associated with challenging Whiteness in using the notion of "goodness" to explore why preservice teachers are perpetually unprepared to teach students of color.

Margaret-Mary Sulentic Dowell then provides a response to, and synthesis of, the case chapters in her chapter titled, "So What? Who Cares? And What's Our Point about Diversity?" In seeking an answer to the volume's title question, *Just how important is diversity work in higher education?*, this chapter concludes that not only is diversity of paramount importance in public higher education, it is of paramount importance in all quarters of public life.

From our editorial perspective, all of the chapters in this volume take up the call to "occupy the academy." In doing so, they recharge our efforts as equity/diversity workers, and reaffirm equity/diversity work. *We shall not be moved.*

Significance

The Role of Dialogue

In *debate*, the goal is to trump others' perspectives by *listening to gain advantage* (Clark, 2003; Nagda & Zúñiga, 2003; Schoem & Hurtado, 2001; Tannen, 1999). In *discussion*, participants typically offer their perspectives on a common topic in a manner more akin to a *serial monologue* than to the deliberative exchange of ideas (Clark, 2002, 2003; Nagda, Gurin, & López, 2003; Nagda & Zúñiga, 2003; Schoem & Hurtado, 2001; Schoem, Hurtado, Sevig, Chesler, & Sumida, 2001). This work seeks to engage readers in *dialogue*, where the communicative goal is to *listen to understand*, but not necessarily to come to agreement. In fact, the goal is to build comfort with, and skill for, continuing engagement, especially when disagreement persists (Clark, 2002, 2003; Lawrence, 2005; McPhail, 2003; Nagda, Gurin, & López, 2003; Nagda & Zúñiga, 2003; Schoem & Hurtado, 2001; Schoem, et. al., 2001; Tannen, 1999). In short, we see dialogic conversation as the practice of a democracy that is more dedicated to solving real world problems, than to the mere maintenance of political ideologies or affiliations. Accordingly, we present the ensuing case studies in this volume as a form of dialogue, and for dialogue, simultaneously: They engage readers in dialogue, and they can be used by readers to foster dialogue beyond their boundedness.

The ultimate aspiration of this work is that it will be of particular benefit to equity/diversity workers (and related constituents/stakeholders) who have experienced assaults on their work and/or are concerned about their local or the national climate for diversity. By engaging in dialogue on common equity/diversity related challenges that have emerged in a variety of educational workplace settings, especially since the election of President Obama, our hope is that efficacious strategies for responding to these challenges can be developed and implemented locally, collectively amassing global impact (Gurin, Gurin, Dey, & Hurtado, 2004; McLaren, 1997; Nagda, Gurin, & López, 2003; Nagda & Zúñiga, 2003; Sleeter, 1996; Tough, 2008).

Moving from Margins to Center:
From Occupiers to Collective Owners

As editors, we see 'the work' *of and in* this volume as being in alignment with the spirit and tactic of the Occupy Wall Street protests, generally recognized as having begun in New York City's Zuccotti Park and to be continuing across the country and around the globe. The occupation at the heart of these protests is about taking over space, for a period of time, within larger environmental contexts the "proprietors" of which ardently endeavor to, at best, remove and, at worst, ignore the presence of the occupiers. And though characterized by the Right as aimless or uninformed, these occupiers are very clear about what they want to achieve and very organized in how they are seeking to achieve it.

The occupiers want concerns about injustice to be heard and respectfully acknowledged, and then for the fabric of society to be stitched anew such that those concerns can be fairly resolved—they want a more just and fair world. The occupiers' approach engages knowledge as power; accordingly, they have created open libraries—*the people's library*—to educate themselves, as well as those who "own" the occupied space, about the conditions of existence engendering the occupation (TRMS, 2011b). Through informed and informing occupation then, occupiers are making a dialectically humanistic form of appeal to those in power about the need for transformative change; the need to radically alter the local and global political and economic machinery that renders some people *cogs in* and others *owners of* the machinery. Imprisoned within the machinery is all people's humanity: Whether cog or owner, the machinery dehumanizes us all.

In sum, this volume makes plain that equity/diversity workers are largely occupiers in academia. And while the case studies in this volume attest that college and university equity/diversity workers have learned to negotiate, survive, and even thrive in their work against great odds, it is clear that they have done these three things in greatly varied measure, and that the weight of most equity/diversity work still remains largely survival in nature. Only when academia rebuilds its institutional foundation with equity, diversity, inclusion, and social justice as its cornerstones will equity/diversity workers become collective owners of academic life. Likewise, only when society welcomes those on the margins into the center will Wall Street protests become All Street celebrations.

Stories from the
Chief Diversity Officer Frontlines

Bailey W. Jackson

THE CASE STUDIES IN THIS FIRST SECTION focus primarily on the role of the Chief Diversity Officer (CDO) in relationship to various campus and community diversity stakeholders, as well other institutional stakeholders. The scholar-practitioners who author these cases provide current accounts of what change work in equity- and diversity-oriented systems in higher education looks like.

CDOs typically have campus-wide responsibility, but often not the authority to carry this responsibility out, or only the authority to carry it out in some places/ways (e.g., in diversity programming, but not equity policies). While CDOs are often perceived to have a 'view from above,' they often sense presidents, chancellors, regents, trustees, donors, the media, and elected officials 'looking down' on them. At the same time, others on campus and in local neighborhoods tend to 'look to' CDOs to 'do it all.' Across all of these views exist myriad assumptions about hierarchical power that are rarely true, especially when it comes to diversity work in public higher education; thus, these views reveal a general lack of understanding of the depth and breadth of diversity work (especially staffing and funding challenges), especially the political pressures that come to bear on campus CDOs as they engage the work.

Generally, the CDO's function is to carry out the institution's diversity goals *on behalf of and under the supervision of* those to whom she/he typically reports, *for* the campus community at large (students, faculty, staff, alumni, and off-campus community members). What those goals are and how they are carried out expresses an institution's interest in, and commitment to, becoming a Multicultural Organization (MCO). For some institutions, the

CDO is seen as the person who is only responsible for making the institution 'look good' with respect to equity, diversity, and even social justice, but without making much structural change in the policies, practices, culture, and traditions of the institution. Using a CDO to keep the institution 'out of trouble' is the a priori concern for an institution that is not dedicated to becoming an MCO. For those institutions that are more evolved in terms of their multicultural cognizance, the focus of the CDO role is not only concerned with developing and implementing initiatives that will increase compositional diversity, improve campus climate, and cultivate understanding for some, but dedicated toward systemic change efforts designed to ensure equity, fairness, and social justice for all. Supporting a CDO (often along with an internal or external diversity change committee or team) in regularly designing, carrying out, and assessing multifaceted, institution-wide diversity plans is the a posteriori desire of an institution eager to become an MCO.

The process of Multicultural Organization Development (MCOD) will vary depending on the MCOD stage of the institution. Institutions in the earlier stages of MCOD (Exclusionary, White Male Club, and Equal Opportunity Compliance) are unlikely to have even established a CDO position, or if they have, this position is largely figurehead in nature. Institutions in the later stages of MCOD (Affirmative Action, Redefining, and Multicultural) are more likely to have a CDO position and to have begun to think critically about how to best situate and support this position to ensure the success of diversity efforts on campus. Institutions at the most advanced stages of MCOD will often augment the responsibilities and resources ascribed to the CDO to extend institutional services to the local community hosting the campus. By locating the cases in this section on the MCOD continuum, from Exclusionary to Multicultural, while no single case sits squarely in only one stage, there is a perceivable developmental progression from Case 3, to Case 1, to Case 2, to Case 5, to Case 4. The key ingredient fueling this progression is genuine leadership commitment to, and political and economic support for, the CDO, coupled with an understanding that the work of the CDO must be fully integrated into the fabric of the entire institution.

1

Extra, Extra, Read All About It!

Diversity Soul-ed Out (and Sold/Out) Here

Christine Clark

Institutional Background

THE UNIVERSITY OF ACME, LOCAL AREA (UALA) was established in 1957 in what is now the urban Southwest (UALA, 2011). It is an accredited comprehensive research university enrolling 28,000 students and employing 2,900 faculty and staff. It is a part of the ACME System of Higher Education (ASHE), composed of seven other institutions, the system Flagship University, a Research Institute, a four-year State College, and four Community Colleges, most of which also offer some baccalaureate degree programs (UALA, 2011). UALA is located in the city of Local Area, which is in the Southern part of the state of ACME.

State geography plays an important role in public higher-education funding and related politics (Bowers, 2006; Driggs & Goodall, 1996; Moerhing, 2000, 2007; Moerhing & Green, 2005; Rothman, 2010). The University of ACME, Flagship was established 50 years prior to UALA in the northern part of the state. At that time, the city of Local Area did not yet exist. Accordingly, the state capital and related infrastructure were established in the North, where state population density was most concentrated. However, beginning in the early 1950s and continuing until 2007, the city of Local Area experienced unprecedented growth of all kinds. By the 1970s, state demographics made Local Area the only urban area in the state, which remains true today. While the current recession has had a devastating impact on Local Area's economy, causing a significant slowing of growth but not yet a decline, Local Area remains the most populous area in the state (with 22 percent of the entire state population) and the most diversely so (31.5 percent Latina/Latino, 11.1 percent Black, 6.7 percent Asian, 5.5 percent mixed, 0.7 percent Indigenous, and 47.9 percent White) (U.S. Census Bureau, 2011a, 2011b). Despite these demographic realities, there has not been an equitable shift in the allocation of state or higher-education funding from the North to the South, which has been, and continues to be, a source of tension for state leaders, especially those in the UALA administration. The proportional underfunding of UALA and the overreliance of the Local Area economy on tourism has made it difficult for UALA and for Local Area to build the infrastructure necessary to develop an educationally and professionally diversified community. There is some evidence that this reality has been carefully, politically engineered and reengineered to cultivate dependency on the tourist industry, even by largely working-class locals (Bowers, 2006; Driggs & Goodall, 1996; Moerhing, 2000, 2007; Moerhing & Green, 2005; Rothman, 2010). Accordingly, Local Area has the lowest level of education per capita in the nation (AECF, 2011; AEE, 2011; Luna, 2009; Zuckerbrod, 2007), and sound efforts to change that fact have met with somewhat surprising resistance.

At the same time, Local Area is home to a small number of extremely wealthy individuals who, because of the youngness of the state and, therefore, its remarkably flat political hierarchy, have unprecedented influence in business and government. Not surprisingly, these individuals are, in small numbers, neoliberal at best, and largely politically conservative, a mix of 'old guard' and Tea Party Republicans, and conservative Libertarians (Driggs & Goodall, 1996). One such individual, a lawyer who became a media mogul, has had significant, ultimately negative, influence on diversity in public higher education in the state, especially at UALA. This case chapter focuses on this influence.

Case Study Method

This case chapter uses Case Study Method (CSM), specifically the work of Yin (1994), Stake (1995), and Denzin (1984) to explore and explain the lived experience of diversity at UALA during the Obama campaign, election, and first-term period. While the analysis in the volume as a whole relies on broad *pattern matching* (the shared lived experience of diversity across the institutional cases), the analysis in this chapter relies on a specific form of pattern matching called *explanation building* (Yin, 1994). In explanation building, the analysis in this one case is built through the explanation of the lived experience of diversity at UALA itself. In building this explanation, the analysis emerges and is, therefore, codified. Said another way, if the data generated in this case resonates with readers' lived experience of diversity in public higher education, greater understanding of this experience is realized (Stake, 1995).

The main sources of evidence used to build the explanation herein are archival records, direct observation, and participant observation (Denzin, 1984). In linking this explanation to the rest in this volume, this case makes use of *investigator triangulation* to further establish its cogency. The additional engagement of Critical Race Theory (CRT), both in this case and across all the cases in the volume, lends also to *theory triangulation* in the revelation of shared interpretative results.

Critical Race Theory Framework

This case also uses CRT in its explanation building. Specifically, this case uses the concepts of *interest convergence* (Bell, 1992), *Whiteness as property* (Harris, 1993), and *expansive versus restrictive policy* (Crenshaw, 1988) to elucidate the lived experience of diversity at UALA.

According to CRT, interest convergence occurs when something is permitted that serves the interest of people of color, so long as it also serves the interest of Whites (Bell, 1992). However, at the point of perceived interest divergence for Whites, permission is revoked, regardless of the impact on people of color. In this case, the development of a progressively oriented, campus-wide diversity initiative is supported by even wealthy, conservative Whites until that initiative (implicitly and explicitly) outlives its usefulness to White hegemonic interests and especially when it is perceived to challenge the efficacy of those interests.

Related to the idea of interest convergence is Whiteness as property. Harris (1993) describes the idea of Whiteness as property by arguing that light skin privilege (the assumption of Whiteness) affords one advantages that operate like property rights do in daily life. Essentially, Whiteness functions as a form of currency in the lives of people perceived to be White. As currency, Whiteness has exchange value or value on which one can trade to acquire something in return, often without conscious knowledge that a trade has even been made. In this way, there is also a *transparency* in Whiteness; that is, White people often cannot 'see' or do not acknowledge their Whiteness to the extent that it affords them exclusive and unearned rights. Given that Whiteness can be assumed and not actual (based on European ancestry), it is clear that the property rights flowing therefrom have some transferability. Further, this transferability can extend beyond the assumed-to-be-White to those who are clearly 'not White' in certain limited circumstances. But, in both instances, the transfer of these rights occurs only when it serves the self-interest of Whites. For example, in

this case, members of minority groups are rewarded (financially and position-
ally) for conformity to White norms, even in the provision of campus-wide
diversity services, while others are punished (through isolation or demotion)
for their nonconformity.

To a lesser extent, Whites are also punished for nonconformity to these
norms. Because Whites are buoyed by Whiteness, even when they are punished for challenging its hegemony, the effect of their punishment is not as
great as that experienced by people of color. Jackson and Holvino (1988)
describe an organization, like UALA, that operates in this way as being at
the *White Male Club* or second stage in their five-stage continuum of Multicultural Organizational Development (MCOD), ranging from intentionally
Exclusionary organizations (e.g., the Ku Klux Klan) to explicitly *Multicultural*
ones. At this second stage, an organization like UALA welcomes members of
other groups (i.e., not White men) as long as they adhere to the preexisting
White male culture of the organization.

Finally, Crenshaw (1988) describes the relationship between expansive
and restrictive policy and law as a key element of CRT. Expansive policy
and law seeks to extend to all people what their restrictive counterparts
ascribe only to Whites. Restrictive policy and law go hand-and-hand with
Whiteness as a property right and interest convergence in that they also
support exclusivity for Whites. In this case, restrictive diversity efforts are
ultimately favored over expansive diversity efforts, for example, those efforts that focus on process (e.g., building a welcoming campus climate for
diversity), rather than those that seek results (e.g., improving tenure and
promotion outcomes for historically underrepresented racial and ethnic
minority faculty).

CDO Generation 1.0 'On Blast'

The city of Local Area received unprecedented attention from Democratic
candidates pursuing the party's nomination for the 2008 election. There were
many candidate visits to the city and to the UALA campus, and both the city
and the campus hosted a candidate debate. This preelection activity, particularly the increasing momentum that the Obama campaign was building, created the sense that there was a door opening through which diversity efforts
could move forward in a significant way on the UALA campus, and maybe
also on other ASHE campuses in the southern part of the state. Perhaps
ironically, part of this optimism was tied to the increasingly vocal "support
for diversity" being expressed by the state's media mogul-turned-system-
chancellor as the Obama era was unfolding in ACME.

While the mogul's multimillion dollar "gift" to the system served as his qualification for securing this role, he touted his business savvy as key for "turning around" some real, some perceived, and ultimately, some invented problems in the system's functioning. Concerns equity advocates might have otherwise expressed about the efficacy of the "process" by which the mogul became chancellor were atomized by his increasingly widely publicized (especially on his own local television station) desire to 'do the right thing,' especially for key Latino stakeholders in the city of Local Area.

Unexpectedly, UALA's president—ten years into that role—became the target of attack by the chancellor for what was characterized as her, at best, indifference to diversity in her campus leadership. It is of note that this president, also a scholar in her field, has a sophisticated understanding of diversity stemming from its grounding in that field. What this president may have lacked was a willingness to give dedicated time, and visible attention, to the concerns of racial and ethnic minority constituents, on and off campus, again, especially to specific Latino community leaders. Leveraging the growing divide between the president and these leaders, the chancellor very publicly and swiftly fired the president. As a result, the chancellor simultaneously named himself "defender of diversity" while padding his media empire.

The search for a new UALA president began concomitant with a push to establish a campus Chief Diversity Officer (CDO). A new president was hired with the mandate to establish and fill a cabinet-level, campus-wide diversity position. While this new president was openly politically liberal, thus generally supportive of the mandate, his leadership style was *so* hands off that once the position was filled, he did not express his support for the work of diversity (or, really, for the work in any other area of campus life) in a manner that would buoy its long-term success. Nonetheless, this president, in contrast to his so-called antidiversity predecessor, was—at least by the implication of the circumstances surrounding his hire—touted as a prodiversity president.

Interest Convergence

While it is clear that interest convergence played a huge role in the founding of the CDO role at UALA, it is not clear if any of those interests were actually sincerely committed to campus diversity work or, more importantly, to meaningfully increasing educational access and success for students from underrepresented groups. *When a person (or group of people) believes she/he is acting as (and is understood by others to be acting as) a diversity advocate for students from her/his own underrepresented group, does that necessarily mean that she/he is? That is, can the stated 'diversity' interests of people of color actually operate as White interests, or at least in the individual self-interest of certain people of color seeking individuated status in White spaces under the auspices of promoting diversity for the greater good of the underrepresented group? Further, can diversity be leveraged—perhaps even without the full consciousness of those who leverage—to undermine diversity? Said another way, can diversity be used as a vehicle through which some people of color leverage individual self-interest?* If all interests in the diversity equation ultimately serve individual self-interest, by default they serve only the hegemonic group interest of Whites. This renders Bell's (1992) interest convergence thesis somewhat inert, even if some underrepresented people ultimately derive some benefit, because the nature of the convergence is based on some false interests. This reveals an inequitable diversity reality where people of color (and White allies) have to behave better than nonallied White people— they have to operate in accordance with a revolutionary ("we") ethic in the context of reactionary ("me") societal structure—to bring about structural change within social institutions. In *Pedagogy of the Oppressed* (2000), Freire describes this reality as a function of *false generosity,* manifest as follows:

> The oppressed must not in seeking to regain their humanity . . . become in turn oppressors of the oppressors, but rather restorers of the humanity of both.
>
> This, then, is the great humanistic and historical task of the oppressed: to liberate themselves and their oppressors as well. The oppressors, who oppress, exploit, and rape by virtue of their power; cannot find in this power the strength to liberate either the oppressed or themselves. Only power that springs from the weakness of the oppressed will be sufficiently strong to free both. Any attempt to "soften" the power of the oppressor in deference to the weakness of the oppressed almost always manifests itself in the form of false generosity. . . . In order to have the continued opportunity to express their "generosity," the oppressors must perpetuate injustice as well. An unjust social order is the permanent fount of this "generosity" which is nourished by death, despair, and poverty. That is why the dispensers of false generosity become desperate at the slightest threat to its source.
>
> True generosity consists precisely in fighting to destroy the causes which nourish false charity. False charity constrains the fearful and subdued, the "rejects of life" to extend their trembling hands. True generosity lies in striving so that these hands—whether of individuals or entire peoples—need be extended less and less in supplication, so that more and more they become human hands which work and, working, transform the world. (pp. 44–45)

While a difficult circumstance emerges when White allies are not supported by the people of color with whom they profess allyship, this circumstance must also be anticipated. Equity and diversity work seeks to create avenues for access even if those who take advantage of the avenues later engage in activities that threaten continuing access to them (e.g., Clarence Thomas). Clearly then, White equity and diversity workers must continue the work with ally consciousness even when the reference point for their allyship is elusive. All equity and diversity workers must do the work, because they understand its importance independent of how any "Others" respond to it. The work is not done to please or garner approval from members of underrepresented groups. Of note, however, is how alienating and otherwise lonely the work can be.

*   *   *

The search for UALA's first CDO began in the fall of 2006 and was completed by the spring of 2007. Just prior to the selection of the CDO, the campus announced the hire of two African American men as deans of the Law School (named for the media mogul) and the College of Education. These hires, coupled with the perceived role the "Latino community" played in creating the context for the establishment of the CDO position, created a sense that the CDO hire would/should be a Latina or Latino. Finalists for the position included one Latino who withdrew from consideration following the campus interview amid speculation that he was not willing to play "stakeholder politics" (give special dispensation to the Latina/Latino community once hired). This left two African American men and one White woman in the finalist pool. As the remaining applicants were still sufficiently diverse and all easily met the advertised qualifications for the position, advocacy efforts to have the search reopened to find additional Latina/Latino applicants were not successful. Ultimately, the White woman was chosen.

Whiteness as Property Part 1

While the White woman was chosen with a clear majority of support from all parties formally and informally involved in the search, there was still a sense that the selection of a White person as the first CDO represented something less than a successful outcome. Recognizing this, the new CDO joined the UALA community determined to prove that racial and ethnic disparity issues would figure prominently in her leadership priorities—that she could/ would represent minority community interests. Theologian James H. Cone, author of *A Black Theology of Liberation* (1986), argues that:

> If whites expect to be able to say anything relevant to the self-determination of the black community, it will be necessary for them to destroy their whiteness by becoming members of an oppressed community. Whites will be free only when they become new persons—when their white being has passed away and they are created anew in black being. When this happens, they are no longer white, but free. (p. 97)

But, critical pedagogist Peter McLaren, in *Becoming and Unbecoming White: Owning and Disowning a Racial Identity* (1999), cautions:

> Becoming non-White is not a "mere" choice, but a self-consciously political choice, a spiritual choice, and a critical choice. To choose blackness or brownness merely as a way to escape the stigma of whiteness and to avoid responsibility for owning

whiteness is still very much an act of whiteness. To choose blackness or brownness as a way of politically disidentifying with White privilege and instead identifying and participating in the struggles of non-White peoples is an act of transgression, a traitorous act that reveals a fidelity to the struggle for justice. (p. 43)

UALA's first CDO—CDO generation 1.0—sought to affirmatively choose Blackness and Brownness. *But what does this choice look like in the daily professional practice of a CDO? Was CDO 1.0 able to remain faithful to this choice? Even if she were faithful, would this choice be recognized or valued by her colleagues and/or by campus and community stakeholders? How would she know for sure if it were recognized? Finally, who would benefit from this choice and in what ways, and who might even be hurt by it?* One advantage that Whites may have over people of color in engaging in social justice struggles is that in being conditioned as White people they expect advantage, not disadvantage. Thus, they operate from an intrinsic posture of habituation to access, belonging, and entitlement. Even if people of color firmly believe that they have a right to everything that White people do, they may still unconsciously or subconsciously act with greater trepidation in seeking to secure it. By the same token, Whites may be disadvantaged in seeking to be effective allies to people of color in these struggles, because in being conditioned to expect advantage, they are less likely to have developed the kind of resilience necessary to persist in social justice struggles in which successes do not come easily or quickly. This is akin to what DiAngelo (2011) describes as *White fragility*. Fortunately, in being conditioned by disadvantage, people of color are more likely to sustain struggle in the face of continuing and pervasive resistance. In seeking to choose Blackness and Brownness as a White CDO, CDO 1.0 may have opted to, at once, occupy and navigate a wilderness borderlands space.

*   *   *

CDO 1.0 came to the campus with a strong academic background in diversity—both specifically and broadly defined. She also had previous campus-wide and senior (but not cabinet level) diversity leadership experience at another, more prestigious, public research institution. During the interview process, CDO 1.0 was forthright in characterizing her philosophy of campus-wide equity and diversity work as decidedly progressive, and specifically one that considered past and continuing power imbalances in promoting social justice. She carried this forthrightness into her work as CDO 1.0. But perhaps even before this dispositional orientation made CDO 1.0 a target for attack, the growing likelihood that Senator Obama would be elected 44th president of the United States did.

In late October of 2008, the UALA campus was abuzz with student—Democrat and Republican—political activity. As CDO 1.0 walked across campus, a political science student approached her to ask if she had seen the blog of a Republican state legislator attacking her. She had not, but went immediately to her office to review it. With some fear and some amusement, CDO 1.0 discovered the state senator's attack to be largely motivated by the erroneous assumption that she and another diversity-focused academic with the same first and last name were the same person. As that other academic's research interest was in lesbian identity, the state legislator launched his attack on CDO 1.0 from a homophobic point of entry. But he did not stop there. What ensued was the suggestion that state education expenditures on diversity were a waste of money.

Perhaps sincere, perhaps not, the chancellor had been getting a lot of media attention for his opposition to ACME governor's proposed budget cuts to public education, stating that the cuts would effectively decimate the state's already ailing educational efforts. The state legislator's blog argued that UALA's expenditures on diversity were evidence that the chancellor's opposition to the governor's budget cuts were unfounded. As further evidence of this, he quoted CDO 1.0's salary, which, while high in general, was still at least $20,000 less than all of her cabinet colleagues (among whom all the women earned less than $200,000 and all the men earned more). He also erroneously stated as fact that CDO 1.0 had a big staff (she did not yet have even a permanent administrative assistant), a huge budget (she did not yet have a permanent budget), and a company car (she drove an eight-year-old, personally owned vehicle).

CDO 1.0 forwarded a link to the state senator's blog to her president via e-mail the Friday before Obama-era Election Day. The president then shared the details of the blog with the chancellor during a conversation the two had in 'the president's box' at UALA's Saturday night football game. The following Monday night—Election-Day eve—immediately following the conclusion of the news on the chancellor's television station, the chancellor's son gave an "Editorial Comment" in which he quite literally lambasted the state senator for his insensitivity to diversity and, by association, to the state's diverse residents and their children's educational needs. The next day, the state senator summarily lost his bid for reelection and, momentously, President Obama was elected.

CDO 1.0 was almost as stunned by the turn of local events as she was by Obama's win. She felt defended and affirmed in her work in diversity as never before: Maybe, just maybe, the kind of significant structural changes necessary to reverse persistent and continuing injustices could/would finally be made, not only in public higher education, but in society at large. CDO 1.0 gave it her best shot. Over the next 18 months, she helped bring serious attention to several key (sometimes controversial) equity and diversity concerns at the campus, community, system, and state level; for example, the use of noncognitive variables in admissions, unacknowledged racial biases in tenure and promotion protocols, and the complex relationship between bias incidents and hate crimes policy and law, among others. She also helped establish sustaining frameworks through which these concerns could be engaged and addressed. Most notable in this latter regard, and again with the chancellor's "support," she helped to establish a system-level diversity council.

But, a mutiny in the UALA and ASHE ranks was mounting. By the spring of 2009, mid- and senior-level campus and system leaders were becoming increasingly dissatisfied with UALA's "prodiversity" president. While this president's perceived support for diversity was really not at the crux of the dissatisfaction with him, if perceived indifference to diversity could be used to bring down one president, certainly perceived support for diversity could be used to bring down another one. Capitalizing on the cooccurring rising fear of Obama's "Black Planet," the chancellor, other ASHE leaders, several members of the UALA cabinet, influential UALA donors, and 'old guard' UALA faculty senate representatives began leaking information to various media sources that was designed to concomitantly and, again, very publicly, unseat the president, 'reel in' CDO 1.0, and stifle the work of diversity.

Whiteness as Property Part 2

While CDO 1.0 would acknowledge that she worked fast and pushed hard in ways that alienated some, while endearing others, she might argue that what she helped to bring about—the successes of the work—were actually the source of ensuing attacks on her than the shortcomings of her unapologetic approach. But it is hard to disaggregate CDO 1.0's approach from her Whiteness, especially her White privilege. Despite seeking to choose Blackness and Brownness in her decision making, CDO 1.0 at least subconsciously also chose Whiteness behaviorally. Her ability to assume an unapologetic approach in her work as CDO is, in and of itself, a function of White privilege. In this way, her professional disposition mirrored, on a smaller scale, those of the media mogul.

Drawing on the work of Bentham (1914) in *Theory of Legislation*, and Radin (1982) in "Property and Personhood," Harris (1993) describes property as expectations, and by extension, the expectations embedded in Whiteness as property in this way:

> "Property is nothing but the basis of expectation," according to Bentham, "consist[ing] in an established expectation, in the persuasion of being able to draw such and such advantage from the thing possessed." The relationship between expectations and property remains highly significant, as the law "has

recognized and protected even the expectation of rights as actual legal property." This theory does not suggest that all value or all expectations give rise to property, but those expectations in tangible or intangible things that are valued and protected by the law are property.

In a society structured on racial subordination, white privilege became an expectation and, to apply Margaret Radin's concept, whiteness became the quintessential property for personhood. (p. 1729)

In a verbal confrontation in the summer of 2009, the media mogul expected not only that CDO 1.0 would engage with local media "or else" (in many instances with reporters whom he specifically instructed to seek her out for commentary), but that she would engage them in a specific way—the same way he did: without regard for the consequences of how what he said could be manipulated. His controlling interest in local media, as well as the insulation provided by his wealth, seemingly blinded him from understanding (or caring about) the differential consequences that could come to bear on her had she done the same.

But CDO 1.0 may have at least tacitly expected colleagues with an expressed commitment to the work of diversity—perhaps especially racial and ethnic minority colleagues—to assume a similarly unapologetic approach in doing the work as evidence of their fidelity to the struggle. This expectation suggests that CDO 1.0 may have, at best, temporarily forgotten how Whiteness enabled her behavior and, thus, the differential consequences that would have accrued to her minority colleagues in attempting to behave the same way.

CDO 1.0's reaction to the media mogul's ultimatum illustrates that she did act with some trepidation—that is, despite the buoyancy of her Whiteness, she still had a sense of how deep she could swim. Maybe she did succeed in choosing Blackness or Brownness, at least in a nuanced way. Still, both the media mogul's and CDO 1.0's expectations typify the way Whiteness operates as property. While CDO 1.0, in contrast to the media mogul, recognizes and acknowledges this and that it is a bad thing, she did so in retrospect. Key for her is the development of earlier consciousness and, eventually, an ever-present one. As long as she has to think about mustering this consciousness, Whiteness still operates in her psyche in a manner that precludes her from choosing Blackness or Brownness in a more organically Black and Brown way.

The 'I' in Diversity: CDO Generations 2.0 and 3.0

While CDO 1.0 might have been expected to be (and accepted as) a personal opportunist once granted that 'seat at the [cabinet] table,' she was not expected to be (nor accepted as) an equity and diversity scholar-activist. Accordingly, recognizing that it was likely only a matter of time before she would be asked to return to the faculty following the firing of the "prodiversity" president (the one who hired her), she proactively opted out of her CDO role, assuming a 'senior scholar' position within her discipline, as well as a ceremonial 'founding CDO' title in the fall of 2009.

UALA's provost was appointed interim president. While he vowed publicly to fill the CDO role before the end of the fall 2009 semester, it was not actually filled until late summer of 2010. CDO generation 2.0 was to be selected from among the campus's existing senior *faculty* ranks to avoid reenergizing media attacks about so-called frivolous expenditures on diversity. Quite remarkably, reenergizing the prior conflict between the campus and local African American and Latina/Latino communities in this search process was not only not avoided, it was exploited. While several senior faculty members applied to be considered for the position, the African American male and Latina female selected as finalists were among the most professionally and politically opportunist segments of their respective racial/ethnic communities. Simply having named a third finalist might have mitigated the polemics that emerged in the search process that led the nonselected Latina finalist to threaten a lawsuit, which in turn, caused the selected African American male finalist to begin his CDO stint in a defensive stance.

In 2008, CDO 1.0 asked CDO 2.0 (then an associate dean) to cochair a campus-wide commission on equity and diversity. CDO 2.0 declined the co-chair position, stating that while he was a strong advocate for diversity, he did not have any formal education or professional training in the diversity arena. Accordingly, he did not feel qualified to assume the leadership role. Though after being lobbied by the interim president to apply for the CDO role, any concerns CDO 2.0 might have had about his preparedness for the job appeared to dissipate. To his credit, CDO 2.0 did approach CDO 1.0 to ask her how she would feel about him taking on this role. She expressed support for him and his professional trajectory (encouraging him to become a candidate for this position), but she also reminded him of his previously stated concerns about his academic and practical background for such a role and indicated that it would be hard for her to see him in the CDO role for that reason. It is of note that in the months prior to his hire, CDO 2.0 was in conflict with the newly appointed older, White, and male interim dean in his college. That dean position was the job CDO 2.0 really wanted. And it is possible that CDO 2.0 might have been in line to secure that position had the previous dean not also been a young, Black male who, though brilliant and quite ceremoniously hired, behaved erratically and often without any sound judgment over his less than 18-month term of employment. It is clear that CDO 2.0 became 'guilty by association' with the previous dean, not simply by being one of his associate deans, but by also being young, Black, and male. The appointment of an 'old White guy' as interim dean served as a clarion call to all those impacted by the previous dean's antics that an implicitly aged and raced form of reason would now be restored to the deanship.

The CDO position only became the focus of interest for CDO 2.0 when it became clear he would not only not get the dean job, but that he would also be asked to leave his associate dean position and return to the faculty. Interestingly, CDO 2.0 inherited a second deputy CDO (also previously an associate dean) who had, for a long time, been in conflict with her older, White, male vice president because of her proactive advocacy for students of color in her associate dean role. The picture painted by these two CDO area appointments is that when people of color become "problems" for their White supervisors (and colleagues) for whatever reason, giving them positional promotions in transferring them to the 'diversity office' is an expedient way to solve problems so that the clearly more important academic units can function unfettered by their "problem" behavior and, by extension, the problems of diversity. These are examples of what Bell (1992) calls *racial symbolism*, where so-called symbolic victories are offered in lieu of actual ones.

CDO 2.0 remained in the position for one year, during which time he was in periodic negotiation with another institution that ultimately hired him into a dean role. It is not clear what he accomplished in his year as CDO. As he is known for being a 'feel good' ambassador and an effective conciliator of minority community concerns, it is possible that his role was intentionally uneventful—to quiet the critics of CDO 1.0, at the same time allaying fears of diversity advocates that no replacement CDO would be named and, thus, that senior-level coordinating responsibility for diversity would be lost.

CDO generation 3.0 was appointed almost immediately following the departure of CDO 2.0, and he was appointed from the existing *administrative* ranks. His appointment reflects a relational demotion in, and positional deemphasis of, the role of the CDO. Previously the CDO role was exclusive—the entire portfolio of the CDO was dedicated to diversity. CDO 3.0's previous portfolio as UALA's 'government relations' liaison was combined with the CDO portfolio. As CDO 3.0's area of education and training, as well as professional and political aspirations, lie in the governmental affairs arena, it is clear that the CDO title is simply an add-on for him. Of particular note in this regard, he proudly identifies as a Republican, and he holds a leadership position in a local Latino-focused chamber of commerce.

In the fall of 2007, CDO 3.0 (then in his exclusively government relations role) was hyperbolically delighted to discover in a public conversation with UALA's Chief of Police—held in front of several UALA students—that not only was the Chief also a Latino Republican, but that he would "never vote for someone for U.S. president who could not pass the background check required to become a police officer at UALA" (personal communication, 2007). One of the first acts of CDO 3.0 was to cede the *campus-wide* diversity center, established only in February of 2009, to Student Affairs to become a primarily *student* diversity center. So while the Latina/Latino community finally got "their" CDO, this victory may ultimately be a pyrrhic one. Only time will tell.

Expansive versus Restrictive Policy

The change in UALA's diversity posture and policy from CDO 1.0 to 2.0 to 3.0 reflects movement along the continuum from an expansive conceptualization of diversity work, to a restrictive one (Crenshaw, 1988). In literally moving from a Leftist to a Neoliberal to a Republican CDO, the campus also moved from a diversity agenda that promoted results-oriented structural changes in admissions, hiring, and supplier and other administrative activities, to one that uses progressive language ("social justice") but that concentrates its efforts on student programming and conservative *governmentality* (Foucault, 1986).

Concluding Considerations

It is of note that between the fall of 2007 and the spring of 2011, ASHE lost an unprecedented 62 percent of their state funding (ADA, 2011; State of ACME, 2011). In part, these cuts were a function of the national recession brought on by Wall Street excesses. Local Area still leads the nation in foreclosures, and its continuing utter dependence on tourism, at a time when 99 percent of the nation has no disposable income, has decimated the local economy. Adding insult to injury, ACME has no state income tax, and major corporate businesses headquartered in the state pay less than 10 percent in business tax, while those headquartered elsewhere pay no business tax in ACME at all (Moerhing, 2000; Moerhing & Green, 2005).

But these cuts were also a function of the conservative backlash against Obama and the public sector as "socialist," and against public educators as supposedly incompetent, lazy, and Leftist, but really as cultivators of an educated and potentially progressively engaged and voting citizenry (Giroux, 2011b). The media has been a pivotal vehicle for transmitting this backlash. As this case elucidates, *privately owned* media can, and does, dictate diversity posture and policy in *public* higher education in some astonishingly harsh ways. Racism and other forms of discrimination can cause such extreme cognitive dissonance that people impacted by them are disrupted in their ability to build, join, and sustain coalitions for change, even when those coalitions are in their own political and economic self-interest. These social pathologies can also threaten even a staunch and astute social justice activist—especially if that activist is operating largely in isolation of any significant and staid allyship.

In closing, this case arrives at the dialogic question implied by Carr and Kemmis' work in Critical Action Research (2005): Do we want diversity *in* the school or *for* the school? UALA supports diversity for itself (restrictive policy, e.g., superficial image promotion), not for those in it or that it serves (expansive policy, e.g., sincere operational transformation). Accordingly, the school's diversity "values" change on a dime, from being leveraged for "we" to being leveraged for "me." What UALA and other public higher-educational institutions may not realize is that in selling and soul-ing out diversity, they are also selling and soul-ing out academia. The same media that exploits diversity for its value in making "conflict news" for profit is also hostile to facts, data, research, validity, integrity, scholarship, knowledge production, intellectual life, critical thinking, and a life of the mind. The *FoxNews*ification of the academy flows directly from the academy's collusion with media to reduce the work of equity and diversity in higher education to mere hospitality work. If that's the situation, in the spirit of the Occupy Wall Street protests, can I get a . . . Mic check: MIC CHECK! It's time to clean house: IT'S TIME TO CLEAN HOUSE!

2

Balancing Act

A Contextual Case Analysis on Recentering Diversity in the Midst of Social and Economic Fluctuations

Katrice A. Albert and Marco J. Barker

Historical Overview and Institutional Context

ACME State University (ASU) is the state of ACME's public flagship and top-tier university, with a Carnegie classification of high research and civic engagement activities. The university has land-, sea-, and space-grant federal designations, and boasts an enrollment of over 28,000 students and 4,200 faculty and staff (ASU, 2011a, p. 1; ASU, 2011b, para. 1). The ethnic minority and international student enrollment is approximately 20 percent (ASU, 2011a, p. 1). The largest ethnic minority representation is African American or Black at 9 percent (ASU, 2011a, p. 1). The state of ACME has an African American population over 30 percent (U.S. Census Bureau, 2011c, p. 1). Like many public Predominantly White Institutions (PWIs) in the southeastern United States, ASU has a historical legacy of ethnic minority racial exclusion (1950s), resistance toward desegregation (1960s–1970s), and demonstrated slow movement toward minority access (1980s–1990s) (Prestage & Prestage, 1988).

Given the racial disparities between state demographics and participation in higher education, universities and colleges in the state were forced to pay closer attention to these discrepancies when compelled by federal action. Between 1981 and 2004, ASU was issued a federal consent decree and a settlement agreement in *United States of America v. State of ACME* (1987). As a result, the federal government required the ASU System to take several race-conscious actions with respect to admissions and enrollment, the awarding of scholarships, and other activities to attempt to remedy the effects of institutional segregation on racial and ethnic minorities. ASU was thrust, at best, or forced, at worst, into strategic outward action around campus diversity. These actions were intended to, and in fact did, ameliorate some of the disparity in the proportionality of Black students in the state relative to those on predominantly White campuses, including ASU. In 1998, ASU's accrediting council found that diversity efforts (i.e., enrollment, curricula, faculty representation, outreach, and leadership) did not meet basic standards and required ASU to develop remedies to address the council's finding. Therefore, in the late 1990s, ASU created a senior-level administrator position dedicated to: (a) creating a vision for campus diversity; (b) developing an organizational structure with allocated resources (e.g., financial, facilities, technical, human capital); and (c) establishing a strategic plan to enhance diversity with measurable outcomes. The Office of Diversity and Outreach (ODO) was subsequently formed to support this role.

The purpose of this chapter is to provide a senior-level, institution-wide perspective on the challenges associated with advancing a diversity agenda at ASU. Specifically, this chapter examines the ways senior-level diversity professionals respond to these challenges, particularly given the economic, political, and social tensions within their institution and relative to state politics. This chapter also presents promising practices that may provide senior- or centrally located diversity professionals with situationally adaptable strategies for effectively navigating culturally tough terrain: *balancing* the quest for greater inclusion and diversity responsiveness, despite institutional pressures and resistance.

Overview of Institutional Case Study

The Diversity and Civic Engagement Organizational and Structural Model will be used to situate this case study (Williams & Wade-Golden, 2008a). Through ASU's adoption of this model, ODO came to be located in the division of academic affairs at ASU, and ODO's Vice Provost and CDO was made a part of ASU's senior executive team. The positioning of ASU's CDO in this manner dovetails with Williams and Wade-Golden's (2007) contention that a CDO must have "positional capital" communicated through an appropriate administrative title in order to be effective (p. 40).

ASU's ODO is the central diversity unit, including offices that focus on community outreach; conflict resolution; gender equity; multicultural and minority affairs; diversity recruitment, retention, and pipeline issues; training and development; and local and statewide capacity building. ODO also oversees stand-alone centers, as well as major university committees that specifically focus on civic engagement and outreach, institutional diversity practices, and women's and gender issues. Finally, ODO provides leadership for the ASU System's diversity council, which governs diversity efforts at its nine-member institutions located across the state.

Despite its extensive supervisory portfolio, ODO consists of less than 12 full-time professional and support staff members. According to Williams and Wade-Golden (2008a), this staffing level is not optimal given institutional enrollment and employment demographics alone, much less given the demographics of the larger community (over 200,000 people) to which ODO's outreach efforts are directed (U.S. Census Bureau, 2011d, p. 1). Despite staffing challenges, ODO has a solid track record spanning over ten years; that is, ODO has been successful despite human resource limitations.

With the onset of regional natural disasters in 2005, and the national financial crisis in 2008, the state of ACME experienced a cruel and unsympathetic downward economic spiral dovetailing with the election of President Obama. Subsequently, ASU has faced major funding cuts and mid-year rescissions each fiscal year (FY) between 2008–2011. While the ASU Budget Committee protected the 'institutional core' (i.e., academic colleges and schools), the committee significantly reduced the budgets of administrative areas. ODO suffered disproportionate reductions compared to other institutional administrative units like student affairs, public affairs, technology, and finance and administration. In sum, ODO had the smallest administrative budget predating this budget rescission period but incurred similar or higher budget cuts.

While enhancing diversity in higher education requires institutional commitment, initiative, strategic approach, and key programming efforts, the allocation of financial resources is paramount in making diversity work (Pollard, 2004). Further, appropriate budgeting for diversity ensures that cultural inclusion is engaged as a basic university core value (Pollard, 2004). Absent financial resources, institutional commitment to diversity comes under attack and diversity management becomes expendable. Unfortunately, this can happen even with appropriate budgeting (where the budget itself becomes the target of attack). While never equitably funded, ODO's pre-2008 budget became a target for cuts when larger financial challenges created the context for questions about the efficacy of its efforts to be raised and considered.

A national survey revealed that while diversity offices had a wide range of allocated budgets, 49 percent reported having less than $300,000 with most of these resources being allocated to skeletal staffing salaries (Jaschik, 2011). Surveyed CDOs noted further that, "When budgets fell in the fall of 2008, diversity programs were slashed" (Jaschik, 2011, para. 5). Thus, major budget reductions experienced by the ODO (and other diversity offices across the United States) can be compared to what is known as *lingchi* or *death by a thousand cuts*, a form of torture originating in Imperial China (Brook, Bourgon, & Blue, 2008). While the experience of *lingchi* in this context is not physical, it can have an especially life-altering, negative impact on those students whose success in higher education is predicated on the presence of campus diversity efforts (e.g., climate), if not altogether dependent on them (e.g., cocurricular support programs).

Although the ODO formed under federal compliance and accrediting pressures, it made significant proactive gains in advancing the university's diversity agenda. Economic instability, however, stifled ODO's growth when institutional decision makers began to question the legitimacy of expenditures on diversity and outreach initiatives instead of other, perhaps higher, institutional priorities.

Methodology

For this analysis, we use a case study approach. According to Yin (2003), case study research allows the researcher to examine a phenomenon with a particular focus on context. Cases present *special contexts and backgrounds* through which researchers explore how these contexts and backgrounds influence the environment (Stake, 2006). This case explores the role of institutional, historical, social, and economical factors in promoting diversity at ASU.

Analysis and Validity

The primary unit of analysis for the case is the university. We explore the internal (e.g., leadership behavior and decision making, institutional data) and external (e.g., communities, state government, social environments) factors impacting efforts of the university's diversity professionals to promote systemic transformational diversity at the institutional level. A secondary unit of analysis is ODO. Data sources include narratives of diversity professionals, observations, and secondary data sets (drawn from institutional, census, and other government data sources). For internal validity, we use explanation building. Explanation building is a "special type of pattern matching" or the formation of connections between the case and "theoretical, significant propositions" (Yin, 2003, p. 120). Additionally, we present *time-series relationships* for greater internal validity (Yin, 2003). Finally, we establish construct validity through the use of multiple sources of data; we also used an external diversity professional to review the study.

Theoretical Frameworks

Three critical theories serve as the frameworks for this case: Critical Race Theory (CRT), Black Feminist Thought (BFT), and Critical Whiteness Studies (CWS). These three theories encapsulate the ways in which diversity professionals, particularly those in the ASU region, experience challenges and resistance to creating transformational change around diversity in the Obama era (campaign, election, and post–first election). The three critical theories are explained in turn.

The central tenets of CRT include revealing *counternarratives* so as to unmask racism "despite espoused institutional values regarding equity and social justice" (Harper, Patton, & Wooden, 2009, p. 390) and "reject[ing] the notion of a colorblind society" (p. 391). CRT also recognizes that racism exists at both individual and systemic levels, and that its elimination must involve efforts to also eliminate other forms of oppression (e.g., ageism, homophobia, religious persecution, sexism, etc.). Another major component of CRT, *interest convergence*, exists when Whites become conscious or unconscious proponents of advancing racial equity for their own self-interest as Whites (Bell, 1992; Harper, Patton, & Wooden, 2009).

Collins (1986) identifies three major components of BFT: (1) self-defining and self-evaluating, (2) exposing interlocking systems of oppression, and (3) valuing Black women's culture. Through self-defining and self-evaluating, two processes occur: the process of "challenging the political-knowledge-validation process" that forms "stereotypical images of Afro-American womanhood" (p. S16); and the process of combating socially constructed forms of dominance by investigating the "intentions of those possessing power to define" (p. S17). By exposing interlocking systems of oppression, connections among race, gender, and class oppression and the importance of these connections are revealed. Finally, BFT requires understanding of the experiences of Black women and how Black women, "create and pass on self-definitions and self-evaluations essential to coping with the simultaneity of oppression and their experience" (p. S21). Collins (1990) captures the essence of BFT in stating: "There is always choice and power to act" (p. 564).

CWS examines how Whiteness and White supremacy operate in everyday life in seeking to unpack, address, and challenge all forms of oppression. CWS reveals the pervasive manifestations of Whiteness and, more specifically, its *language of imposition* (Delgado & Stefancic, 1997b). According to Lewis (2004), studies of Whiteness and race must examine the *history of racialization*, as well as the link between *material resources* (economic, social, and political) and especially ideological power. Delgado and Stefancic (1994) suggest that efforts to change or alter such dynamics of power will be met with a form of resistance they refer to as the *language of encroachment*. This language not only creates the "Other" or the outsider, it also positions the outsider's motive for greater equality as problematic. Common subtextual examples of this language include: (a) *What's so special about you?* (b) *After all we have done for them,* and (c) *I have problems, too* (Delgado & Stefancic, 1994, pp. 1047–1050).

Case Discussion

The election of President Obama stimulated discourse on race and diversity in America and on issues of access, equity, and participation relating to ethnic minorities in PWIs. Obama's election served as a historic moment for a "country that [has] retained a system of legalized racism" and was founded on "White supremacy, Black slavery, and Native genocide" (Wing, 2009, p. 34). The Obama era is associated with high adoption of the colorblind ideology (Wing, 2009), enactment of social policies (Mettler, 2010), and an increase in discussions on race (Asukile, 2009; McKanders, 2010; Walters, 2007), gender (Tax, 2009), multiculturalism (Brown, 2009; McKanders, 2010), and about the need to balance national solidarity and cultural differences (Edgell & Tranby, 2010).

This case analysis captures the essence of specific, instrumental experiences of public higher-education diversity professionals at the senior executive level who remain committed to advancing diversity despite "a thousand" instances of institutional resistance to diversity, including budget rescissions. This analysis focuses on how these professionals have continued their efforts while also operating in the Obama era; an era in which diversity has become a negative euphemism for a Black president, and White financial and political privilege further threatens the implementation and growth of a sustained institutional inclusion agenda.

This case gives special attention to the political savvy and artistry of these diversity professionals as they continue to challenge and expose social injustices while also forming and building collaborative relationships. According to Williams and Wade-Golden (2008a), CDOs must possess the ability to respond to "politically charged or sensitive situations . . . find win-win solutions to difficult problems," build "consensus, accrue buy-in, and reconcile competing interest" (p. 32) and continue to "leverage diversity change initiatives and fuel the diversity change process" (p. 9), all at the same time. At ASU, the CDO seeks to walk this talk.

Colorblindness and Counternarratives:
Unveiling Critical Race Theory (CRT)

Novkov (2008) fears that Obama's successful election would lend credence to the idea that the United States had achieved a postracial and colorblind state in which, "racial subordination was rendered politically unspeakable though still structurally present" (p. 658). This fear is not unfounded. Some Americans have claimed Obama's election to mean that racial equality for all has been achieved; and thus, America's history of racial exclusion can be forever laid to rest. A CRT analysis of Obama's campaign process and election illustrates how the lack of claims to the contrary (counternarratives) and the resurgence of a colorblind ideology seriously challenge diversity efforts.

While ASU celebrates a sanitized history of serving ACME's citizenry, it is imperative for ODO to provide a more critical, revisionist history that high-lights ASU's exclusionary past. While the early 1900s witnessed the admission of ASU's first Latino student and the first group of women to enter as fresh-men, the university did not enroll its first African American undergraduate until the mid-1900s (Prestage & Prestage, 1988). This student stayed at ASU for six weeks before transferring to another institution. Early ASU ethnic minority students experienced a very hostile environment; accordingly, these students' experiences were muted from discussions of the university's rich history, legacy, and tradition. To highlight the counterstories of these trailblazers, ODO actively sought to weave these alums' perspectives into the historical fiber of the institution.

ODO also sought to create a campus climate where student development within affinity groups was prioritized. While specific strategies to enhance ethnic minority participation had measurable outcomes and visible gains, the predominantly White, male executive leadership continued to operate with a colorblind ideology, unable or unwilling to recognize the hidden power struc-tures at the university that perpetuated institutional racism and (their) White male dominance. Obama's election to office reinforced this colorblind ideol-ogy (manifest in the unconsciously biased decisions of senior administrators) by offering a false sense that racial equality had been achieved.

The racially insensitive climate of the state of ACME, coupled with the po-litical aftermath of the national election of Obama, further complicated the work of the ODO. In the disbursement of state monies, the state "neglected" to give additional resources to statewide offices that focused on affinity groups. Given that the state's higher-education governance board is (and has been) 1 percent or less ethnic minority, its lack of attention to people-of-color-focused work is not surprising (Board of Regents, 2011). In addi-tion, the national political sentiment of 'change' and social equity following the election did not transfer to state-level politics, which, in turn, impacted state institutional climate. Adding insult to injury, as the national political sentiment became polarized in the aftermath of Obama's election, polemic posturing across state agencies, including public institutions of higher education, ensued.

Defining and Centering Diversity:
Embracing Black Feminist Thought (BFT)

Questions about hierarchy and representations of identities during the 2008 national election prompted debate between Black and White feminists, but these debates "consistently downplay[ed] the saliency of race" (Tax, 2009, p. 64). But, Obama's candidacy disrupted traditional definitions of race and reinvigorated the image of a multicultural America (Carter, 2009; Marquez, 2009). Obama's blended identity as a multiracial/multicultural person of color, with a unique international heritage, who shared experiences with both Blacks (Jones, 2011; Walters, 2007) and Whites (Brown, 2009) offered a different representation of race in America.

At ASU, the image of ethnic minorities as inadequate also needed to be disrupted and replaced with a different representation. Thus, ODO developed programs and opportunities that, grounded in BFT, were aimed at debunking such stereotypes in order to foster cultural awareness, knowledge building, and skills development and, thus, promote student success. The ODO also fought deficit-laden definitions of students of color by tethering its practices to the Association of American Colleges and Universities' (AAC&U) definition of "Inclusive Excellence" (Williams, Berger, & McClendon, 2005, p. vi), which stresses the benefits of cultural differences on the learning enterprise, and the importance of creating a "welcoming community" (p. vi) on the college campus in promoting student development and learning.

In the course of its advocacy for students of color, ODO also found itself needing to assert its own value and the efficacy of its work to the larger ASU community and leadership. Drawing from BFT (Collins, 1990; hooks, 2000), ODO engaged in conscious self-definition in order to center attention to diversity in all policy and related decision-making efforts. These self-definition efforts accrued central status as a campus leader to the CDO and ensured that the diversity office's role, scope, and mission continued to leverage resources necessary to continue its educational inclusion work (hooks, 2000).

For ODO's diversity professionals, ongoing self-definition means being on the frontlines where we "hav[e] the power to act" in key roles at national, state, local, and varied institutional levels (personal communication, n.d.). Nationally, the ODO is a charter institutional member of a nationwide association for CDOs. Additionally, the CDO chairs regional and statewide diversity task forces. At ASU, diversity and community outreach have been integrated, as major tenets, into the university's new strategic plan because: (a) ODO's diversity and outreach efforts across campus have been successful in creating a campus climate that values these efforts, and (b) the CDO has been able to make diversity and outreach salient in critical conversations with senior administrative and faculty leaders.

In the "Public" Interest: Unpacking Critical Whiteness Studies (CWS) through Imposition, Whiteness, and Interest Convergence

The Obama era, specifically the campaign process, demonstrates the ways in which people of color must navigate their own identity and cultural interests by carefully balancing the notion of diversity as sociopolitically *imposing* to Whites (Berlet, 2009). Scholars have posited that the politics of race and identity acted as a cultural pendulum for Obama's presidential candidacy (Asukile, 2009; Walters, 2007). On one hand, Obama represented a 'diverse' candidate who emphasized issues of cultural inequality in America. On the other hand, Obama refrained from engaging his identity or cultural inequities in his candidacy. Additionally, his candidacy presented him "as a substitute for a traditional or 'real' Black person, as a more acceptable version" (Walters, 2007, p. 9). Through the lens of the pendulum, the central, White hegemonic perspective of what a traditional presidential candidate is expected to be is revealed.

From a political perspective, cultural conservatives began to characterize Obama's policies using the *language of imposition*. For example, his policies were characterized as affording "racial privilege" and "special rights" (Berlet, 2009, p. 58), possibly falling outside of Judeo-Christian belief and, therefore, un-American. More moderate cultural preservationists intimated that Obama's attention to diversity was 'happy talk' or a way to publicly address "racial discrimination and inequality without invoking an explicit language of race" (Edgell & Tranby, 2010, p. 196).

The imposition dynamic emerged at ASU when ODO challenged the role of Whiteness on campus during economic crises. In 2008 when the national economic downturn impacted ASU Whiteness narratives became palpable and intense. To deal with the university's significant budget shortfalls, an exclusively White, majority male, ASU budget committee formed and concluded that the goals of increasing campus diversity and ethnic minority participation were peripheral to the university's central goals, including to the goal of increasing the institution's overall enrollments.

Despite ODO's existing small budget (in comparison to all other administrative areas), the committee reduced ODO's budget at the highest allowable rate every six months (i.e., successive mid-year budget cuts) for three consecutive years. The committee's decision to do this showed no regard for ODO's diversity and outreach efforts, nor any understanding of the vital roles these efforts played in campus life and the university's standing with various off-campus stakeholders. Here Whiteness and related White privilege played an absolute role in resource allocation decisions. Committee members were not active users of the services provided by ODO and, therefore, were unable or unwilling to consider the negative impact of diminishing ODO's services to already-marginalized ASU community members.

From an interest-convergence perspective, ODO is the 'go-to' unit when cultural or racial incidents occur on campus, when goodwill and humanitarian efforts are needed to promote the institution's reputation in the community, when diversity benchmarks need to be established for external accreditation, when demographic diversity impacts institutional funding, and when other matters where the university's standing or reputation are up for review. While in these moments, ASU senior leaders clearly recognize and understand the importance of ODO, they nevertheless continue to view the office as providing services that are, or should be, low to no cost. Any attempts made by ODO to secure equitable resources, even ODO's request for assistance with external fundraising, have resulted in ODO being characterized as "unappreciative," "insensitive to the university's fiscal landscape," and lacking "self-initiative" or an "entrepreneurial spirit." While other administrative units have dedicated fundraising staff, none are dedicated to campus diversity efforts.

Interest convergence also operates within the larger geographic context. When the state of ACME significantly reduced allocations for higher education between 2008 and 2011, state institutions, including ASU, were adversely affected. Resultantly, ASU developed a funding rule restricting the disbursements of funds only to initiatives or efforts *perceived to benefit the entire campus*. In response, ODO formulated small-scale fundraising strategies that included assembling external development teams composed of individuals from community, alumni, and corporate sectors. These teams also included diverse individuals (e.g., in terms of race, gender, sexual orientation, and nationality) specifically selected to also serve as diversity advocates. The team's fundraising focus served the dual purpose of reenergizing the campus' interest in diversity, while these advocates also challenged the institution to invest in inclusive excellence.

Successes and Promising Practices for the Institutional Diversity Office

To succeed in hostile social and economic contexts, it is critical that diversity offices recognize the frameworks through which they work to develop approaches that strategically recenter their offices within their institutions. Despite fiscal, cultural, and political challenges, ODO has redeveloped a diversity agenda that aligns with university goals and nationally tested, resilient practices. In this examination of our own experiences of challenge and rebound, we identify five key strategies that enabled us to sustain our success even in tough times.

Strategy 1: Institutional Mission

Diversity offices must ensure that diversity and civic engagement are part of the institutional mission and/or strategic plan, and that the goals and objectives of the diversity office are in tight alignment with that mission and/or plan. This means that the CDO or, in the absence of a CDO, another significant campus diversity professional must have direct input into the strategic-planning process.

Strategy 2: Courageous Conversations

Diversity officers, especially CDOs, must be vocal about the inequities and hidden barriers that exist on campus in conversations with senior leadership. These conversations must be undertaken in ways that ensure that leaders understand the importance of diversity in higher education. Although sometimes uncomfortable, these conversations must: (a) reveal decision-making processes that reinforce marginalization, and (b) recommend more equitable solutions.

Strategy 3: Historical Relevance

Diversity offices should develop opportunities to connect cultural histories to contemporary issues. Creating this connection has several benefits: (a) members of the institution learn about their own campus history, (b) diversity offices can reengage ethnic-minority or women alums who had negative experiences on campus, and (c) university leadership can communicate or reiterate commitments to centering diversity in campus culture.

Strategy 4: External Development

Diversity development can be leveraged by forming a national diversity advisory board and by developing small-scale alumni events. Advisory boards can push the institution to pursue large-scale funding opportunities for positive national attention, while alumni events create small victories and short-term gains that can, in turn, fuel larger development activities. Diversity offices should connect with their offices of advancement and alumni affairs to discuss opportunities for external development.

Strategy 5: Branding and Communications

Tell the campus' diversity story through marketing and press releases to ensure that diversity offices remain relevant and visible. It is essential that diversity offices form strong, working relationships with public affairs offices to devise realistic promotion strategies as there are often hidden rules that must be followed to get stories featured in popular publications.

Concluding Thoughts

Using critical frameworks of CRT, BFT, and CWS, this chapter illuminates the challenges and possibilities associated with advocating for diversity in a difficult economy and a hostile Obama-era context. Despite facing *death by a thousand cuts*, ASU's diversity professionals found innovative ways to push forward and ultimately assembled advocates, including powerful White allies, who could challenge the institution's draconian fiscal policy toward ODO.

It is our hope that other diversity professionals can learn from the challenges and promising practices we have described in this chapter. We urge our colleagues to develop "sophisticated relational abilities" to successfully challenge social injustice while simultaneously navigating hostile economic and social climates (Williams & Wade-Golden, 2008a, p. 33). To achieve this goal, diversity professionals:

> must possess extraordinary emotional intelligence, charisma, and communication skills. Given that much of the work will require lateral coordination, a CDO must be comfortable crossing organizational boundaries and adapting language and delivery to different audiences. (Williams & Wade-Golden, 2008a, p. 33)

It is important to not become overly discouraged during these difficult times. As diversity professionals in ODO, we experienced marginalization. To counter this experience, we developed effective relational strategies to recenter ourselves and our diversity message within the institution. While we have had successes, there remain many challenges to ensuring that diversity becomes and remains a top priority: This is a quest we will continue to undertake.

3

Deconstructing Hope

A Chief Diversity Officer's Dilemma in the Obama Era

A. Leslie Anderson

Situating the Case

THE HISTORY OF THE UNITED STATES HAS BEEN PROFOUNDLY SHAPED by race, at the same time racism has been marginalized as a significant factor in understanding inequitable educational outcomes in U.S. schools (Ladson-Billings & Tate, 1995). The coding of race as merely a cultural difference, especially in educational settings, obscures the active and embedded mechanisms by which curriculum, pedagogy, and policy are used to maintain racism and institutional racial hierarchies (Winant, 2000; Yosso, 2005). Thus, a critical analysis of race and racism is needed to understand the role of a Chief Diversity Officer (CDO) in higher education, particularly in the Obama era.

By the mid-1970s, legal scholars and activists began to articulate the position that U.S. Supreme Court jurisprudence relative to race actually *legitimized* racism (Delgado & Stefancic, 2000; Matsuda, Lawrence, Delgado, & Crenshaw, 1993). With the election of President Barack Obama as the nation's first president of color, we witness the rise of rhetoric about our society as now postracial, an increase in racial tensions related to a perception that existing power structures are at risk, and an unprecedented number of death threats being directed at a U.S. president (30 threats a day, an increase of 400 percent since G. W. Bush was in office) (Harnden, 2009, para. 1). Grounded in the so-called postracial Obama era, this case study uses Critical Race Theory (CRT) to analyze the development of a CDO position in a public state university.

Single Case Study

The basis for this chapter is a single-case design (Yin, 2003) in which the leadership team of ACME State University (ACME State), and their responses to the development and maintenance of a CDO position, are the objects of analysis. This case study is based on the internal dialogues of the leadership team as the CDO position is developed, as well as perspectives of campus diversity leaders, including the first and interim CDO, as the CDO's office is established.

Context

ACME State is situated in a racially and religiously homogenous rural region in the Midwestern United States; residents of the region self-identify as politically and socially conservative. Historically, the university has taken pride in this homogeneity. As recently as 2010, the enrollment of domestic students of color was under 8 percent, and domestic faculty of color ranks were under 9 percent (ACME State, 2011, p. 1; Anderson, 2011, p. 1). In 2005, like many universities across the United States, ACME State had diversity programming in student affairs and various academic departments, but lacked any cohesive campus-wide structure or communication mechanism that would have allowed these programs to become more than isolated initiatives. That same year a new university president appointed a commission for diversity and charged it with researching and recommending strategies for improving campus climate and increasing demographic diversity. In the fall of 2006, the commission's report echoed the recommendation of other diversity committees on campus: to hire a CDO who would report directly to the president or provost (President's Commission for Diversity, 2006). This recommendation was not acted upon until 2009.

In this analysis, "diversity leaders" refers to a group of four ACME State employees, both faculty and staff members, including the author. This group came together because we recognized that in order to influence administrative leaders to make substantive diversity-related changes on campus we would need to use a more tactical approach, one that necessitated our collaboration. More specifically, we four were motivated by our frustration with ACME State leadership team's lack of commitment to structural transformation, and our belief that such transformation could only be brought about with a strategic plan of action. Our group was not appointed or formally charged by any administrative body; rather, we sought each other out and then worked 'behind the scenes' to ready ourselves to take advantage of opportunities to make structural change in the institution in the moment these opportunities arose. Preparation became a prescient and effective strategy because ACME State's leadership team and governing board demonstrated only tepid support for changing the campus' compositional diversity, and no support for social justice–oriented change. Ultimately, our 'behind-the-scenes' efforts paralleled tension felt by some governing board members and, from there, became a source of enough political conflict that the decision was made to move forward in establishing a CDO position.

Critical Race Theory

CRT is primarily concerned with conceptualizations of race and racism, how groups in power demonize or marginalize other groups in order to justify their exploitation, and which voices or interpretations are considered valid. In this chapter, the development of the CDO's position at ACME State University before and after Obama's election will be analyzed with CRT through the lenses of *colorblindness* and *hegemony*.

Colorblindness

> The slick thing about whiteness is that you can reap the benefits of a racist society without personally being racist. (Powell, spoken in Pounder, Adelman, Herbes-Sommers, Strain, & Smith, 2003)

It is presumed by CRT scholars that racism, defined in both individual and institutional terms, has created and continues to maintain racial disparities in, for example, education, health care, housing, and income across the United States. These disparities exist despite a legal system that purports not only to be race-neutral, but *colorblind* (Bonilla-Silva, 2003). CRT argues that the privileging of *abstract* and *ahistorical* descriptions over *contextual* and *historical* ones enables a deceptive image of justice as (color)blind (Delgado & Stefancic, 2000).

Colorblind attitudes, like those at focus in this case, are those that purport that it is not only *possible* to 'not see race' in a racially informed and charged society, but that it is indeed *preferable* to see everyone as 'an individual.' These attitudes are fueled by conservative weariness with discussions about race (e.g., *Aren't we 'over' this already? Don't 'play the race card!' Treat everyone 'the same.'*) and liberal perspectives about transcending race and judging each person's individual merits. Only from the perspective of CRT is colorblindness challenged at its core: "If minority groups face group-based discrimination, and whites have group-based advantages, demanding individual treatment for all can only benefit the advantaged group" (Bonilla-Silva, 2006, p. 36). Accordingly, colorblindness actually serves to reinforce systemic racism and racist outcomes, which is exactly how colorblindness operates in this case.

Hegemony

> The privilege of writing and teaching history only from the perspective of the colonizer has such profound implications that they are difficult to fathom. As white people, we believe the stories we were taught are true, often failing to question and discrediting those who do. (Kendall, 2006, p. 74)

The idea that current social stratifications are *natural* relative to the social construction and maintenance of race, and particularly racial disparities, is a result of hegemonic narratives. Within culture, hegemony is achieved when certain messages are valued over others, specifically those messages that support and maintain privilege and oppression; hence the need for the CRT construct of *counterstory* (Lawrence, 1995). Chomsky (1997) argues:

> To discover the true meaning of the 'political and economic principles' that are declared to be 'the wave of the future,' it is of course necessary to go beyond rhetorical flourishes and public pronouncements and to investigate actual practice and the internal documentary record. (p. 138)

It is the *stories* of this case that create reality by defining the relationships between and meanings of events, values, and positionalities of dominance and subordination. Accounts known as *counterstories* give voice to nondominant perspectives, and help "shatter complacency and challenge the status quo" (Delgado, 2000, p. 61).

Deconstructing Hope through Colorblindness

In his March 2008 speech responding to Reverend Jeremiah Wright's incendiary comments, Obama delivered a refreshingly forthright speech that became the basis for a national conversation on race, racism, and racial disparities and their antecedents rooted in institutional bias through Federal Housing Administration loans and Jim Crow laws. Obama's message was mixed, however, as his speech also affirmed themes of postracial liberalism and common hopes, praised American progress, and inferred Black irresponsibility (Obama, 2008a). Obama's essential rhetorical 'leveling' of racial struggle became the only fuel needed for White resistance to the continuing need for racial progress to emerge in the form of colorblindness.

After Obama's election, race became both more visible and, simultaneously, more affirmatively dismissed as relevant in national affairs. The election of this *biracial* president gave society permission and encouragement to believe in the *benign nature of race* and to declare racism finally over (Crenshaw, 2011). Media sources attempting to engage the *real* historical significance of the nation's first *Black* president still did not entertain deeper discussions about the persistent significance of race. Nor was there sustained dialogue on the implications of Obama being labeled Black for some purposes, and biracial or White for other purposes. *How could a nation be postracial, while racial disparities continued to persist? And what of the contradiction inherent in the touting of Obama's election as significant because of his race and, at the same time, because it signaled that racism was over?* On the day after Obama was elected, a *Wall Street Journal* editorial opined, "One promise of his victory is that perhaps we can put to rest the myth of racism as a barrier to achievement in this splendid country" (*Wall Street Journal*, 2008, para. 4). ACME State's diversity leaders did not share this sentiment, hoping that after Obama's election the campus climate would become more conducive for deliberate and open dialogue about race and related systems of privilege in the present moment and moving forward.

Unfortunately, after Obama's election, ACME State's White students were heard remarking to Black students, "You got *your* President." The cautionary implication of this remark was clear: Racial problems are over, so discussions of race or its impact are no longer necessary or welcomed. Administrative leaders responded similarly, renewing questions about the need for a CDO. Staff, when asked what the functions of a CDO might be in the Obama era, were unable to articulate any functions beyond the desire to change the homogenous racial demographics of the campus. In response, senior ACME State staff members claimed that pressures from donors (by implication, White, conservative businessmen) suggested that the campus should "not make changes too quickly." Obama's election signaled to many ACME State students, leaders, and funders that the need for a CDO might now be moot, in essence framing not only race, but racism as a past, not present, reality.

For two decades before Obama's election, ACME State leadership supported only silo diversity programming efforts—for example, student-affairs film nights, unit-level recruitment and retention efforts, and campus-wide heritage-month activities—but only limited academic-enrichment initiatives. Numerous campus committees made recommendations to the president that articulated the utter ineffectiveness of this silo approach, and the fatigue suffered by those attempting to sustain it. Many diversity leaders across campus called for a new diversity officer who would report directly to the president or provost. This call was rebuffed by the president, suggesting that he would "need to be convinced" of the value of a CDO position. In spite of being provided with a number of compelling documents, including the Association of American Colleges and Universities' (AAC&U) three *Inclusive Excellence*-themed reports (Bauman, Bustillos, Bensimon, Brown, Bartee, 2005; Milem, Chang, & Antonio, 2005; Williams, Berger, & McClendon, 2005), the president remained firm in his belief that a CDO position was not necessary until 2009.

Accordingly, colorblindness flourished at ACME State. A singular focus on increasing compositional diversity emerged, but ironically, even with this focus the president refused to disaggregate demographic data to learn more about how various student, faculty, and staff populations were actually faring on campus in service to its compositional diversity goal. Our recommendation was for the university to explore whether, for example, retention rates, choice of major, or representation in leadership roles reflected racial differences and/or disparities. Even a climate survey conducted by *a presidential commission* yielded themes that could (and should) have been explored even if only the goal of increasing compositional diversity was sincere. But ACME State leadership was satisfied with simply having conducted the survey because this, in and of itself, could be reported as a diversity accomplishment. Using the findings of the survey as a road map in making more substantive diversity accomplishments was not on the leadership agenda. Despite leadership indifference to the survey results, concerns about the lack of culturally diverse perspectives in course instruction and about students of color having to minimize aspects of their culture to fit in on campus figured prominently. Strong student support for a diversity course requirement also emerged in the results. Of course, ACME State leadership did not assign any administrator or office responsibility for acknowledging, much less responding, to these findings.

Data disaggregation tensions also surfaced in relationship to the differences in historical backgrounds and corresponding educational and employment needs of international and domestic students and faculty of color. The ACME State leadership team's focus on international students' needs vis-à-vis its compositional diversity goal revealed an apparent desire to exclude attention to the different needs of domestic students of color. The team pointed to the combined number of internationally and domestically diverse students on campus as evidence of ACME State's diversity "fitness," thus data was to remain aggregated to surreptitiously reflect a demographic composition that appeared to be more racially diverse than it was. Further, one campus leader chided, "You act like there's a difference between international and domestic diversity" (personal communication, n.d.). The campus did finally disaggregate and report the data on both its domestic and international populations, but services for international students of color remain separate from, and perhaps more valued than, services for domestic students of color.

Colorblindness was also a dominant theme after a report on ACME State students revealed their experiences of racial micro-aggressions on campus. These findings were secured through a confidential national study called *The Voices of Diversity* (Caplan, Nettles, Millett, Miller, DiCrecchio, Chu, 2009) that allowed campus-level data to be culled. The ACME State leadership team dismissed these students' experiences as a function of individual bad behavior, rather than reflective of a larger system of privilege. In a subsequent planning retreat, administrative leaders expressed strong support for diversity efforts being oriented toward the goal of creating *a colorblind campus*. This so-called diversity goal reinforced their own dominant discourse: They could express support for diversity without ever having to acknowledge the systems of power and privilege that create and maintain the racism that makes diversity work necessary.

Even though universities across the country are establishing CDO positions, it is unclear whether the motivation for creating such roles is to bring about substantive change or merely to enhance public relations (Gose, 2006). ACME State's motivation was always the latter: to establish a senior-level diversity office to proffer the *appearance* of sincere commitment to diversity, while simultaneously structurally *distancing* the CDO from her/his own hierarchical power by: (a) forcing the CDO to convince other senior leaders (ostensibly her/his leadership *peers*) of the benefits to the campus of engaging any ideas related to diversity, and (b) by underfunding and understaffing the CDO's office relative to other senior-level offices.

Perhaps a benefit of Obama's election was that more progressive ACME State leaders could leverage largely White fear of appearing racist by not supporting diversity in seeking support for establishing the CDO position. At the same time, ACME State's leadership team was not willing to engage evidence of the need for the position—it refused to disaggregate data in order to affirm the experiences and voices of people of color on campus. The leadership team also ignored the mentorship needs of various underrepresented populations in the university community, failing to support opportunities for their advancement as students, faculty, and staff. Ultimately these dynamics came to a head and the CDO position was established, but as an interim appointment and with a vague, watered-down job description. ACME State's leadership team reduced the role of the person in this position to that of a pseudo 'ombudsman' who would simply consult with other campus leaders. Consequently, the CDO would be a figurehead lacking the necessary authority, personnel, or budgetary support to make the systemic change those who had fought to establish the position had desired.

Relentlessly Reasserting the Power of White Hegemony

> If we see race or gender as irrelevant characteristics, we have to question why white men, with very few exceptions, head all of the major institutions in this country. Either race, class, gender, sexual orientation, and physical disability are relevant to an individual's ability to gain power and access to power, influence, and resources, or all people of color, women, gays and lesbians, people with disabilities, and working-class people are personally deficient. (Kendall, 2006, p. 107)

Historically, ACME State's administrative leadership team has been composed of Whites, predominantly White men. The team was unresponsive to its racial and gender homogeneity as a matter of concern for campus diversity leaders. The team saw its composition as having evolved *naturally*. It did not see its composition as deficit in representation or related voice, much less as potentially compromising its commitment to 'ethical leadership.' When perspectives that questioned the efficacy of the team's hegemony were raised, the team's response was to silence the questions and shame the questioners (or their messenger). Four examples will illustrate this pattern of oppressive behavior and its continual reassertion of White hegemony. These examples will be delineated under the headings of: leadership communication styles, determination of relevance, strategic disconnection from power, and refusing to implement faculty accountability.

Leadership Communication Styles

Communication in ACME State's leadership team meetings often contained subtle, power-structure reinforcing messages. When these communicative messages were brought to the attention of the team by the CDO, the CDO was treated with contempt and derision. It was clear that the team had little interest in examining its leadership style, decision-making process, or agenda items relating to the work of the diversity office. One of the team members remarked, "You have offended every single person [fifteen total] in the room" (personal communication, n.d.). Hegemony is easily maintained when there are few spokespersons for diversity-related issues, and when leaders respond to even those spokepersons with anger.

Determination of Relevance

ACME State's diversity leaders recommended the adoption of a common reading for faculty that explored the impact of privilege in higher education (Kendall, 2006). The recommendation included a request for higher administration to role model the importance of this reading (and, by extension, diversity efforts in general) by leading faculty in the discussion of it. The leadership team took the recommendation under advisement. A week later the team rejected the reading, saying that it was not academic and, therefore, not relevant. ACME State diversity leaders repeatedly initiated follow-up discussions with senior leadership about privilege, systemic racism, and the ways systems of privilege undermine efforts to recruit and retain diverse populations of students and faculty. Privately, ACME State leadership just as repeatedly and quickly dismissed these conversations about systemic privilege, while simultaneously publicly touting their commitment to diversity.

Strategic Disconnection from Power

As the inaugural CDO was completing a full year of employment, the university went into a strategic planning cycle. ACME State's diversity leaders were successful in bringing concerns about educational access and success, data disaggregation, campus climate, and diversity-training requests into the strategic-planning conversation, though few of these concerns made it into ACME State's newest strategic plan. The plan gives no authority, direct responsibilities, or funding to the CDO, thus, no pathway for the CDO to achieve even the institution's stated diversity goals. As a result, the CDO's role is undermined and, along with it so too is the potential for real social change on campus.

Refusing to Implement Faculty Accountability

Though the ability to teach using a *culturally responsive pedagogy* is paramount in positively changing the curricular core of the campus, ACME State's leadership team would not require faculty to demonstrate competence with diverse populations, or make diversity-related criteria a mandated part of faculty evaluation and promotion processes (Gay, 2010). 'Faculty rights' were touted as the reason such requirements and mandates could not be made. This had the effect of centralizing of power to maintain the institutional status quo, serving, once again, to invalidate efforts toward transformative change.

Reconstructing Hope through Assessments and Strategies

This chapter illustrates the neoliberal, colorblind, and hegemonic perspective of ACME State in its approach to diversity, equity, and inclusion. While ACME State has more recently instituted several apparent changes with regard to diversity, including improving the CDO's institutional authority and responsibility, it is still not clear whether ACME State's establishment and tenuous support of their CDO role will lead to meaningful structural change. Instead, it could actually *ghettoize* diversity by limiting the institution's overall commitment to diversity, thereby further reinforcing its colorblind and hegemonic paradigms (Williams & Wade-Golden, 2008b). While Williams and Wade-Golden (2008b) argue that erroneous fear of ghettoizing campus diversity efforts has been an institutional leadership argument *against* the establishment of a CDO position, as this case illustrates, the *establishment* of a CDO position can be used by leadership toward the deliberate end of ghettoizing diversity efforts as well.

ACME State's 'town and gown' relationship has been strengthened. Key community leaders have become actively engaged in ACME State's diversity progress. Through the lenses of economic development and community vitality, city leaders have looked to ACME State for leadership on diversity development. This campus–city relationship was initiated during the first year of the CDO position with the hope that community support would bring additional strategic pressure for diversity change at ACME State over time. In the years since the CDO–community connection was first made, these external demands may finally be bearing fruit.

A number of other indicators suggest there is hope for ACME State's progress on diversity and inclusion: Domestically diverse student enrollment is beginning to increase, as are employment numbers for faculty of color; the CDO's office has been restructured to house vital campus offices and functions related to diversity; and, the university has moved from an interim to a permanent CDO appointment, and the permanent appointee's training and background offer added hope that continued progress will include meaningful, structural change.

In order to demonstrate that these changes are structurally meaningful, ACME State's leadership team still needs to demonstrate a willingness to explore systems of privilege and oppression, in order to learn how they impact students, faculty, and staff. They also need to actively seek out and express the value of input from people from underrepresented groups in their decision-making processes. In so doing, employee evaluations and student learning outcomes might begin to reflect appreciation for social justice and, in turn, the diversity office might become more adequately staffed and funded.

Reconstructing hope for ACME State requires transparency in leadership action, intentional diversification of the leadership team, and an explicitly stated focus on the value of education to *emancipate and empower* (Yosso, 2005). The dilemma of a CDO in higher education has become more complex in an Obama-era world. Colorblindness as a diversity goal has been refueled by the presence of a family of color in the "White" House, all the while White racial hegemony continues to operate. It is this hegemony that enables ACME State leaders to reject the history, experiences, and voices of persons of color, as well as to hold tight to policies and practices that fundamentally privilege Whites and, conditionally, others if they remain silent about the persistent negative realities of people of color (including their own).

In higher-education communities, everyone is responsible for diversity. Concerns about educational access and success, campus climate, representational leadership, student learning outcomes, and institutional commitment to structural change should be campus-wide concerns. Each of these concerns must be examined through a lens that: (a) recognizes the impact of history on decision making; (b) seeks to dismantle the systems of privilege that built even public higher education into the self-perpetuating, exclusive enterprise that it is; and (c) values the voices of underserved populations. When this happens, "hope" becomes more than a four-letter word; it becomes the catalyst for transformation.

4

Transforming Lives and Communities

Case Study of a Diversity and Community Engagement Portfolio at a Flagship Institution

Gregory J. Vincent, Sherri L. Sanders, and
S. Kiersten Ferguson

Overview

ONE OF THE MOST COMPREHENSIVE AND INNOVATIVE PORTFOLIOS of its kind on a university campus, the Diversity and Community Engagement Portfolio (DCEP) at the University of ACME, Flagship (UA, Flagship) presents a unique case study of diversity in higher education. This chapter provides an in-depth exploration of the portfolio divisional model at a large public research institution, utilizing relevant research literature on Critical Race Theory (CRT), the role of the Chief Diversity Officer (CDO) and related organizational archetypes, as well as the Multi-Contextual Model for Diverse Learning Environments (MCMDLE). Despite encountering challenges, including institution-specific historical and legal ones, as well as those relating to the development of a new diversity-oversight unit for previously decentralized campus-diversity efforts, the portfolio continues to make great strides in creating a more diverse and inclusive campus in a post-*Grutter* (2003) world.

Background

Situated within a large metropolitan area in the Southern United States, UA, Flagship is a selective public research university. With more than 50,000 students and over 20,000 faculty and staff members, the university is a national leader in both research and teaching (UA, Flagship, 2011a, para. 2). Despite having been segregated longer than it has been integrated, the university's

2010 incoming freshman class was diverse and the most diverse in its history (UA, Flagship, 2010). In the mid-2000s, the president of UA, Flagship emphasized the university's commitment to diversity and inclusion by establishing a vice presidential DCEP with a multimillion dollar budget. The DCEP aligned varied offices, funding streams, and work processes to establish one of the broadest units of its kind in higher education. The portfolio includes more than 50 subunits, programs, and projects that structurally span the university in order to target the different aspects of diversity and community engagement that ensure a diverse faculty, staff, and student body. The portfolio is organized into three areas: (1) academic diversity initiatives, (2) campus diversity initiatives, and (3) community engagement.

Case Study Context

According to Stake (1995), illustrative cases are one type of descriptive case study. They seek to describe and explain what is happening in a situation and why, in order to paint a situational picture. Illustrative case studies are also typically representative of important variations. This case study undertakes an in-depth analysis of DCEP in order to provide an illustration of an effective portfolio divisional model at a large research institution. This case analysis locates UA, Flagship's CDO position within an organizational framework for CDOs, defines the content of the DCEP portfolio, and analyzes the DCEP portfolio using various dimensions of the MCMDLE.

Critical Race Theory (CRT) Framework

In delineating the work of the DCEP in this case, four elements of CRT are used, very briefly, in conjunction with four of the seven dimensions of the MCMDLE. CRT's *interest convergence, permanence of racism,* and *racial symbolism* (Bell, 1992), as well as *cultural subordination* (Kennedy, 1990) introduce the discussions of the MCMDLE's historical legacy of exclusion/ inclusion, compositional diversity, psychological dimension, and behavior dimension, respectively.

Obama-Era Context

In locating this case study in the larger Obama-era context, it is important to note that President Obama's stated educational priorities consistently focus on increasing access to higher education and raising college-graduation rates. In 2011, President Obama articulated that "America will only be as strong in this new century as the opportunities that we provide . . . to all our young people—Latino, Black, White, Asian, Native American, everybody" (para. 4). Despite this national context, many universities continue to encounter obstacles to increasing diversity on campus. But the DCEP is a success story illustrating how nurturing inclusion and access on campus, while connecting intellectual resources with community needs, serves the priorities of a public research institution. By establishing a CDO portfolio equal in substance to other vice presidential portfolios, UA, Flagship president communicates the importance of diversity and community engagement to the university's core mission.

The Portfolio Divisional Model and the
Chief Diversity Officer (CDO)

Williams and Wade-Golden (2008a) identified three vertical, organizational-structure archetypes or models: (1) collaborative officer, (2) unit based, and (3) portfolio divisional. Each of the archetypes provides a "template for how an institution might design the vertical capabilities of the [Chief Diversity Officer's] role" (p. 17). The collaborative officer model tends to have a small support staff and few, if any, direct reporting units, relying on collaborative relationships and lateral coordination to accomplish its work. While the unit-based model also focuses heavily on collaborative relationships and lateral coordination, it has more staff, at both administrative and mid-level professional levels. These two models represent the most frequently used CDO role archetypes in higher education.

The portfolio divisional model contains characteristics of the collaborative officer and unit-based models, including lateral coordination, collaborative relationships, and direct reporting units; it is also vertically integrated. Nationally, of CDOs with portfolio models, 69 percent are at the vice presidential, associate vice presidential, vice provost, or vice chancellor ranks; further, 90 percent of portfolio divisional models exist in large institutions, those with at least 10,000 undergraduate students (Williams & Wade-Golden, 2008a, pp. 16, 38). Williams and Wade-Golden suggest 10 potential units that may report directly to the CDO in a portfolio divisional model. These units include: multicultural and minority affairs, international affairs, student support services, campus cultural centers, Ethnic and Gender Studies, retention and pipeline initiatives, community outreach, training and development, equity and compliance functions, and campus research centers (p. 20). Williams and Wade-Golden also identify several potential benefits of the portfolio divisional model including: (a) increased leadership capacity, (b) coordination of diversity at a high administrative level, (c) enhanced opportunities for synergy among portfolio units, (d) maximized impact across the campus and community through economies of scale, (e) consistent diversity leadership across the university, and (f) additional opportunities for linking diversity initiatives across campus (p. 23).

The Diversity and Community Engagement Portfolio (DCEP) at the UA, Flagship

The DCEP model is a portfolio divisional model. In the mid-2000s, UA, Flagship's president elevated the university's commitment to diversity and inclusion by promoting the CDO to a vice presidency and shifting the work process of the CDO from a collaborative to a portfolio model. Following the augmentation of the CDO's role and level of responsibilities, DCEP developed its infrastructure. During this portfolio development process, DCEP brought existing units from other vice presidential portfolios across campus to create the new units that came to form DCEP.

Of the 10 potential units Williams and Wade-Golden (2008a) identify for a portfolio divisional model, DCEP includes seven: multicultural and minority affairs, student support services, retention and pipeline initiatives, community outreach, training and development, equity and compliance, and various research centers. Additionally, DCEP has three large auxiliary units including a foundation for mental health that awards millions of dollars in grants and scholarships, an interscholastic league that spans the state, and a research-based demonstration elementary school. The portfolio also targets different aspects of diversity and community engagement to: (a) ensure a diverse faculty and areas of scholarship, (b) create a more inclusive campus culture, (c) support underrepresented students from prekindergarten to graduate and professional school, and (d) establish mutually beneficial partnerships with the community.

The Association of American Colleges and Universities (AAC&U) (n.d.) defines inclusion as:

> the active, intentional, and ongoing engagement with diversity—in people, in the curriculum, in the co-curriculum, and in communities (intellectual, social, cultural, geographical) with which individuals might connect—in ways that increase one's awareness, content knowledge, cognitive sophistication, and empathic understanding of the complex ways individuals interact within value systems and institutions (para. 7).

In many of his campus addresses, the university president reiterates his commitment to inclusion and the role diversity plays in furthering the mission of the university. He notes, "America draws much of its strength from its diversity—diversity of color, certainly, but diversity of culture, ideas, points of view, and skills as well. They not only make America strong—they are the *sine qua non* of university life" (Powers, n.d., para. 1). It is precisely this kind of support from senior leadership that makes it possible to meaningfully foster a diverse and inclusive campus community that truly benefits all members of UA, Flagship's community. DCEP does this by focusing on creating and maintaining richly diverse and inclusive learning and working environments across campus.

For students, the benefits of a diverse and inclusive learning environment are well documented in the research literature. These benefits include increased cognitive development, educational outcomes, leadership skills, cross-cultural understanding, and readiness for a globalized society (Antonio, Chang, Hakuta, Kenny, Levin, & Milem, 2004; Bowman, 2010; Chang, Denson, Saenz, & Misa, 2006; Gurin, Dey, Hurtado, & Gurin, 2002; Hu & Kuh, 2003; Hurtado, 2005; Milem, Chang, & Antonio, 2005). For faculty and staff, the benefits of a diverse and inclusive campus community have not yet been as thoroughly explored in research. Preliminary research suggests that benefits may include amplification of scholarly perspectives and pedagogical techniques (Aguirre, 2000; Antonio, 2002; Cooper & Stevens, 2002; Moody, 2004; Stanley, 2006a; Stewart, Malley, LaVaque-Manty, 2007; Umbach, 2006; Valian, 2004).

DCEP seeks to strengthen the university's academic and engagement missions to transform the lives of students, faculty, staff, alumni, and the community by fostering a culture of excellence committed to social justice. To achieve this vision, DCEP identified four strategic goals to guide the division's work over the next five years. These goals focus on achieving greater community engagement, and disciplinary and representational diversity within the university. The goals are to:

1. Advance efforts to create a more inclusive, accessible, and welcoming culture on campus;
2. Cultivate mutually beneficial community–university partnerships that further the mission of the university to serve the state of ACME and beyond with an emphasis on historically and currently underserved communities;
3. Create a successful pathway for first generation and underrepresented students as they progress from prekindergarten through graduate and professional school; and,
4. Serve as a national model for the creation of knowledge and best practices for diversity and community engagement through innovative scholarship, teaching, policy development, programs, and services.

DCEP and the Multi-Contextual Model for
Diverse Learning (MCMDLE)

Utilizing the MCMDLE (Hurtado, Alvarez, Guillermo-Wann, Cuellar, & Arellano, 2012) and CRT (Bell, 1980; Delgado & Stefancic, 2001; Greene, 2009; hooks, 1994; Taylor, Gillborn, & Ladson-Billings, 2009), we will now explore how race and other forms of identity continue to be significant in historical and cultural contexts at UA, Flagship. Hurtado, et al. (2012) provide a useful, multidimensional framework for understanding and describing the campus climate for racial and ethnic diversity in higher education. The key dimensions of the MCMDLE are interdependent, relate to internal and external campus contexts, and require ongoing attention. These dimensions include: (a) governmental and policy forces, (b) sociohistorical forces, (c) the historical legacy of exclusion and inclusion, (d) compositional diversity, (e) organizational structure, (f) a psychological dimension, and (g) a behavioral dimension. For the purposes of this case study, the framework is expanded to the more inclusive (i.e., race and beyond) definition of diversity at UA, Flagship, to focus on: (a) the historical legacy of exclusion and inclusion, (b) compositional diversity, (c) a psychological dimension, and (d) a behavioral dimension. Legal actions, challenges to admissions policies, and difficult economic times notwithstanding, DCEP continuously strives to move from a diverse compositional community to an inclusive campus culture where people actively and intentionally engage with diverse individuals, groups, ideas, and perspectives.

Historical Legacy of Exclusion/Inclusion

As an example of CRT's *interest convergence* (Bell, 1992), UA, Flagship's president articulates the desire to address diversity issues concomitant with: (a) increasing the campus's stature among other universities, and (b) creating social and political leaders. Specifically, the university president has said, "We cannot profess to be a great public university unless we educate a diverse group of leaders to guide the state and the nation into the future" (Powers, 2006, para. 31). However, the campus's history of segregation and subsequent desegregation provides a complex backdrop for its current diversity efforts. The university has been segregated longer than it has been integrated, and during the 1950s and 1960s, the university struggled a great deal to desegregate educational facilities, academic and cocurricular programs, residence halls, and athletics.

Like many university campuses in urban settings, UA, Flagship also borders an underserved neighborhood. Tensions between the university and the surrounding community have been tense at times, particularly in the 1960s and 1980s when the university's growth encroached upon neighborhood land. DCEP works closely with this and other proximal neighborhoods to establish and sustain mutually beneficial partnerships through: (a) a community-engagement center, (b) a research-based demonstration university elementary school for underserved families, and (c) community-recognition events.

Housed in a space rented from an African American church in the local community, the community engagement center promotes and coordinates services, learning opportunities, and research. Lower-performing schools have historically been located in the neighborhood immediately adjacent to the university; these schools have had high teacher turnover and dropout rates. To address this need, the university elementary school was located within the historically underserved community to serve not only first-generation and lower-income students, but the larger community as well. As an open-enrollment campus with a lottery-based admission system, the school enrolls students from prekindergarten through fifth grade. In addition, the university elementary school partners with UA, Flagship's college of education and other neighborhood schools through the college's urban education program. The program shares research-based, good practices in instruction with teachers in partner schools, and provides training and mentoring support to preservice teachers. DCEP and the president's office at UA, Flagship also recognize outstanding community members and organizations through annual leadership award events held at cultural centers in the community, which, in turn, further break down barriers. While UA, Flagship's historical legacy of segregation continues to affect even the current campus climate and diversity, DCEP continues to promote a more inclusive campus and is connected to community through these key initiatives and partnerships.

Compositional Diversity

Due to the *permanence of racism*, universities across the country, including UA, Flagship, have to make concerted efforts to compose a diverse population of students (Bell, 1992); that is, such populations will not emerge on these campuses of their own accord. *Compositional diversity* refers to the numerical representation of individuals from diverse social identities, in this instance, on a college campus (Hurtado, et al., 2012). DCEP coordinates and creates initiatives on campus and within the community, including recruitment and retention programs, that support achievement of a compositionally diverse student, faculty, and staff at UA, Flagship. Since the 1980s, UA, Flagship's outreach centers have served thousands of middle- and high-school students from low-income communities across the state by offering precollege preparatory workshops and academic enrichment programs on college campuses. The outreach centers' mission is two-fold: (1) to expand the pool of students who intend to go to college, and (2) to improve the number of admissible outreach students applying to the university. Of the students participating in the outreach programs in 2010–2011, 71 percent of the seniors were admitted to UA, Flagship, 50 percent of whom enrolled at the university for the fall 2011 semester (UA, Flagship, 2011b, p. 22).

Located within DCEP, the Scholars Program maximizes the academic success and social connections of underrepresented students at the university; 90 percent of program participants identify as first-generation college students, students from disadvantaged socioeconomic backgrounds, students of color, students with disabilities, and/or students with other needs (UA, Flagship, 2011c, para. 1). The program offers smaller class sizes in many math and science courses, coursework in critical thinking and college life skills, academic advising, individual counseling, peer mentoring, class registration assistance, tutoring, and cocurricular opportunities. The Scholars Program served almost 300 incoming freshmen in 2010–2011, with a first year retention rate of 92 percent (UA, Flagship, 2011d, p. 12).

In addition, the university's commitment to diversity continues to grow through an innovative thematic faculty hiring initiative which has resulted in more than 30 faculty hires and visiting professorships in colleges and schools across the campus, including fine arts, education, law, and architecture (UA, Flagship, 2011b, p. 9). The thematic hiring initiative utilizes unique partnerships between DCEP, the provost's office, academic departments, colleges, and schools across campus to attract and retain faculty members in areas of scholarship that are underrepresented in the university.

Psychological Dimension

Psychological dimension refers to individuals' perception of the learning and working environment on campus (Hurtado, et al., 2012). A UA, Flagship policy on racial harassment, established during the late 1980s, came to be viewed by students of color as a *racial symbol*, because no real consequences accrued to those violating the policy (Bell, 1992). Consequently, campus racial tensions reached a critical point in the early 1990s. A series of racial incidents at campus fraternities in 1990 led to marches on fraternity houses and to the state capital. Students also protested these incidents at a speech being given by the university president; the speech was halted by shouts from student protesters. In the late 1990s, a university law professor's racially and ethnically biased comments led to a campus rally and over a thousand students marched on the law school following the rally.

In the years following these incidents, the university has made great strides in improving campus climate. In the early 2000s, the university president created a task force to make recommendations about how to respond to continuing racist incidents on campus; for example, the egging of the campus' Reverend Martin Luther King, Jr. statue, and student organization parties arranged around racially and ethnically stereotypical themes. Another task force recommendation was for the UA, Flagship president to create a CDO position to lead an office for diversity and equity that would implement and monitor progress on all of the task force's other recommendations. A CDO was hired.

The subsequent promotion of the CDO position and creation of the DCEP reaffirmed and augmented the university's commitment to inclusion. Student-driven initiatives led the campus to erect statues of Cesar Chávez and Barbara Jordan, as they had previously with the Reverend Martin Luther King, Jr. statue. These accomplishments altered the campus' visual landscape, positively affecting the sense of whom that landscape represented. The long-standing Confederate statuary that many students viewed as a painful reminder of the state's history of segregation and discrimination was offset by the addition of statues of civil rights leaders. Another example of the university's commitment to diversity included the renaming of a residence hall previously named after a professor who played an active role in the Ku Klux Klan.

Behavioral Dimension

Because of UA, Flagship's painful history of segregation *and* integration, nondominant groups on campus have struggled not only psychologically but also behaviorally to overcome what Kennedy (1990) describes as *cultural subordination. Behavioral dimension* refers to the frequency and quality of formal and informal interactions among individuals and groups on campus (Hurtado, et al., 2012). Despite past challenges, the university's commitment to diversity continues to grow through innovative campus and community initiatives. DCEP plays an integral role in providing and promoting novel education and training around diversity and inclusion through the gender and sexuality center, multicultural engagement center, institutional equity practices, and diversity education initiatives. Through the gender and sexuality center, Peers for Pride, a peer facilitation program for academic credit, trains student facilitators to lead workshops about sexual orientation and gender identity. The multicultural engagement center provides diverse educational opportunities and support services, including student leadership institutes and summits, excellence awards, as well as annual events that foster awareness, dialogue, and community around varied social identities. Institutional equity practices support the development and maintenance of a nondiscriminatory work environment by providing an array of compliance interventions, including ombuds and counseling functions. The diversity education initiatives unit supports diversity educators in the promotion of learning that examines multiple identities from critical perspectives. In addition to providing community and university programming and consultation services through innovative partnerships, the Social Justice Conversation Series is a professional-development opportunity for DCEP leadership to meet in small-group cohorts to build awareness around, as well as discuss, social justice issues like ableism, ageism/adultism, classism, heterosexism/transgender oppression, racism, religious oppression, and sexism. The series serves as a model to the university and community by communicating that building awareness of, and improving dialogue skills around, social justice requires continuing education for *everyone*, including DCEP leadership and personnel.

Concluding Discussion

In order to make excellence inclusive, universities must "create synergy within and across organizational systems through the alignment of structures, politics, curricular frameworks, faculty development policies, resources, symbols, and culture" (Williams, Berger, & McClendon, 2005, p. 3). As the previous discussion illustrates, at UA, Flagship, the leadership and related support offered by the president has been essential for making the kinds of real and lasting changes that are necessary for inclusive excellence to take root and continue to grow on campus. In addition to elevating the CDO position to the vice presidential level and creating the comprehensive DCEP, the president of the university made diversity one of his four strategic priorities from the outset of his tenure as president. Likewise, in his state of the university addresses, diversity is a consistent and key focus: He reiterates how a supportive institutional mission affirms the importance of diversity, thereby ensuring a culture for student success.

Despite historical and legal challenges faced by the university and DCEP, DCEP's impact continues and traverses the campus and community in areas of scholarship, support for underrepresented students from prekindergarten to graduate and professional school, and mutually beneficial university–community partnerships. Advancing efforts to create a more inclusive and welcoming culture at UA, Flagship has been a challenging and long-term process. In extending this transformational change, the university continuously reexamines its long history of segregation and discrimination, at the same time implementing initiatives that ensure that diversity and inclusion are a natural part of the campus culture.

5

Southern Predominantly White Institutions, Targeted Students, and the Intersectionality of Identity

Two Case Studies

Allison Daniel Anders, James M. DeVita, and
Steven Thurston Oliver

Locating the Cases

C AMPUS CLIMATES REMAIN CHILLY for lesbian, gay, bisexual, and transgender
(LGBT) individuals on many campuses, despite specialized services
aimed at counteracting homophobia and heterosexism (Evans, 2002; Hinrichs & Rosenberg, 2002; Renn, 2010). Typically these services fail to address
the intersections of LGBT identities with other aspects of identity (e.g., race,
gender identity and expression) that have been shown to significantly impact
the experiences of LGBT students in higher education (Strayhorn, Blakewood, & DeVita, 2008). Using the concept of intersectionality (Crenshaw,
1991a, 1991b) and document analysis (Glesne, 2006), two "diversity workers"
from the University of ACME, Flagship-A (UAA) and a Chief Diversity Officer (CDO) from the University of ACME, Flagship-B (UAB), discuss campus
climates and daily life at UAA and UAB. The authors articulate the special
importance of grassroots mobilization and resource-procurement efforts for
students who embody multiple targeted identities.

Intersectionality

In her work in Critical Legal Theory and Critical Race Theory (CRT) Crenshaw (1991b) analyzes cases that required plaintiffs to argue discrimination
based on a single categorical axis of identity. In particular, Crenshaw criticizes
the courts for forcing Black women to interpret discrimination based only

on race or only on gender, but not both. In refusing to allow Black women to allege discrimination based on experiences that were raced and gendered, the courts denied the reality of the multiple intersections of discrimination in the everyday lived experiences of Black women. Crenshaw argues, "Because, the intersectional experience of discrimination is greater than the sum of racism and sexism, any analysis that does not take intersectionality into account cannot sufficiently address the particular manner in which black women are subordinated" (p. 58). Crenshaw's (1991b) use of intersectionality "highlights the need to account for multiple grounds of identity when considering how the social world is constructed" (p. 94). Separately, racism and sexism do not account for the raced and gendered discriminatory experiences of Black women. Similarly, homophobia alone does not account for the discriminatory experiences of a Black woman who also identifies as a lesbian.

Crenshaw (1991a) identifies political and structural intersectionality in her work. Political intersectionality addresses the fact that a political goal or agenda informed only by one dimension of identity ignores other social-justice goals based on another targeted social identity. For example, an anti-racist agenda may not include critique of systemic inequities perpetuated by patriarchal policies. Similarly, a feminist agenda may fail to address systemic inequities perpetuated by racism. Similarly, structural intersectionality addresses the policies, practices, and strategies of a given institution and the consequences of those structural components on individual experience.

Though Crenshaw believes intersectionality could be one way to recognize difference and still organize politically to affect change, she argues that, "ignoring difference *within* groups contributes to tension *among* groups" (1991a, p. 1242). Crenshaw critiqued the deployment of monolithic categories in identity politics, and the authors argue here that the use of "LGBT" to refer to multiple individuals and no less than four distinct communities (i.e., lesbian, gay, bisexual, transgender) erases the everyday lived experiences of multiple targeted identities. The authors agree with Crenshaw that in the pursuit of political and structural equity one must consider the intersectionality of targeted individuals.

Despite some support for lesbian and gay rights from the Obama administration, grassroots organizing efforts at UAA and UAB are better situated in the politics of their shared geographic region and on their respective campuses. Unfortunately, these more local contexts have given rise to devastating policy impacts on students, staff, and faculty members who navigate multiple targeted identities. Accordingly, the authors argue that resource distribution in higher education must take intersectionality into account when addressing student, staff, and faculty needs, because, for example, LGBT communities are not only White and middle class (DeVita, 2010; Renn, 2010).

In the following sections, the authors recount some of their experiences as diversity workers at two flagship universities located in the southeastern United States. Navigating neoconservatism and homophobia at their respective institutions and in their state legislatures, they articulate the need for more comprehensive support services for LGBT individuals in public higher education. Both case studies point to the efficacy of bottom-up grassroots organizing efforts for improving support services, and to the importance of affirming student, staff, and faculty intersectional identity (Scully & Segal, 2002). In comparing and contrasting experiences across two institutions, this chapter offers two singular case studies as well as a cross-case study (Denzin, 1984).

Case Study One: University of ACME, Flagship-A

Campus Climate

The University of ACME, Flagship-A (UAA) is a large, public, research-intensive university located in an Appalachian area of the southeastern United States. The institution is predominantly and historically White, and the student body is strongly Christian despite the public status of the university. Though the campus climate was described as unaffirming, unfriendly, and unwelcoming by students, faculty, and staff, campus leaders have cautioned against the pursuit of any diversity agenda that includes equality for LGBT faculty and staff for fear of retribution from state legislators. Campus-climate concerns have been confirmed by several UAA sources, including the Campus Climate Subcommittee Final Report (2008). Included in the report were the following troubling statistics: Over half of all openly LGBT-identified students had been harassed because of their identity, and nearly three-quarters of all African American and Black students had experienced racism on campus. The overwhelming majority of these and other targeted students believed that UAA's poor climate contributed to their feeling unwelcome, inhibited their ability to fully engage with others, and contributed to psychological distress.

Diversity Work on Campus

Although there are several initiatives directed at ameliorating the negative campus climate at UAA (e.g., Black Cultural Center and Safe Zone program), there is no CDO charged with the task of improving climate for targeted populations or with leading diversity initiatives that recognize the importance of intersectional identity for targeted students. This means that at UAA there are no administration-led collaborations designed to bring about inclusive university policies for targeted students, staff, and faculty, such as, domestic partner benefits, 'equal opportunity hire' salary lines dedicated to women of color, or special programming initiatives for LGBT Christians. Such campus leadership would help the campus to achieve political intersectionality (e.g., agenda setting), and structural intersectionality (e.g., the development of new institutional policy priorities). The 2010 report from UAA's Commission for LGBT People best characterized diversity work on campus in this way:

> LGBT students, faculty and staff, as well as the entire university community, face a reality of tension if not contradiction. Our shared, essential goals of inclusion, of justice and of doing the right thing are held in an environment of fiscal constraints, and we are ever mindful of the limitations imposed by place, time and politics. The accomplishments of the past three and one-half years (establishment of the commission itself, inclusion of sexual orientation and gender identity in the university's non-discrimination, admission and complaint policies and procedures, Safe Zone training and the opening of the Resource Center [all of which were initiatives undertaken by "diversity workers" voluntarily, that is *above and beyond* their regular duties], as important and significant as they were, may well have been the 'low hanging fruit' of a longer and more profound effort to secure full inclusion and equality for LGBT students, faculty and staff. (p. 3)

Diversity Worker Anders

In 1996, I began working in residence life as a graduate advisor at a flagship university in the Midwestern United States. At my first staff meeting with resident advisors, a courageous young woman disclosed her family's negative responses to her coming out as a lesbian and the contrasting, supportive response she received from her friends. Her story taught me to anticipate the possible needs of LGBT youth, to establish a critical and inclusive space for resident advisors, and to seek institutional support for targeted students. But at the time there was no institutional support for such things. Months after that meeting, I became a facilitator of workshops offered across campus to residence life staff members on LGBT community concerns. In the fall of 1998 when overt antigay incidents took place on campus, having Safe Zone curricula developed, immediately identifiable allies, and trained workshop facilitators available on campus was indispensable in quickly and effectively responding to these incidents.

Deeply impacted by the experiences targeted students endured on college campuses, I chose to study issues of diversity and multiculturalism. When I finished my doctorate in 2007, I began work as an assistant professor at UAA where I coupled my commitment to eradicating discrimination against targeted youth with research on theories of power in political and social contexts.

In conversations with other diversity workers on the UAA campus, I found connections across our past professional experiences and research and service interests. In sum, we shared specific interest in working to combat systemic inequities in K–12 and higher education that affect targeted youth. Through these conversations, I also learned about the state of affairs on UAA's campus regarding LGBT issues that led me to accept an appointment as the faculty chair of Safe Zone. In this role, I began facilitating Safe Zone trainings with an assistant director in residence life. Together we reviewed and expanded existing Safe Zone training curricula, and then planned four faculty and staff trainings, and two undergraduate trainings, for the 2010–2011 academic year. As a trainer, I found myself bearing witness to concerns about heterosexism and homophobia that were strikingly similar to what I had heard 12 years earlier as a graduate advisor. Hearing the staggering breadth of discriminatory comments by which members of the UAA were targeted, I recognized that UAA was at least a decade behind most campuses in establishing resources that, among other things, fostered inclusive discourse around issues of diversity for LGBT individuals. This experience reinforced my commitment to the Safe Zone program and inclined me toward grassroots organizing to bring about campus equity.

In the fall of 2010 and 2011, my colleague and I conducted a Train-the-Trainers workshop for students, faculty, and staff interested in becoming new Safe Zone program facilitators. Subsequently, these newly trained facilitators conducted multiple Safe Zone trainings for faculty and staff, and undergraduates. Since that time, over 150 UAA faculty and staff and over 80 UAA students have participated in Safe Zone trainings.

Although the Safe Zone grassroots initiative led to some positive climate change at UAA, the persistent lack of a campus CDO significantly inhibits the development of more comprehensive diversity programming. Further, absent even lower-level diversity-dedicated personnel means that this programming is undertaken only informally and only by diversity workers who chose to labor for campus equity without institutional recognition and usually on top of their primary campus responsibilities. Distanced by different department affiliations and campus roles, these workers volunteered their time to address the outrageous daily expressions of homophobia and heterosexism on campus. In sum, these workers committed themselves to bottom-up diversity work.

Diversity Worker DeVita

For two years at a small, private liberal arts institution located in the Northeastern United States, I was Coordinator for LGBT Initiatives, responsible for running all aspects of the office. Collaboration across campus was strongly encouraged, and initiatives aimed at supporting LGBT students often integrated other aspects of diversity, such as race, socioeconomic status, and religious orientation. As an alumnus of the institution, I did not openly identify as gay until I obtained my bachelor's degree, because of my concerns regarding campus climate. This status gave me a unique perspective on LGBT life on campus and a personal investment in the office's success.

Moving forward, to supplement my personal experiences and broaden my leadership skills in LGBT-focused work in higher education, I took advantage of several professional development opportunities. I attended the Social Justice Training Institute (SJTI) and several student-affairs conferences. I also sought out mentorship from colleagues in student affairs and LGBT student programming at UAA, on other campuses, and outside of higher education. These opportunities led to my involvement in other diversity initiatives.

Despite my personal and professional diversity-training experiences, when I enrolled in my graduate program at UAA in 2006, I found it difficult to become engaged in diversity work on the campus. In fact, when I interviewed for a graduate assistantship with the Office of Minority Affairs, discriminatory remarks about my experiences and related identities left me questioning my decision to attend the institution. When asked about how a White male could work in diversity programming with students of color, I described my prior experiences advising student organizations like the South Asian Cultural Club, African Student Alliance, and a Lambda Student Alliance. The snickers and cock-eyed looks that ensued gave me pause. In so doing, I employed the same facilitation strategies with the *interviewers* that I had previously used with students to get them to examine multiple aspects of their identity: As an example, I offered my experiences as a White, gay male. The search committee chair, a senior administrator and director of the office, dismissed my response and took the opportunity to "educate" me about campus priorities: Black–White issues only. The chair further cautioned me against LGBT-focused work, arguing that pursuing this work would alienate students of faith. In this instance, the search committee: (a) singularly defined diversity issues as "race," to the exclusion of other targeted identities, thereby ignoring the concept of intersectionality; and (b) reified a dominant discourse in the United States, in this instance Christianity, thereby reproducing not only Christian privilege, but the privilege of the evangelical Right. As a result, LGBT students, non-Christian students, and LGBT-identified Christian students were all summarily excluded from even the *diversity* discourse at UAA.

In my subsequent experiences at UAA, I continued to be cast as an outsider. The Office of Minority Affairs minimized LGBT topics by ignoring the fact that LGBT students can be people of color and/or people of faith. My initial frustrations with the office and the larger campus were compounded by the lack of LGBT visibility, much less LGBT-related programming. After working for two years to find and build rapport with other, more intersectionally focused diversity stakeholders across campus, I joined a grassroots effort to improve campus climate for negatively targeted, and largely neglected, populations. My professional status as a graduate research assistant afforded me access to administrators who agreed to collaborate with me to develop LGBT-related initiatives (e.g., Safe Zone trainings and even a dedicated resource center), as well as a summer bridge program directed toward improving educational access and success of "at-risk" (e.g., racial/ethnic minorities, first-generation, low socioeconomic status) students at UAA.

Case Study Two: University of ACME, Flagship-B

Campus Climate

University of ACME, Flagship-B (UAB) is a large, public, research-intensive university located in a small city in the southeastern portion of the United States. UAB is a predominantly and historically White institution located in a state where the relative lack of racial diversity challenges the institution's ability to establish a critical mass of minority populations among faculty, staff, and student ranks. Similar to UAA, UAB suffers from the off-campus perception that students of color are unwelcome on campus. The historical foundation for this perceptional legacy is closely tied to state legislative decisions. Specifically, the state was very slow to desegregate public spaces and establish laws that would allow African Americans access to educational advancement and employment in the mining, textile, and agricultural industries. As a result, there was a mass exodus of African Americans from the state, a loss from which the state has yet to recover. During a recent focus group, a Black male student described the continuing impact of the state's racist legacy on his public educational experience this way:

> I don't feel like they care about us. Like if you go to . . . I have been to a couple of teachers this semester, and it's like they're more surprised that if a black kid is coming to them. . . . They look at us like we're just space in the seat. Like they just look at us, like what are you here for? Like you're gonna fail out anyway, so just keep moving. (personal communication, n.d.)

For students of color who also self-identify as LGBT, the environment at UAB is, at best, one of cautious uncertainty. Conservative political views and the pervasiveness of right wing and fundamentalist Christian ideologies make UAB a difficult environment for anyone to come out of the closet. Further, only the most confident LGBT students, faculty, and staff risk being open about their multiple marginalized identities. Using Crenshaw's (1991a) ideas about political intersectionality, student organizational staff and advisors have been able to work with students around honoring multiple targeted identities, thereby providing student organizations opportunities to broaden and, therefore, strengthen their organizational agendas. As a result, these organizations have been able to affect campus policy positions, programming foci, outreach efforts, and resource allocation.

Diversity Work on Campus

UAB's decision to elevate its CDO to the level of a vice president was intended to signify its commitment to addressing present and historical diversity challenges. In its three-year existence, UAB's Office for Institutional Diversity (OID) has engaged deans across campus in dialogue around diversity, especially the inclusion of diversity within every unit's strategic plan.

In 2009, OID and the Office for Institutional Research conducted a "Climate for Learning" survey that sought to better understand the ways in which race impacts student perceptions of UAB. The survey found that Black students were far more likely than White students to perceive disparate treatment on the basis of race. Additionally, White students were far less open to diversity and engagement across differences than were Black and Hispanic students.

In response to these findings, OID developed training modules for faculty and staff to raise their awareness about racial *microaggressions* (Davis, 1989), the presence of *stereotype threat* (Steele, 1997), and strategies for *culturally responsive pedagogy* (Gay, 2000). While the conversation around diversity and inclusion at UAB has most frequently centered on issues of race, gender, and socioeconomic status, OID has been intentional about weaving LGBT issues throughout the fabric of its work, especially in acknowledging and honoring the multiple targeted identities that students may have. An LGBT Task Force composed of faculty, staff, and students also recommended the following: (a) development of supportive services for LGBT students, staff, and faculty; and (b) educational programs for the entire campus community. One task force member described the rationale for the recommendations this way:

> While our focus obviously is supporting the LGBT members of our UAB family, we are also serving the entire campus community. As an institution of higher education, our duty is to prepare all of our students for the diverse workforce they will enter. If one student leaves our campus without ever having engaged in conversation about LGBT issues, we have not fulfilled that duty to its fullest potential. (personal communication, n.d.)

Diversity Worker Oliver

For years as an African American working in higher education, I often resisted being engaged in diversity work for fear of being professionally pigeonholed. I had similar fears when it came to making decisions about the focus of my doctoral work, because I did not want to be seen as someone who could only work on "Black" issues. Ultimately, I heeded the words of one of my mentors who often said, "If you don't do this work, then who will?" I came to the conclusion that diversity work was my passion and the place where I could have the most influence for the greater good. In my current role as Assistant Vice President for Institutional Diversity, I often make the point that diversity work is broad, ever evolving, and necessarily includes everyone. I work hard to create spaces for students to examine their biases, explore their areas of privilege, and devise ways to function as an ally for many communities as we collectively work towards ending the oppression of all communities.

As an undergraduate, I attended a politically liberal institution where the LGBT student organization was one of the most active and vocal groups on campus. Years later, I served as scholarship manager for the Pride Foundation in Seattle; in this role I coordinated the largest LGBT student-focused scholarship program. These experiences impressed upon me the need for campus support for LGBT students. I was very pleased that when I approached my supervisor about creating an LGBT Task Force at UAB, her response was to "run with it!"

Once assembled, the LGBT Task Force quickly identified that the establishment of an LGBT center, staffed with a full-time professional dedicated to the provision of LGBT-focused education and support programs, would be the Task Force's initial priority. The Task Force was particularly concerned that undergraduate LGBT students lacked institutional support and, therefore, were asked to assume positions of critical leadership for the campus' LGBT initiatives (e.g., supporting their peers' identity development) that arguably should be the responsibility of the institution, not the students.

Interestingly, it was the search for members for the LGBT Task Force that enabled me to see just how challenging the environment at UAB was for LGBT faculty and staff in addition to LGBT students. The LGBT community was largely invisible on campus, forcing me to rely on 'word of mouth' to find individuals who were either openly gay or willing to risk being perceived as gay and, therefore, willing to serve on the Task Force. During this search process, I also learned that it was risky for junior faculty working toward tenure to be identified as LGBT or LGBT-supporters on campus.

As a part of its work, the Task Force conducted focus group sessions. In these sessions, UAB LGBT undergraduate students shared that the religiously and politically conservative nature of the campus and surrounding community was the primary source of the negative experiences they had. Reconciling sexual identity with their respective faith traditions surfaced as another recurring theme in the focus groups. In response to these findings, the LGBT Task Force sponsored a forum entitled "LGBT Issues and the Church," which featured clergy from local LGBT-affirming congregations who offered spiritual counter-narratives and alternative explanations of religious texts purported to negatively reference LGBT people.

Since this forum was held, students have shared that some LGBT students of color do not feel included in the mission and actions of the LGBT-focused undergraduate student organization. So while some progress has been made for the LGBT community and their allies, there is still work to be done. Clearly, LGBT students of color need more specific support to explore the intersections of their multiple targeted identities. The complex interplay of identities at focus here are those to which Crenshaw (1991a) refers in her conceptualization of *intersectionality*. In isolation of one another, sexual orientation and race fail to account for the embodied experiences of, and qualitative differences across, for example, a Latina who identifies as lesbian, a Black male who identifies as gay, or a White transgender person who identifies as straight.

Implications

As our UAA and UAB case studies reveal, to visibly establish equitable leadership, service, and support for LGBT and other negatively targeted students on campus requires diversity workers to, in varied measure, harness their experiences of outrage, employ grassroots organizing strategies, and procure resources by leveraging top-down institutional governance. As Pascoe (2007) asserts in his research on masculinity and heteronormativity in a U.S. high school, students navigate not only dynamics of gender expression, but also dynamics that are classed, raced, and sexualized. Applying understandings of *intersectionality* (Crenshaw, 1991a, 1991b) to decision-making practices in student life is, therefore, clearly paramount, particularly on campuses saturated by histories of racial discrimination and related violence, as well as mainline and fundamentalist Christian ideologies.

Typically, research on LGBT populations has addressed issues of their visibility, identity development, and campus climate concerns (Renn, 2010). In seeking to extend these foci, the authors introduced the importance of political and structural *intersectionality* (Crenshaw, 1991a; 1991b) in improving experiences for LGBT people in higher-education contexts. While on some campuses social-justice action and/or university leadership have created a comprehensively inclusive, LGBT-friendly environment, this is largely not the reality at UAA, and is not yet fully the reality for UAB. For flagship universities in regions marked by both political and religious conservatism, the awakening progressive transformation at UAB offers some hope. LGBT advocates at UAA reference the proactive pursuit of equity for the LGBT community and the establishment of equitable benefits at UAB in committee meetings, commission meetings, and informal employee-activist conversation as evidence that local change is possible. These cases can stand alone or together in illustrating the power of grassroots work and the important role that intersectional consciousness can play in that work. Together these cases capture the potential value of nurturing regional cross-campus alliances in advancing intersectional equity goals.

Stories from the
Mid-Level Administrator Frontlines

Bailey W. Jackson

THE LAST CASE STUDY IN THE FIRST SECTION and all the case studies in this second section focus principally on the broad roles of Mid-Level Administrators (MLAs), some of whom are also faculty, working across myriad campus contexts. The practitioner-researchers who author these cases offer real-time, on-the-ground narratives of what equity- and diversity-directed change work involves at office, unit, departmental, and campus-wide levels.

MLAs may have campus-wide responsibility (e.g., sexual harassment prevention and diversity training), or they may only be responsible for a single department's or division's efforts (Queer Studies, etc.) or for a particular dimension of diversity (e.g., race-conscious hiring, or programming for women). Both campus-wide and dimension-specific responsibilities can derive from, or be designed to support, a larger institutional change plan. Thus, MLAs characteristically have a 'view from the middle,' looking from above, below, and across while simultaneously being looked at by other campus constituents from these same vantage points.

MLAs' contexts for carrying out their work can be within departments, units, divisions, or colleges, or out of a senior administrative office with institution-wide purview (including the office of a Chief Diversity Officer). Their work can focus on protecting the rights and safety of those who are commonly the targets of social injustice (underrepresented members of protected class groups)—often called 'equity work.' More often their work focuses on promoting awareness, knowledge, and understanding of differences broadly considered—commonly referred to as 'diversity work.' Accordingly, the MLA often wears multiple hats as investigator, mediator, conflict resolver, facilitator, trainer, and educator.

The authority MLAs have is usually limited; their units might oversee complaints of discrimination and harassment, but not be empowered to sanction senior administrators no matter the violation, or their offices may be responsible for vicarious liability reduction through the provision of required sexual harassment training, but still be unable to compel faculty to complete the training. Still, there is a hope that the work of MLAs will influence those in supervisory positions (at all levels within the institution) to make policy and procedural changes that can move quadrants of the institution, and eventually the institution as a whole, farther along the Multicultural Organization Development (MCOD) continuum from Exclusionary to Multicultural.

Because the MCOD process fluctuates in relationship to an institution's stage of MCOD, institutions in the first three stages of MCOD (Exclusionary, White Male Club, and Equal Opportunity Compliance) often limit the transformative impact that diversity work can have on campus by relegating it to the purview of one, entry rank MLA in a single office with oversight responsibilities focused only on dorm life, or only on secretarial and trades support-staff orientation. Institutions in the last three stages of MCOD (Affirmative Action, Redefining, and Multicultural) are more likely to distribute responsibility for diversity work to several MLAs at multiple ranks of employment (entry, middle, and supervisory), and to ensure the work is specialized to campus function (student, academic, administrative affairs) and geared to constituent needs (e.g., first-year undergraduates, international graduate students, adjunct instructors, tenure-track faculty, administrative supervisors, academic administrators). All of the cases in this section describe institutional movement along the MCOD continuum from Exclusionary toward Multicultural, in some instances jumping two stages forward at one moment, and a stage backward at another. Case 9 articulates the movement of a single institution through the first five stages, and into the sixth. Case 8 describes an institution's struggle to move through the second stage. Case 10 illustrates campus forward movement from the second to the fifth stage, backward movement to the second stage anew, and then forward movement to the fifth stage once again. Case 7 delineates the dynamics of an institution in the third stage relative to its location within a campus system at the fifth stage. Finally, Case 6 elucidates an institution stalled between stages four and five, struggling to maintain forward movement. These cases illustrate the challenges associated not only with initiating MCOD, but in continuously sustaining its movement toward lived multiculturalism.

6

The Myth of Institutionalizing Diversity

Structures and the Covert Decisions They Make

Mark Brimhall-Vargas

"We cannot exercise power except through the production of truth."

—Michel Foucault (1980b, p. 93)

Diversity Caught in the Middle:
The University of ACME, Flagship Context

THE UNIVERSITY OF ACME, FLAGSHIP (ACME) is a large public institution of higher education located in the mid-Atlantic region of the United States. At one point in its history, the university refused to admit African Americans, going so far as to pay the tuition of potential admits to other institutions to maintain a "Whites-only" campus (Clark, 2005). Today, the campus has largely embraced the idea of diversity to counteract the negative image it had during its overtly discriminatory past. In many ways, this history has created two competing images of the university with respect to diversity, and paradoxically, both are true. On the one hand, the university has made remarkable strides in its efforts to diversify the campus writ large. For example, the current undergraduate student body is composed of 34 percent students of color, with African American students constituting 12 percent and Asian American students constituting 15 percent. The university is also first in the number of doctorates granted to African Americans, and parity has been achieved between male and female bachelor's degree and master's degree recipients since 2001 (ACME, 2010, p. 9). Conversely, the institution lags behind similar institutions in terms of the dedicated resources to the populations mentioned above. An example of this is that, to this day, the university does not have a women's or a multicultural resource center, nor is there any current, serious effort to bring either one of these about.

An initial explanation for these competing images suggests that the university has been particularly sensitive to the need to raise external, nonstate support resources at a time of fiscal constraint and ongoing right-wing attacks toward public-educational expenses. As higher education increasingly comes under fire from the political Right, the process by which ACME has defended itself involves moving presumed tangential concerns (like diversity and equity, but also humanities, education, social sciences, and the liberal arts) lower on the list of priorities, or compromising them completely when financial resources are very tight. Conversely, those academic areas at ACME that directly reflect emerging business or national security interests have gained human, fiscal, and physical space resources, as well as influence over the university's priorities and direction even during this time of fiscal constraint. Examples include the expansion of *global* contractual relationships with China and the Middle East, while efforts to preserve and carry out the local land grant mission to *local* communities are neglected.

It is within this dynamic that diversity and equity efforts on campus are now squeezed. But the truth of the matter is that diversity and equity efforts on campus were never founded on the premise of increasing university access to emerging global capital markets, nor were they ever adequately resourced to succeed in any meaningful and large-scale way in their domestic focus. Because campus diversity offices are aware of the new resource priorities, they now preoccupy themselves with a desire to *add (not replace)* an international focus to their work, ultimately spreading out their mandate and thin resources even further.

It is also important to recognize that the competing images of ACME stem from the fact that the people in the institution are much 'farther along' than the structures of the institution, creating a perpetual drag effect on diversity and equity efforts on the campus. This chapter seeks to assess the structures of diversity implementation at ACME, not the sincere personal commitments of those persons involved in those structures. Indeed, my experience suggests that diversity practitioners and scholars at ACME are genuinely concerned about realizing a transformative vision of diversity at the institution. I scrutinize the structural implementation of those diversity efforts instead, because I propose that the results may be structurally predetermined despite the genuine efforts of those involved.

Use of Case Study

To analyze ACME, I start with a premise that case studies should *by definition* rely on "multiple sources of evidence, with data needing to converge in a triangulating fashion" and pay strict attention to "prior development of theoretical propositions to guide data collection and analysis" (Yin, 1994, p. 14). In terms of the *theoretical proposition*, I make use of Critical Race Theory (CRT) as explanatory of the behavior in and potential outcomes of this case. Sources of evidence include my own experience as a diversity practitioner at ACME, ACME's stated diversity plan for the next decade, and its current organizational norms regarding the creation and maintenance of structure.

Specifically, I use a single-case design with multiple, embedded units of analysis to explore the larger institutional pattern (Yin, 1994, p. 40). These multiple units of analysis include my own diversity unit, where I have been a diversity practitioner for approximately 15 years, the larger constellation of diversity units organized under the new Chief Diversity Officer (CDO), and the new campus-wide Diversity Advisory Council (DAC), to be implemented in the near future. I use a single-case design to make sure that I am allowing for interaction across the various units of analysis in an "integrated system" where "the parts do not have to be working well, the purposes may be irrational, but it is a system" (Stake, 1995, p. 2).

In viewing these various units of analysis, I recognize the speculative nature of assessing a diversity structure as it moves into the future with a new administrative head. I agree, however, with Merriam's (1998) assertion that:

> Speculation is a key to developing theory in a qualitative study. Speculation involves 'playing' with ideas probabilistically. It permits the investigator to go beyond the data and make guesses about what will happen in the future, based on what has been learned in the past about constructs and linkages among them and on comparisons between that knowledge and what presently is known about the same phenomena. (p. 190)

The key here is that the freedom to *speculate* is still being checked by two self-policing standards. As the researcher, I must connect: (1) the speculation to past constructs and linkages, and (2) to rational comparisons of existing knowledge. Thus, I rely heavily on past experience to inform future speculation about the structural analysis that follows. I also rely on my own subjectivity within the context of ACME. Indeed, that subjectivity is a strength in this case study process, because "subjectivity is not seen as a failing needing to be eliminated, but an essential element of understanding" (Stake, 1995, p. 45).

Two Critical Lenses: Sociology of Knowledge and Critical Race Theory

A problem arises when I consider the structure of ACME using case study method. Specifically, the requirement of triangulation of evidence asks me to consider the location of knowledge, within or outside the system, and whose perspective actually counts as valid or reliable evidence in this analysis.

I resolve this question through the use of Critical Theory in the sociology of knowledge by asserting the value of what Geertz (1983) calls *informal knowledge*. Geertz validates this location of knowledge as connected to, and representative of, the knowledge ordinary people develop to deal with their everyday lives (Gramsci, 1971). In other words, my own perspective is one which contains information on the way an average diversity practitioner's knowledge is developed to deal with the university circumstances as they are, especially if those circumstances come in an intertwined mixture of good and bad. And by naming my own experience, I participate in the "insurrection of subjugated knowledges" and expand on what is considered possible in the current status quo (Foucault, 1980b, p. 81).

Coupled with the sociology of knowledge, I connect my own experience with my observations of larger patterns of oppression described in CRT. As a Critical Race Theorist, Lawrence (1992) has stated the need to privilege the perspective of those directly involved in any situation. He says: "The Word . . . embraces positioned perspective. It recognizes the impossibility of distance and impartiality in the observation of a play in which the observers must also be actors" (p. 2252).

This analytical approach suggests the need to be sensitive to the particular ways that the experience and outcomes related to race indicate larger patterns of oppression within a system or group. Specifically, I seek to make use of my own counterstory to explore several facets of established CRT: (a) a tendency in higher education to engage in *imperial scholarship* (Delgado, 1984), (b) the *dilemmas of serving multiple masters* (Bell, 1976), (c) *interest convergence* (Bell, 1992), and (d) the *permanence of racism* (Bell, 1992).

From Imperial Scholarship to Imperial Organizational Development

At the highest level of analysis in the institution, ACME has recently hired a new CDO to move the institution's diversity efforts forward, and, in my estimation, this person will likely do a very good job *as that job is conceived and constructed*. Though this person is very bright, skilled in diversity work, and has the academic credentials to garner respect throughout the institution, the frame into which the new CDO is placed is somewhat limited in title and overt power. It is this limitation and the way that limitation came about that I seek to narrate. Foucault (1980a) illustrates the purpose of a structural narrative as illuminating the distinction "between structures (the thinkable) and the event considered as the site of the irrational, the unthinkable, that which doesn't and cannot enter into the mechanism and play of analysis" (p. 113).

Thus, to name this phenomenon, I borrow from the work of Delgado (1984) and his concept of *imperial scholarship*, which describes the practice of White academics doing research on people of color without reference or serious engagement of the work of academics of color with contrary perspectives. In the context of this case, I translate imperial scholarship into Imperial Organizational Development (IOD) to describe the way in which senior-level administrators at ACME quietly made decisions about the CDO position in a way that supplanted the overt recommendation of campus experts (people of color, women, LGBT (lesbian, gay, bisexual, and transgender) individuals, and people with disabilities) for their own, more palatable version.

Though senior administrators clearly have the right to make decisions about positions in the institution, Delgado's (1984) objections stem from the notion that their decisions may be: (a) faulty, and (b) self-interested. Referencing two groups of people, A and B, where A is a disempowered group and B is the empowered group, Delgado states: "While the B's might advocate effectively, they might advocate the wrong things. Their agenda may differ from that of the A's, they may pull their punches with respect to remedies, especially where remedying A's situation entails uncomfortable consequences for B" (p. 567). This is exactly what happened to the CDO position at ACME.

The diversity steering committee in charge of developing the strategic plan for diversity made recommendations for the CDO position that explicitly stated the committee's desire that the position be a new vice presidency in order to ensure the person hired into the role would have political clout and resources. The recommendation stated: "The president will appoint a chief diversity officer (preferably a vice president with faculty rank) who reports directly to the president and is a member of the President's Cabinet" (ACME, 2010, p. 14). Instead, the leaders of the institution chose to modify the very first goal within the institution's diversity strategic plan by demoting the CDO from a potential vice presidency to an associate vice president under the provost. During the time this recommendation was being discussed and quietly vetted, it was no secret that many senior leaders, including several other vice presidents, objected to the idea that the CDO would be a vice president. Perhaps these objections stemmed from perceived turf issues, a fear of a potential loss of resources/offices into the new CDO's jurisdiction, and/or jealousy that the CDO would also be organizationally one step from the president. Regardless of individual motives here, I believe that Delgado's (1984) conclusions about imperial scholars apply. He says:

> I reject conscious malevolence or crass indifference. I think the explanation lies at the level of unconscious action and choice. It may be that the explanation lies in the need to remain in *control*, to make sure that legal change occurs, but not too fast. (p. 574)

In essence, senior leaders, with no academic expertise in diversity or equity, supplanted the first recommendation of a committee of campus diversity experts *that they charged.* Consequently, the CDO position was established with less formal power than was originally recommended.

This decision created a sense of ambiguity around accountability for change across campus. *Who is ultimately responsible for success of the institutionalized effort?* The strategic plan for diversity suggests that there are many collaborative arrangements between the CDO and the new DAC, but does not specify who is actually in charge. In one section, the DAC is said to "advise" the CDO, putting the CDO in a subservient role.

> The university will create a campus-wide diversity advisory council with representatives from all divisions, schools/colleges, graduate and undergraduate student bodies, and other appropriate units, to play a key role in *advising* the chief diversity officer regarding diversity decision-making, planning, and training [emphasis added]. (ACME, 2010, p. 15)

Yet in another part of the document, the CDO appears to have an executive role with a coequal legislative body, much like a governor and legislature: "The chief diversity officer, *in consultation with* [italics added] the Diversity Advisory Council, should develop measures to monitor and evaluate the success of plan goals and strategies" (ACME, 2010, p. 27). Elsewhere, both the CDO and the DAC are both described in terms that indicate an overt lack of formal power to move forward processes over which they are assumed to have responsibility. Instead, power and authority seem vested in nonequity/-diversity experts and broad constituencies across campus—people *outside* the entire diversity and equity structure:

> Their success will depend, in part, on their ability to *seek the advice and counsel* of expert and engaged faculty, staff, and students from across campus as they pursue these goals; their *willingness to support* bold initiatives; and their *acceptance* of patience and flexibility in finding ways to achieve their goals [emphasis added]. (ACME, 2010, p. 27)

The issue is that the senior leaders at ACME have primarily concerned themselves with the procedure through which a CDO, or an accompanying DAC, would pursue the work, as opposed to both the outcomes of that work and the connection of those outcomes to the authority necessary to bring them about. Unfortunately, this appears to be consistent with the model of a CDO as *only* a collaborative leader currently most in vogue in higher education (Williams & Wade-Golden, 2007).

Serving Two Masters: One Visible, the Other Invisible

Concurrent with the arrival of the new CDO, the new strategic plan for diversity at ACME seeks to replace the existing Equity Council (EC). This is of note as the primary responsibility of EC members is unit-level oversight of search and selection processes. The EC would be replaced with the new DAC, the responsibilities of which far exceed those of the EC. Specifically, the new DAC members are selected and charged as follows: "Units represented on the diversity advisory council will appoint diversity officers who will be responsible for providing diversity education and training, overseeing climate assessments, and supporting diversity-related recruitment/retention, programming, and evaluation efforts within the unit" (ACME, 2010, p. 15).

That the EC is being replaced with the DAC and its more robust mission is not surprising. This body was not always perceived as helpful in resolving equity concerns on campus. The questions this change begs however are: *Why is the EC being replaced at all? If it is ineffective, what made it ineffective? And what is the potential impact of replacing a body primarily charged with **equity** functions with a body primarily charged with **diversity** functions?* The answers can be found in the structural history of the EC member selection process.

Though an associate vice provost chairs the EC, EC members do not report to, and are not supervised by, the chair. Instead, EC members are appointed by heads of their respective units to provide oversight of equity concerns *within* the unit. In essence, they are appointed as watchdogs to their own supervisors and coworkers, and they are asked to perform this function on top of their existing job functions and with no supervisory oversight by the EC chair—the person with actual responsibility for equity on campus. The result is that some unit heads appoint employees who have genuine interest in and/or expertise appropriate to the EC, while others appoint employees who know nothing about equity and are sometimes hostile to the very mission of the EC. For example, some members of the EC spoke overtly *against* recognizing sexual orientation as a protected category in the campus' Code on Equity, Diversity, and Inclusion (then called the Human Relations Code) during senate hearings on the matter a number of years ago. Regardless of the predisposition of the EC member, the work of the EC has always placed several dilemmas before its members: (a) they may "visibly" report to the EC chair, but their actual performance reviews are conducted by those unit heads who appointed them to the EC and, therefore, function as their "invisible" equity supervisors; and (b) all the work for the EC is done as an add on to their respective work functions and, thus, frequently receives much less attention than someone who would be singularly dedicated to equity work.

Bell (1976) describes this situation as one where the individual EC member *serves two masters*, not unlike when civil rights attorneys found themselves caught between attempting to represent the interests of their Black clientele and (White) professional procedures in their field. Of this situation, Bell's concept suggests that the EC members will find themselves in a similar "lawyer-client relationship" dilemma where "it is difficult to provide standards for the attorney and protection for the client where the source of the conflict is the attorney's ideals" (Bell, 1976, p. 472). To punctuate the point, Bell cites Luke 16:13: "No servant can serve two masters; for either he will hate the one, and love the other; or else he will hold to one, and despise the other" (p. 472). Thus, it was the structural selection process that made the EC an ineffective body, even when it included membership who were genuinely concerned with equity and worked tirelessly to bring it about.

The new DAC only compounds the dilemmas of the EC as: (a) DAC members no longer have authority resting in equity law and policy, instead they must rely on convivial relationships to be successful in their DAC roles; and (b) the scope of DAC member responsibilities has ballooned to now include diversity-related training, education, recruitment, retention, and evaluation/ assessment efforts. Given that EC members struggled against the weight of competing structural forces arrayed against them, it is far less likely that DAC members will be able to effectively undertake these tasks while similarly reporting to two masters: the visible, but not supervisory CDO, and the invisible, and ultimately more powerful, immediate supervisor and their appointer to the DAC.

Interest Convergence: When the Diversity Tab Does Not Get Paid

In the lowest level of analysis, my own office at ACME is an exemplar of what happens when diversity rhetoric meets the harsh reality of diversity under-resourcing. The Office of Diversity and Equity (ODE) (a pseudonym), one of the few offices on campus charged with both diversity and equity functions, is often called upon to meet new challenges on the diversity frontier *with* faculty, staff, *and* students, while also being available to conduct discrimination complaint intakes *for* faculty, staff, *and* students based on protections in the campus' Code on Equity, Diversity, and Inclusion (ACME, 2010). In other words, the ODE is asked to be all equity and diversity things to all people on campus.

To meet this mandate, ODE has a history of having been supported with up to nine full-time staff, upwards of nine graduate assistants, and numerous undergraduate students, some who worked in the office on financial aid funds.

Over time, however, this support has dwindled to the point where ODE now has four full-time staff and a half-time graduate assistant. Despite the steady decrease of personnel to address campus-wide mandates on both diversity and equity fronts, the burden of responsibility to meet these needs has not ebbed. Resultantly, steady and predictable job intensification has ensued leading staff members to ceaselessly leap from one new project to another, all the while maintaining steady service provision in compliance intake, sexual harassment prevention training, and intergroup dialogue programming.

The experience of ODE over the past decade points to another CRT concern known as the *interest convergence dilemma*. In this dilemma, diversity efforts are supported only insofar as they are in the current interest of the group in power (Bell, 1992). Once those interests diverge, however, support dwindles. Bell (1992) says:

> When whites perceive that it will be profitable or at least cost-free to serve, hire, admit, or otherwise deal with blacks on a nondiscriminatory basis, they do so. When they fear—accurately or not—that there may be a loss, inconvenience, or upset to themselves or other whites, discriminatory conduct usually follows. Selections and rejections reflect preference as much as prejudice. (p. 7)

ODE's interests aligned with administration interests when it was necessary for the institution to have an office that was technically responsible for every facet of diversity on campus. When that impossible mandate was not swiftly achieved, however, ODE was seen as comparatively expensive to other offices with a much more focused mission.

To compensate for this loss of resource support, ODE has sought to institutionalize some of its programs in the hopes that other units would be interested in subsuming them, even if for these other units' own interests, as opposed to the existing campus-wide ones. In theory, such an approach would then allow ODE staff to focus their attention elsewhere. The acceptance of ODE's intergroup dialogue program courses as meeting the cultural competence requirement in the campus' general education curriculum could, again theoretically, be seen in an example of this institutionalization effort. The university's strategic plan for diversity even made specific mention of the program and the need to continue its growth and success in the manner that its incorporation into the general education curriculum communicates. This plan states: "The university will continue to support intergroup dialogue programs that expose students to the identities, backgrounds, cultural values, and perspectives of diverse students, and that enhance their communication, intergroup relations, and conflict resolution skills" (ACME, 2010, p. 22). In being institutionalized in the general education curriculum and supported by existing campus diversity rhetoric, ODE staff assumed that additional campus resources would eventually flow to support the program, especially given its campus-wide popularity, even if those funds were temporary at first. While the campus, through the previous provost, initially agreed to fund half of the program for three years, after this provost left, his successor immediately took back that commitment, only agreeing to continue it through its then current year. Ultimately, it would seem that even a successful diversity office and/or program is only "supported" when it is as cost free as possible to do so.

Structures in Opposition as the Permanence of Racism

Though this case chapter may appear to leave little hope for significant institutional change, the realities this chapter delineates have not, in fact, demoralized diversity and equity effort at ACME. Cautious optimism continues to exist on campus because those scholars/practitioners dedicated to social justice have refused to quietly disappear into obscurity. Despite the institution's business-related interest convergence, these scholar/activists' efforts have brought about the establishment of a bona fide CDO position. Thus, ACME has responded to its internal diversity stakeholders by institutionalizing higher-level oversight of processes that have often resulted in inequity, discrimination, and a lack of inclusion. In this sense, diversity efforts have gained traction.

Yet, as my assessment in this case suggests, the new CDO is not structurally situated within the institutional hierarchy to ensure success, nor the success of campus diversity efforts. Though the CDO position is permanent to the extent that it is now a part of this hierarchy, it continues to be operationalized in a disempowered David versus Goliath–like manner relative to the institution's "traditional" permanent structures. Clearly, it is these traditional structures that actually steer the institution's true interests; thus, it is not surprising that these structures face little resistance when they avoid meaningful diversity and equity interventions that most other quadrants of the campus are required to engage. As a result, meaningful diversity-related change does not occur even though diversity efforts have been institutionalized. In short, as diverse players become more permanent members of the team, the traditional rules of the game are changed making the game more difficult for them to play well, much less win.

This case chapter lends credence to the idea that the institutionalization of diversity offices, programs, personnel, and efforts is not enough to secure the social justice outcomes the institutionalization may be perceived by some to imply. Without a corresponding de-institutionalization or intentional scaling back of the entrenched, and heavily resourced, structures of dominance and invisible decision making, the institutionalization of diversity creates merely a stalemate. In this stalemate, a largely unchanged, though perhaps annoyed, larger, stable, academic structure exists in connected stasis with a smaller, struggling, and ultimately disempowered diversity structure.

In considering this notion of stalemate vis-à-vis Bell's (1992) notion of *permanence*, I am also reminded of Bell's insistence that social justice advocates embrace *racial realism*—an understanding of the permanence of racism in the American body politic. In the context of higher education, this means that any *seemingly* permanent (stalemate) change in the rules in a progressive direction requires a corresponding and *actually* permanent (permanence) response: When a new player scores a goal, the referees will compensate by devaluing the worth of the goal in order to maintain the competitive advantage of the status quo. So, even when a CDO is appointed, she/he is unlikely to have the staffing and other resources that other senior staff members enjoy. This is the reality of the new CDO at ACME in the Obama era: Institutionalized gains, rooted in the real struggle of real people, do little to change the 'on the ground' realities for diversity. I fear that these efforts will ultimately produce what Bell (1992) has characterized as "another instance—like integration—that Black folks work for and White folks grant when they realize—long before we do—that it is mostly a symbol that won't cost them much and will keep us blacks pacified" (Bell, 1992, p. 18).

Coda

As I consider the future of ACME, I realize that much of its current institutional structure is created and supported by people who believe it to make sense; to, in fact, be rooted in "common" sense. Thus, this analysis is offered with a compassionate nod toward common sense. At the same time, this analysis also seeks to remind people that common sense is obviously informed by traditional (White) institutional power. As Hall (1988) puts it, "Common sense is itself a structure of popular ideology, a spontaneous conception of the world, reflecting the traces of previous systems of thought that have sedimented into everyday reasoning" (p. 55). My genuine desire is for a more socially just future at ACME which requires *uncommon* sense.

7

Swimming up Mainstream

Facing the Challenges to Equity, Diversity, and Inclusion on a University of ACME, Regional Campus in Obama's Era

Virginia Lea, Hollace Anne Teuber,
Glenda Jones, and Susan Wolfgram

Our Case Context

EQUITY AND DIVERSITY WORKERS KNOW THAT THE EXACT PROCESS for creating the conditions for equity, diversity, and inclusiveness to flourish is illusive. In this case study, we have taken the perspectives of colleagues and students who are underrepresented in higher education and constructed a composite minority account in attempting to build a *thick*, holistic picture of diversity at University of ACME, Regional (ACME, Regional) (Merriam, 1998). While we are mindful of the negative connotation the term "minority" carries in a society that values majoritarianism, our use of this term refers, broadly, to members of our campus community who are Black, Hispanic, American Indian, or Hmong (whose ancestors originated from Laos, Vietnam, or Cambodia), as well as those who are underrepresented by virtue of their status as women or as lesbian, gay, bisexual, transgender, or queer (LGBTQ), or by socioeconomic class, ability, or age.

We engage Critical Multicultural and Cultural Studies Theory (CMCST) to illustrate how powerful race, gender, class, and other master narratives can be produced and reproduced through Whiteness, dominant worldviews, and liberal discourse. CMCST derives from Critical Race Theory (CRT) and Critical Theory (CT). Cultural Studies (CS) is grounded in CT via literary criticism (During, 2003) and Critical Multiculturalism (CM) emerging from the application of the CRT's sociopolitical lens to multicultural education (McLaren, 1997). While CMCST is not a formally codified theory, the manner in which we use it herein draws from the work of Steinberg (2001) in examining the ways in which racism, classism, sexism, and other forms of oppression inter-lock in the academy.

We are concerned with the *daily struggle* against oppressive narratives and practices. We use metaphor and conscious listening as methodologi-cal tools to create counter narratives in exploring this concern. We identify the hegemonic processes through which administration and faculty seek, intentionally, to enhance what some see as the "problem" of diversity on our campus, and we assess the effectiveness of these processes. Three interrelated contexts—political, administrative, and social/cultural—are used to build our case. Our analysis reflects the direct impact of both national and state politics, and other significant political forces on educational and workplace dynamics at ACME, Regional.

The Political Context: We Needed Revolution, Not Reform

> The age of Obama has fallen tragically short of . . . a revolution in our priorities, a re-evaluation of our values, a reinvigoration of our public life and a fundamen-tal transformation of our way of thinking and living that promotes a transfer of power from oligarchs and plutocrats to everyday people and ordinary citizens. (West, 2011)

In the age of Obama, we are witnessing the opposite of West's revolution. The United States Department of Education (USDE) has reported out data from thousands of school districts that demonstrate that students across the country do not have equal access to a rigorous education (NCLB, 2002, based on ESEA, 1965). Simultaneously, the USDE promotes educational policies that are being challenged on the basis of their effectiveness (Delpit, 2006; Kozol, 1991; Ravitch, 2010). What constitutes PK–12 education is determined by a series of interlocking, historical mechanisms of power, the outcome of which is that the quality of children's schooling is generally determined by the zip code in which they reside. That method distinguishes not only postal mail assortment, but also the sorting of individuals into second and third classes by predetermining educational quality, status, and attainment based on their particular zip code (Coles, 2001). This sorting process is associated with the appallingly low school graduation rates of 40 to 50 percent for students in major U.S. city urban schools, exacerbated by a Black male student high-school dropout rate of 52 percent (Grey, 2008, para. 2; Lilley, 2010, para. 1).

From primary and secondary public schools, these inequities spill upward into institutions of higher education like ACME, Regional. Even with federal student-loan programs, young people from poor families and/or families with low occupational status, especially from African American, Latina/Latino, and Native backgrounds, have had disproportionately less access to higher education (Education Trust, 2010). There are "more African Americans under correctional control today . . . than were enslaved in 1850" (Alexander, 2010, para. 5). *What would be the societal response if 53 percent of White male students dropped out of school and ended up in prison?*

The largely fictional American dream narrative is about social mobility. As long as people *feel* they have a fair shot at building a better life—by working hard and playing by the rules—the dream remains alive. Particularly in times of economic turmoil and high levels of social inequality, many people rely on the belief that education provides the best means to upward mobility. Unfortunately, being born into economic and/or racial privilege is the most direct and reliable path to success. Federal and state economic policies, and related corporate malfeasance, have led to further diminishing public services and corresponding increasing disparities between rich and poor (Rose, 2007). Socioeconomic status largely dovetails with racial and ethnic segregation given that a disproportionate number of poor people are also people of color (Pebley & Sastry, 2004). This apartheid affects revenue bases, the level of services that cities or counties are able to provide, public health and child welfare, school delinquency and academic problems among youth, and a host of other related issues, all of which have great consequence for an institution like ACME, Regional (Lea, 2008).

The Administrative Context

Hegemony . . . is a whole body of practices and expectations; over the whole of living. . . . It is in the strongest sense a culture, but a culture which has also to be seen as the lived dominance and subordination of particular classes. (Williams, 1977, p. 110)

To understand the daily struggle—how equity, diversity, and inclusion outcomes have played out with respect to contradicting notions of liberal rhetoric and hegemonic economic priorities at ACME, Regional—a review of system and campus administrative history is required. In 1988, the University of ACME System acknowledged the disparity of access and opportunity for minority, low-income, and underrepresented groups. The Board of Regents adopted a 10-year initiative called *Design for Diversity* that focused on seven specific goals to "improve educational quality and access for all students so that they are equipped with the necessary personal and professional skills to be successful in their lives and to help our state remain economically competitive" (University of ACME System, 1988). This neoliberal plan continued until 1998 when *Plan 2008: Educational Quality Through Racial/Ethnic Diversity*, a new system-wide initiative, was implemented by the Board of Regents, providing another 10-year framework aimed at removing barriers associated with race, ethnicity, and economic disadvantage (University of ACME System Board of Regents, 1998). This plan, like its predecessor, refocused the seven goals from the original plan to create academic and economic opportunity for minority students' success and persistence through graduation. While this plan increased minority student recruitment and enrollment throughout the system, core change never fully materialized. ACME, Regional's campus branding changed from a comprehensive to a polytechnic campus; concurrently, in an effort to focus resources on increasing the overall number of students of color (recruitment), services dedicated to actually support minority student success were reduced (retention).

In 2008, the University of ACME System moved to a more inclusive concept of diversity, thus focused efforts on increasing the visibility of, for example, Women's Studies, as well as cultural group development initiatives like multicultural and LGBTQ student services. The system was now looking beyond *Plan 2008* and for a more all-encompassing plan, accordingly it adopted a new infrastructure change process committed to *integrated and sustainable change through intentional action*. The upper-level administration of ACME System has a history of quickly adopting the most recent initiative promoted by the Association of American Colleges and Universities (AAC&U) so, not surprisingly, the new change process was referred to as *Inclusive Excellence* (IE) and modeled after the framework laid out in AAC&U's then-new monograph titled, *Toward a Model of Inclusive Excellence and Change in Postsecondary Institutions* (Williams, Berger, & McClendon, 2005). The IE plan was disseminated to regional campuses laying out the system's new equity, diversity, and inclusion priorities in this manner:

> Inclusive Excellence is a planning process intended to help each institution establish a comprehensive and well-coordinated set of systemic actions that focus specifically on fostering greater diversity, equity, inclusion, and accountability at every level of university life. The central premise of Inclusive Excellence holds that colleges and universities need to *intentionally integrate their diversity efforts into the core aspects of their institutions*—such as their academic priorities, leadership, quality improvement initiatives, decision-making, day-to-day operations, and organizational cultures—in order to maximize their success [emphasis added]. (University of ACME System, 2009)

The IE change model continued the seven goals of *Plan 2008*, but extended the focus of them to multiple groups (i.e., beyond race). In theory, IE would help University of ACME System institutions dismantle group-specific silos; silos that were indeed evident on the ACME, Regional polytechnic campus.

As the IE change process began at ACME Regional, a series of equity, diversity, and inclusion-related setbacks on campus occurred. ACME Regional announced a *two-year* position development and hiring process for an Assistant Vice Chancellor that would have a joint appointment as Director of Diversity. The person hired into this position would then spearhead the implementation of the new IE plan on campus. But the announcement demonstrated that the campus administration had no clear understanding of IE as an organizational change model; in particular, the kind of person the administration was looking to hire was not someone with senior-level experience in diversity work. Academic silos remained in operation, and by the end of the second year of the position development and hiring process, it became apparent to those directly involved in the process that a skilled professional, with specific background in developing and implementing positive change outcomes for equity, diversity, and inclusion, was what was needed for the new plan to work.

In early 2010, a search for an Assistant to the Provost for Diversity Affairs was conducted, seemingly without input from campus diversity leaders, but failed to produce a hire. After reevaluating why the search failed, the position title and responsibilities were reconfigured with input from campus diversity leaders. The new search announcement, posted in late 2010, elevated the position to an Assistant Vice Chancellor for Equity, Diversity, and Inclusion. The process by which the position description was changed as well as what the changes made to it signaled, for the first time, that campus administration really cared about the IE change model—that it was not just words on a page, rather it was an important and meaningful *human* change process. The daily struggle had finally paid off. The spirit of hope that the system's actions in this regard cultivated led campus offices to willingly dedicate campus funds to hire this new CDO and ready to respect the authority of the person selected for the job. A national search was conducted, and early in 2011 finalists were interviewed.

In January 2011, immediately following the election of an ultra conservative governor, the budgets of the already-compromised public sector in the state of ACME were severely crippled. The effects were devastating statewide, and included abandonment of ACME, Regional's search for an Assistant Vice Chancellor for Equity, Diversity, and Inclusion. The campus administration's low prioritization of equity, diversity, and inclusion resurfaced. In spite of ongoing rhetorical commitment to the IE process, actual commitment to it was relegated to the back burner. ACME, Regional's strategic planning process, Focus 2015, articulated only the campus Chancellor's diversity priority: to implement plans to increase enrollment, retention, and graduation of minority students. Twenty-three years after ACME System announced its focus on compositional diversity in *Design for Diversity*, ACME, Regional was reannouncing its focus in this area and this area alone, ensuring that campus equity, diversity, and inclusion efforts would remain in silos, not integrated throughout the campus. Hegemonic thinking on ACME, Regional's polytechnic campus has relegated campus-wide responsibility for diversity change to the Chancellor's deficit-based approach and located it within the campus' strategic planning process. Any real hope for meaningful and sustainable campus-level change has been summarily compromised. The daily struggle continued.

Social and Cultural Context: Focus on the Classroom

To understand the daily struggle to meet real equity, diversity, and inclusion goals at the department/classroom level within the context of a top-down hegemonic system, a review of campus faculty history is required. ACME, Regional faculty and students are hungry for the realization of the meritocracy story that President Obama has implied he represents (Obama, 2008b). This story is predicated on the idea that the playing field is level and neutral, thus if one works hard, the merits of that hard work will result in achievement of the American dream.

In ACME, Regional classrooms, most students express a belief that it is possible to go from 'rags to riches' through hard work; students cite icons such as Oprah Winfrey and President Obama as evidence of this possibility. While they may inspire millions of people, Winfrey and Obama inadvertently perpetuate the myth that if they can raise themselves out of humble origins, then anyone can. With this myth deeply impressed in their hearts and minds, ACME, Regional students are hard-pressed to recognize the invisible structures of power that operate to perpetuate class stratification—that keep most Americans in the same social strata their entire lives.

While the intent of CMCST at ACME, Regional is to develop student critical consciousness, the meritocracy narrative works against this consciousness from taking hold. The pervasiveness of the meritocracy narrative bars students from developing the critical consciousness necessary to seeing the actually unjust nature of society, concomitantly compromising realization of ACME System's larger "inclusive excellence" mandate. First-year composition and Women's and Gender Studies program courses at ACME, Regional are two academic areas where the daily struggle to develop student critical consciousness is most daunting.

Hegemonic institutional structures are slow to change; consequently, they do not easily make space for bottom-up commitment to CMCST to permeate campus life. Further, the polytechnic branding of ACME, Regional has changed the nature of its academic offerings to students, as well as many faculty members' expectations of student performance. In ACME, Regional's writing program, hegemonic institutional structures make it difficult for faculty to agree to the shared use of a critical pedagogical framework. Further, the polytechnic focus of the campus means no English major is offered; instead, faculty members teach only composition courses. Because of the scarcity of positions nationally for English faculty members to teach in their primary area of interest and expertise of literature, many faculty members teach composition courses as introduction to literature, thus compounding their opposition to teaching writing alone, not to mention from a critical pedagogical framework.

A critical pedagogical framework can certainly be used to teach literature; the literature texts chosen for students to read could offer students insights into the injustices of American capitalism (Berlin, 1993). However, faculty opposes this idea as well because teaching students to look at the world through such literature is challenging. Students have emotional and intellectual reactions to this content that requires a higher level of engagement from faculty. CMCST sees the production of knowledge as a political practice. As a part of this practice, CMCST explores forms of power including race-, class-, and gender-related power; institutional power; and the power dynamics embedded in colonialism. This practice leads students from agency to action (Hall, 1997). Accordingly, faculty members have to be prepared for the daily struggle of student resistance to counterhegemonic narratives, as well as student engagement of these narratives over time. Teaching becomes about much more than content learning, it becomes a path to student self-determination and liberation from oppression.

While faculty resistance to CMCST in writing courses might be anticipated, its resistance in Women and Gender Studies courses might come as a surprise. While ACME, Regional's Women's and Gender Studies program is rooted in the feminist and progressive movements of the state of ACME going back many years, as a result of ACME governor's 25 percent budget cut to state higher education, this program is fighting for survival (WSC, 1999). Consequently, while program faculty members are committed to the use of a critical pedagogical framework in their courses, their preoccupation with funding has meant curricular and instructional concerns get back-seated.

Ideas from the Tributaries:
How Do You Mainstream a Diversity Priority at a
Predominantly White Polytechnic Institution Despite a
Hostile National and State Political Climate?

In 2001, ACME, Regional received the Malcolm Baldrige National Quality Award for performance excellence and quality achievement. To promote itself relative to this award, ACME, Regional leadership imposed (top-down) a policy that led to adoption of a campus-wide applied learning model in 2002. Adoption of the model turned the institution into a 'laptop campus.' In 2007, the 2002 policy was further enjoined by a 'sustainability' policy. Unlike its previous lukewarm commitments to equity, diversity, and inclusion priorities, ACME, Regional leadership's commitment to the applied learning and laptop campus priorities were immediately strong and sustained over time, illustrating that the administration does provide start-up and long-term resources (personnel and funding) to initiatives they value, especially those that are also valued by conservative politicians in the state and nationally.

This chapter's title references "swimming up mainstream." Our discussion within this chapter focuses on the "daily struggle" of equity/diversity workers. Mainstream runs downhill, and equity/diversity workers swim upstream within the mainstream. Taken together, we envision equity/diversity work like one might envision a salmon's spawning journey. While the institution may not recognize it, we, equity/diversity workers, bring rich tributaries of knowledge and experience into the academy. If these tributaries were unobstructed (e.g., if access was undammed), and then supported to flow into the mainstream current of the academy, mainstream knowledge and experience would become a multicultural tidal wave of positive change for all institutional members. Instead, these tributaries continue to be siloed, at risk of becoming isolated oxbow lakes.

ACME System funding has enabled: (a) the *Infusing Diversity across the Curriculum* ACME, Regional faculty-led workshop to continue its work to help campus faculty integrate elements of diversity into their courses; and (b) the ACME, Regional's Women's and Gender Studies program to continue, and even expand, its offerings to promote greater inclusion (for example, the study of race and class through the gender lens). But such system support also precludes campus leadership from having to commit resources to these efforts, and ultimately from having to make and honor an institutional commitment to actualizing IE, despite system directives. Racial and Ethnic Studies course requirements, revised in 2007, will finally be implemented in 2012. A campus and community unity day, Festival of Humanity, proposed in 2007, will not be implemented until 2013. A long-needed LGBTQ coordinator position has finally been funded, but only half time. While faculty and staff members of the campus's Pride Alliance and student members of the campus's Gender and Sexuality Alliance made compelling arguments for how a full-time position could be funded, campus leadership opted only for the half-time position. Individual faculty research provides insight into the ways hegemonic barriers to economic, cultural, and academic equity and inclusion impact minority students on the ACME, Regional campus. While this disjointed pattern of engaging equity and diversity continues at ACME, Regional, without a substantive institutional commitment to these efforts, the broader campus community only understands equity and diversity as the problems of a few, not as important enrichment priorities for all. While this renders them simply a nuisance in the minds of many, in continuously reengaging them, we ensure, at least for now, they will be a nuisance that does not go away.

Conclusions

After more than 20 years of trying to realize genuine equity, diversity, and inclusion on the ACME, Regional campus, we still feel we are swimming upstream against the current of resistance to meaningful change. The new ACME, Regional IE mandate does not seem to promise such change: It is framed through liberal discourse and predicated on Whiteness and middle-class life as "normal." But the mandate is not only negatively influenced by hegemonic processes internal to the university, but also by related political and economic hegemonies operating in our state and the country as a whole. A maelstrom of hegemonic narratives encircle the mandate ensuring that it will never advance beyond Nieto's (1994) *tolerance level* of multiculturalism at ACME, Regional. As a result, the mandate encourages superficial acknowledgments of underserved populations in a largely 'heroes and holidays' fashion. In this way ACME, Regional serves the perceived, but not actual, interest of these populations, while simultaneously expecting them to quickly as-*swim*-ilate into the mainstream culture of the institution.

There is no urgency for radical change in the current hegemonic political and economic climate. Bell (2004) has suggested that the history of the United States is replete with governmental actions that offer a measure of redress for the discriminatory practices of the past, but then weaken or abandon these actions when they threaten to restructure society against the perceived interests of the mainstream. We see this same practice at ACME, Regional—the opening and closing dams that periodically allow, but mostly prevent, the flow of equitable, diverse, and inclusive tributaries into the mainstream. As a result, while engaging students in critique of hegemonic narratives is an educational process that should emanate from the tributaries into the mainstream, this process is blocked by the silt that is race- and class-based oppression. While our "swimming upstream" imagery might suggest that our work to bring about equity, diversity, and inclusion is futile, we do not believe that it is. Even if making meaningful top-down structural change to the existing system is beyond our reach at the moment, our bottom-up work *is* making a difference in the lives of some students and faculty members. We are, at the very least, taking some of the neoliberal and ultra conservative toxicity out of the water, with the hope that more underserved students and faculty may become party to the progressive educational pool. It is worth the swim.

8

The Search for Questions and Tellings of Silenced Students

Douglas J. Loveless and Bryant Griffith

Coherence and Context

DIVERSE INDIVIDUALS INVOLVED IN TEACHING AND LEARNING sometimes characterize education as an unpredictable search for coherence. Because all people come from richly varied backgrounds, effective learning involves serious mutual exploration of those differing backgrounds in educational settings (Lankshear, Snyder, & Green, 2000). Educational *coherence*, consequently, involves engaging in a shared discourse community where all members of the community actively choose to communicate, question, and share pursuit of academic and social goals (Borg, 2003; Weiner, 2007). Educational coherence should not be misconstrued as eliminating difference by replacing the search for coherence with a push to silence and enforce conformity with the dominant group on those who are different from it.

This chapter discusses the experiences of diverse individuals at ACME A&M University, Regional (A&M, Regional), an institution of higher education near the border between Mexico and the United States. Grounded in a Critical Race Theory (CRT) framework and employing Case Study Method (CSM), we examine barriers to coherence, collaboration, and the expression of diverse ideas in the effort to illustrate how individuals overcome such barriers, and use their distinct narratives to engage in *self-authorship* in the teaching and learning process (Bhabha, 1990).

The Obama Era

We live in a continuously conflicted, but also transforming, society. Diversity issues garner more attention as all people increasingly interact with others who are different from themselves through geographic mobility and/or expanding forms of communication.

The outset of the Obama era brought hope for social and educational reform (Suoranta & Vadén, 2007). Yet, while more racially, ethnically, gender-, and religiously diverse perspectives have gained currency during the Obama era, the status quo continues to marginalize racially, ethnically, gender-, and religious-minority ones (Duncan-Andrade & Morrell, 2007). Inclusion is not about merely inviting *the Other* into educational endeavors, as such invitations imply a dominant and subordinate relationship that deepens *Otherness* (Bhattacharya, 2009). To accept such an invitation also means stepping into a role in which one's way of being and thinking is considered merely tolerable. Approaching inclusion in this way achieves diversity in appearance only.

However, issues of marginalization are not unique to the Obama era. Dewey (1902) was aware of marginalization tensions in warning teachers not to give in to the false dichotomy of *either* assimilating students with a classical curriculum, *or* respecting their lived experiences through a more broad-based one (Doll, 1993). Over 100 years later, McLaren & Kincheloe (2007) revisit that false dichotomy and pose the question: *Where are we now?* In response, Steinberg (2007) suggests that we are entrenched in an educational system that requires challenge of conservatives, liberals, "and just about everybody else who just doesn't get it" (p. ix). Steinberg's response suggests the need for critical pedagogy. Not only does such pedagogy not force teachers and students to conform to the dominant narrative, it encourages passionate engagement in discursive disagreement. Critique, despite its messiness, is the fabric of democracy.

Critical Pedagogy and Critical Race Theory (CRT)

We start with a foundational assumption: To be human is to be diverse. All individuals are diverse in multifaceted ways. When the term "diversity" is used to indicate the presence of one particular set of human narratives and characteristics (cultures collectively) within a larger, privileged set, it marginalizes people and reinforces the privileged cultures that label certain people as "normal" and others as "strange." Because each person and all peoples represent distinct lived experiences, we are troubled by the oversimplification of these experiences embedded in stereotypes of racial, ethnic, gender, religious, and other communities. We are especially troubled by the manifestation of these oversimplifications even in progressive educational practices, like critical pedagogy. Accordingly, we employ CRT to challenge critical pedagogy's class-determinist theory of reproduction, and theory of oppression/liberation as "universal." We do this by engaging CRT emphasis on localized critique (Weiner, 2007). In educational settings, individual experiences of racial (and other forms of) oppression vary with corresponding variations in cultural signifiers and related performative acts by inscribing both Whiteness and "non-Whiteness" (Denzin, 2007). Herein, we use CRT to examine the ways in which race is staged, as well as the ways in which racism plays out in daily life.

Case Study Method (CSM), Critical Theory (CT), and a Research Typography Process

The purpose of this institutional case study is to explore issues of diversity in the educational experiences of *individuals* at A&M, Regional (Hatch, 2002; Madison, 2005; Merriam, 1998). We want to understand how students and faculty approach internal and external *borders* that limit their engagement as equal participants in learning and teaching processes (Anzaldúa, 1987). We also want to understand how students and faculty use *individual* narratives and discourses to break imposed silences (Bhabha, 1990; Borman, Clarke, Cotner, & Lee, 2006; Duke & Mallette, 2004). Thus, the questions guiding this study are:

1. *How do individuals at A&M, Regional describe their involvement in education learning and teaching processes?*
2. *How do individuals at A&M, Regional describe possibilities for their vocal engagement in education as equal participants?*

According to Stake (1995), CSM enables examination of participant interaction in a natural setting. We use CSM to analyze the diverse perspectives and behaviors of individuals within A&M, Regional, as well as the institutional reactions to the different experiences these individuals brought to campus. Additionally, we draw from Critical Theory (CT) as an epistemological *and* methodological framework to critique "existing economical, social, or political arrangements" that limit diverse ideas at A&M, Regional (Bredo, 2006, p. 23). We also use CT to suggest what forms an encouraging and liberatory environment for silenced students at A&M, Regional might take (Madison, 2005).

Though A&M, Regional is identified as an Hispanic Serving Institution (HSI), and while we consciously acknowledge the importance of race, ethnicity, and nationality, in this case study we also undertake an even more disaggregated (localized) examination of diverse ways of being and knowing. Specifically, we examine how A&M, Regional's *institutional* practices position *individual* students, and then explore the ways those practices and positions influence oppressive and/or transformative actions in classrooms and the larger campus environment.

Data collection methods include classroom observations of interactions among students and faculty members, conversations with students and faculty members, and reflection on notes taken during and after both (Brenner, 2006). In our data analysis, we examine student and faculty perceptions of their individual experiences of, and institutional reactions to, diversity at A&M, Regional. We identify patterns in these perceptions in order to determine themes to (re)present using a *research typography process* (Drucker, 1994; Loveless, 2011). In this process, research participant (student and faculty) and researcher (our) roles merge to collaboratively create the typography using a web-based program called Wordle (www.wordle.net). Both the means by which the typography is created (process) and the actual typography created (outcome) become reflective spaces in which those involved in the research (participants and researchers) reciprocally represent and discuss perceptions, in this case perceptions of diversity at A&M, Regional (Perloff, 2010; Suoranta & Vadén, 2007). Important themes are represented as key terms or words in the typography; these words act as typographical language (vehicles of communication between and among participants and researchers). The relative perceived importance of these words determines their size, with larger words representing the themes perceived to be most important. Once the core typography is generated based on the important themes identified during data analysis, we (participants and researchers) annotate some words and add others to reflect additional nuances in student and faculty perceptions of diversity at A&M, Regional (see Figure 8.1).

This method of (re)presenting data is undertaken to encourage readers of the research to participate in the interpretive aspects of it. Accordingly, before reading the following sections of this case, interact with the typography as interpretive art and respond to the following questions: *What do you think as you look at it? How does it make you feel? What does it mean to you? How real or realistic do you think it is? What possibilities does it suggest?* Further, because interpretive explanations in arts-based inquiry have the effect of limiting the preinterpretive impact of the art, we ask you to try and hold onto your initial reactions to the typography as we explain how it (re)presents diversity at A&M, Regional (Percer, 2002; Perloff, 2010).

Figure 8.1

(Re)Presentation of Findings

As individuals involved in educational processes at A&M, Regional interact, they "perform" intricate rituals that honor their distinct cultures, while also "acting" educated in the manners defined by privileged cultures within the classroom. Figure 8.1 represents this dramaturgy. Thus, we contend that diversity at A&M, Regional can be viewed in two primary, but opposing, ways: through the lens of racial and gender narratives (customary diversity orientations), *or* through the lens of ontological and epistemological narratives (ways of being and knowing).

Individuals involved in learning and teaching processes at A&M, Regional adapt their behaviors to the privileged culture of schooling. They speak on "acceptable" topics, from a "rational" range of perspectives, using "appropriate" language forms. These topics, perspectives, and language forms are often very different from individuals' background cultures. Once adaptations to the privileged culture become internalized, these individuals become "Othered" at home and in their home culture.

The juxtaposition of vertical and horizontal text in the typography represents the struggle within individuals when they are required to behave differently at school than they are expected to behave at home. Individuals often commented on having to act "educated" at school and "uneducated" at home in order to avoid ridicule in both settings. An A&M, Regional undergraduate student noted, "At school I am careful how I speak; I worry about my accent, so I don't say words I know are difficult for me to pronounce. I also try to use words that will impress my classmates and professors" (personal communication, n.d.). An A&M, Regional doctoral student stated:

> You know, after a time here, I had to be careful how I spoke when I went home. My friends would say "Who do you think you are trying to act smart in front of us?" ... I felt like everyone was waiting for me to abandon my heritage. (personal communication, n.d.)

To be accepted, these students consciously shifted their discourses to fit their surroundings. They often became very adept at moving back and forth between both ways of being, a linguistic form of situational adaptation Ogbu (2008) calls *code switching*. Unfortunately, along with this adaptational skill come feelings of being only partially accepted, or completely unaccepted, at home and on campus.

The large block font in the typography represents how concerns about "fitting in" with family and school remain at the forefront of individuals' thinking about diversity at A&M, Regional. The most visually contrastive word in the typography, *culture*, represents the assumption that there is one acceptable

(White) culture. Further, individuals at A&M, Regional perceive the ability to move between different cultures as dishonest; they feel as though they are in some way or another pretending to fit into each culture they traverse. This feeling has the effect of marginalizing what should actually be centered as an impressive skill: multicultural adaptation or the ability to negotiate interactions in more than one culture simultaneously. *Shame*, the least visually contrastive word in the typography, is represented this way to illustrate that the emotion of shame is masked or 'below the surface.' Individuals at A&M, Regional feel shame that in adapting to campus culture they no longer feel they fit into their own racial, ethnic, gender, or religious ("non-White") cultures.

We (participants and researchers collectively) intentionally crossed out one word in the typography, *silence*. Basquiat, a street artist who incorporates text in his artwork, argues that he crosses out words so the viewer sees them more (Davis, 2010). Accordingly, we cross out the word silence to emphasize it. A&M, Regional silences individuals by not acknowledging or representing the discourses students bring with them to the campus. At home, these individuals silence themselves in order to remain accepted/acceptable members of their families and/or communities. One A&M, Regional graduate assistant explained how silence mediates diversity by saying, "Sometimes, it is better to just not say anything at all and avoid the whole problem . . . or talk about things that don't really matter" (personal communication, n.d.). While silence can also be a powerful form of voice (Rodriguez, 2011), at A&M, Regional, silence primarily means adapting one's voice to speak in manners that are acceptable to status quo: speaking on preapproved content, from dominant points of view, using academic vocabulary. Freire (1970) refers to this kind of learning and teaching as representative of a *banking model* of education in which teachers perceive students to enter classrooms as empty receptacles into which they, the teachers, must make deposits of knowledge. Freire contrasted the banking model with a *problem-posing model* in which teachers engage students in learning through a process of critical questioning that builds on students' *a priori* knowledge in empowering them to *read the word and the world*.

Discussion

Consciously engaging racial, ethnic, gender, and religious differences, as well as *border-crossing* ways of being and knowing, in learning and teaching brings *chaos* to education (Anzaldúa, 1987; Griffith, 2007). Education's default position is to exclude difference under the auspices that doing so offers continuity: *but continuity for whom?* A&M, Regional recruits cultural "Others" into a cultural "normative" educational setting; simultaneously A&M, Regional purports to welcome "Others" while subjugating their "Other" ways of being and knowing. As our typography illustrates, despite the physical appearance of diversity at A&M, Regional, there is paucity in the expression of diverse experiences and ideas.

Affirming diverse experiences and ideas is not easy. Attempting to reconcile (neutralize) challenges between external and internal forces only undermines substantive, progressive change efforts. Only through open, ongoing engagement with the tensions embedded in and across cultural, experiential, and intellectual diversity will affirmation of diversity come to be understood as unifying. Achieving such understanding requires everyone to: (a) step outside socially constructed borders that keep *us* in and *Other* out, and (b) recognize that institutional and local dynamics of power impact who the terms "us" and "Other" describe. In describing how communication takes place in communities that divide and separate people like A&M, Regional, Bakhtin (1981) uses the concept of *ideological becoming*. He states: "The importance of struggling with another's discourse, its influence in the history of an individual's coming to ideological consciousness, is enormous" (Bakhtin, 1981, p. 348). Bakhtin seems to be suggesting that critical thought and expression are not owned by a particular racial, ethnic, gender, or religious group, nor manifest universally across all members of a particular such group.

Within the realm of education, Kincheloe and Steinberg (1997) suggest that *critical complexity* and *progressive pedagogy* open minds to unheard voices. Thus, through the clash of opposing experiences of, and ideas about, existing social spaces comes the power to create new social spaces in which all forms of diversity are truly affirmed (Pratt, 1991). Once those spaces exist, drift toward consolidated power and authority will be rejected in favor of multiplicity of voice and action. We "need to unite, and acknowledge that [the issues facing different communities] can be best resolved if they are tackled as intimately interrelated issues" (Anyon, 2005, p. 175).

Conclusion

In education, a focus on coherence facilitates acknowledgment, discussion, and critique of diverse ways of being, which in turn encourage the development of understanding of what is possible in human existence. The search for coherence is not, however, meant to oppressively enforce conformity of some peoples to the privileged standard of other peoples regarding what being educated means. Coherence seeks to bring about the mutual exploration of all peoples in educational settings in ways that support all our lived experiences and related thinking about the world. The goal of educational coherence is increased communication across individuals, and within and across the diverse communities individuals represent.

Stifling disagreement precludes dialogue, which limits human understanding leading to dehumanization. An important role of institutions of higher education, like A&M, Regional, is to prepare students to develop the disposition to meaningfully interact with each other. To accomplish this goal, institutions have to create educationally coherent spaces. Such spaces embrace cultural "Others" as well as their experiences and ideas, while simultaneously seeking to dismantle the discriminatory practices that create and perpetuate their "Otherness." It is the complexity within coherence that creates new possibilities for a diverse world.

9

The Evolution of a Campus

From the Seat of the Civil War to a Seat on the Freedom Rides

Shaunna Payne Gold and Leah K. Cox

Framing the Case

Multicultural Organization Development (MCOD) is an inherently difficult process, but the difficulty of the process can be exacerbated when initiated on the site of one of the greatest Civil War battles in American history (Jackson, 2006; Jackson & Hardiman, 1994). The Battle of Fredericksburg was fought in December 1862 between Lee's Confederate Army of Northern Virginia and the Union Army of the Potomac (Salmon, 2001). The University of ACME (ACME), a small public liberal arts institution, now sits on the site of that battle, a site where a major Confederate victory was won and where Union forces incurred more than 10,000 casualties. Historically, in the particular area of the southern United States where ACME is located, environments have been racially charged, and racial incidents have been common.

As a result of this challenging historical backdrop, ACME is known, jokingly, to residents of the community adjacent to the campus as the "University of Mostly Whites." But a period of campus turmoil during which there was frequent turnover in the university's president, coupled with the growing possibility that the United States would elect its first Black president, created the context for ACME to make unexpected diversity gains. Using the concept of *inclusive excellence* as a foundation, ACME developed campus-wide diversity, equity, and inclusion initiatives (Williams, Berger, & McClendon, 2005). This chapter tells the unique story of ACME's *warming climate*, and its concomitant warming relationship with the community that surrounds it.

Purpose of the Study

This chapter is organized as an *intrinsic* case study (Stake, 1995). This case engages the question: *How do members of Generation O, as students of ACME, experience MCOD immediately before, during, and after the election of President Barack Obama?* To answer this question, this case uses multiple data collection techniques: critical, emancipatory, focus group, interview, observation, and documentation review.

Theoretical Framework and Methodological Techniques

The core concern of this case is the power relationships among students, faculty, staff, and administrators on the ACME campus. These relations can support or inhibit the process of MCOD. Therefore, we assume a *criticalist* posture in this research that is informed by six basic assumptions:

1. All knowledge is fundamentally informed by power relations that are social in nature and historically constituted;
2. Facts can never be isolated from the domain of values or removed from ideological inscription;
3. Language is central to the formation of subjectivity, including conscious and unconscious awareness;
4. Certain groups in any society are privileged over others, constituting an oppression that is most forceful when subordinated groups accept their social status as natural, necessary, or inevitable;
5. Concern for only one form of oppression, at the expense of others, is counterproductive, because oppressions are interconnected; and
6. Mainstream research practices are generally implicated, albeit often unwittingly, in the reproduction of systems of class, race, and gender oppression (Kincheloe & McLaren, 1994, pp. 139–140).

Criticalist research and Critical Race Theory (CRT) are connected through a shared focus on historically, institutionally, and socially embedded power relations. CRT "is based on the understanding that race and racism are the products of social thought based on power relations" (Gillborn & Rollock, 2011, para. 2).

As criticalist researchers, we work within an emancipatory research paradigm that seeks to transform research and practice concerning cold- and warming-campus environments. Oliver (1992) notes that:

The development of [the emancipatory research] paradigm stems from the gradual rejection of the positivist view of social research as the pursuit of absolute knowledge through the scientific method and the gradual disillusionment with the interpretive view of such research as the generation of socially useful knowledge within particular historical and social contexts. The emancipatory paradigm, as the name implies, is about the facilitating of a politics of the possible by confronting social oppression at whatever levels it occurs. (p. 110)

We use an emancipatory research paradigm to execute Case Study Method (CSM) in describing ACME's extraordinary process of institutional change through the lens of MCOD (Jackson, 2006; Yin, 1994).

In constructing this case, we mine data from several sources. Through a focus group, we question recent ACME alums about their campus experiences. As students, these alums were actively involved in multicultural activities, student organizations, and initiatives. Two of these alums are recipients of the campus' Citizenship Award for Diversity; one alum participated in study abroad; and during one alum's four-year tenure on campus, the university was led by four different presidents. Additionally, through in-depth, semistructured interviews, we question the current university president, a former provost, and two current senior-level administrators who, combined, have more than 25 years of service to the university. We also rely on our own observation of campus phenomena. Finally, we review documents, including policies, study reports, memoranda, meeting agendas, letters, personal notes, student newspapers, and local newspapers. CSM uses data triangulation to bolster the salience of its findings. Accordingly, this case uses multiperspectival analysis and considers the voices and perspectives of various individual actors, relevant groups of actors, and the interactions among various entities within the university context (Tellis, 1997).

Defining Campus Climate and Multicultural Organization

To assess the warming climate at ACME, we examine five dimensions of campus climate:

1. *Historical legacy of inclusion/exclusion;*
2. *Compositional diversity*, including mission and resistance to desegregation;
3. *Psychological dimension*, for example, perceptions of racial/ethnic tension, perceptions of discrimination, and attitudes and prejudice reduction;

4. *Behavioral dimension*, including social interaction across race/ethnicity, degree of intraracial and cross-racial campus involvements, classroom diversity, and pedagogical approaches; and
5. *Organizational/structural dimension*, for example, campus definitions of merit, diversity of curriculum, admissions policies, tenure policies, organizational decision-making policies, budget allocations, and other policies/procedures (Hurtado, Milem, Clayton-Pederson, & Allen, 1998, 1999; Milem, Chang, & Antonio, 2005).

We also use a concise definition of a multicultural organization to anchor our discussion of ACME's warming process:

> The multicultural organization (MCO) is an organization that has within its mission, goals, values and operating system explicit policies and practices that prohibits anyone from being excluded or unjustly treated because of social identity or status. A multicultural organization not only supports social justice within the organization; it advocates these values in interactions within the local, regional, national, and global communities, with its vendors, customers, and peer organizations. (Jackson, 2006, p. 142)

Finally, we used a six-stage model of MCOD to track ACME's warming progress. Briefly, these stages are: *exclusionary, "the club," compliance, affirming, redefining,* and *multicultural* (Wall & Obear, 2008). Characteristics of these stages are discussed in greater detail in the narration of the case.

Stage 1: Exclusionary Organization

Jackson (2006) describes an *exclusionary organization* as at the first stage of MCOD. An exclusionary organization is a culturally immature organization that openly maintains the dominant group's power and privilege, deliberately restricts membership, and is intentionally designed to maintain dominance of one group over others. As a monocultural organization, its discriminatory and exclusionary actions are celebrated and considered appropriate.

Originally named ACME College in 1908, the university began as, and remains, the only public coeducational institution named for a secular woman (ACME, 2011). Created primarily to train White women as teachers, ACME College became a branch of the, at that time, all-male University of ACME, Flagship in 1944. ACME College housed a robust undergraduate curriculum and was known for excellence in teaching women in a residential setting. Despite its focus on women, exclusionary organizational characteristics describe at least the first 36 years of ACME College's history.

Stage 2: "The Club"

In 1972, ACME College made the historic decision to become coeducational (ACME, 2011). This decision began the campus' momentum toward becoming a *club organization*. While ACME College continued to maintain the almost exclusive privilege of those who have traditionally held institutional power and influence—White people—it began to allow a trickle of access to individual members of historically subordinated groups, mostly African American women, in a token fashion. This still highly restrictive access to the organization reinforced the monocultural norms, policies, and procedures, thereby maintaining existing power structures.

The state legislature voted to make the college into a university in 2004 (ACME, 2011). Doing so outwardly acknowledged the institution's master's degree program offerings and increased enrollment in its College of Graduate and Professional Studies. Though technically welcoming to a limited few people of color, club organizations continue to function with a 'business as usual' mindset. Very few cultural norms, policies, or procedures changed, even though these practices have the effect of continuing to make the few new members of 'the club' still feel largely excluded. At this stage in ACME's organization history, a few matters related to diversity, equity, and inclusion periodically arose on campus.

Stage 3: The Compliance Organization

In 2007, immediately prior to Obama's election, a critical incident took place in a campus residence hall that quickly highlighted ACME's lack of preparedness to effectively respond to concerns of diverse student, faculty, and staff populations on a predominantly White campus. The university's housekeeping staff discovered an 8.5" x 11" sign on a community refrigerator depicting a White man with his arm around a sobbing African American man with the caption, "Slavery Re-Instated: Catch Yourself a Strong One." The university president stated, "It's one of the ugliest, most awful things I've ever seen. I got choked up just looking at it" (Dumville, 2007, para. 8). After expressing how livid he was at the students who posted the sign, he said, "I wanted to see them thrown off campus. I don't think they belong here" (Dumville, 2007, para. 2).

The incident highlighted that the university lacked a bias policy, a process to report racial incidents, and a means for sanctioning unacceptable behavior. The students, faculty, and staff were thrown into turmoil, and the larger community began to voice its disapproval of ACME's lack of readiness for, and overall inexperience with, diversity. Just a few days after the investigation of the incident was concluded, the president admitted, "I've found weaknesses in our system that my report will address," and later took steps to meet with affected groups, including the housekeeping staff (Dumville, 2007, para. 4). He expressed empathy by saying, "I want to apologize to [the housekeeping staff] for what they've had to endure because of the actions of a few. I have a gay son. I've seen what persecution can do, and be like" (Dumville, 2007, para. 33).

A newly appointed interim president began moving the university in a new direction, focusing on the ideals of diversity and inclusiveness. A first order of business was to establish a bias incident reporting structure. In 2008, but before Obama was elected as the first African American president of the United States, the ACME's Board of Visitors approved a bias incident reporting policy making the university a *compliance organization* for the first time in its history.

A compliance organization shows its dedication to diversity, equity, and inclusion by seeking to end at least some of the discrimination that is inherent to an organization at the club stage by providing somewhat more access to some additional members of previously excluded or ignored groups. Still, there is very little change in organizational culture, mission, or structure. The compliance organization stops short of proactively challenging dominant groups' offensive actions and behaviors toward oppressed groups.

Stage 4: The Affirming Organization

Following the approval of the bias incident policy, but still prior to Obama's election, ACME continued its implementation of diversity, equity, and inclusion initiatives.

Two Campaign Stops: Clinton, Obama/Biden

In 2008, ACME was abuzz with the sentiment of hope for change as Generation O began to make its presence known through the Young Democrats student organization. This activity led to President Clinton and then-Senators Obama and Biden visiting the ACME campus (Cave, 2008). These visits were politically charged, contributing more electricity to an already emotionally charged campus climate. This energy propelled the campus from a compliance organization into an *affirming organization*. An organization at this stage works to create an organizational culture that values and seeks out the benefits of diversity (Jackson, 2006; Williams, Berger, & McClendon, 2005).

While the campus would likely have continued its diversity initiatives in the absence of the Clinton and Obama/Biden visits, such initiatives were spotlighted and, therefore, thrust forward by these visits. When asked if the Clinton and Obama/Biden visits changed the climate of the campus in any way, most members of the campus community suggested it had little direct impact. For example, former provost of ACME responded:

> Every college, university, and institution that could handle the visit was much more likely to have a high profile presidential candidate. We were not unique. I do think that [the visit] generated a sensibility among the students of a higher level of cognizance of certain issues. (personal communication, n.d.)

ACME's assistant vice president of human resources concurred saying that she could not measure any real direct impact of the visit on campus climate.

Yet members of the surrounding community, who once felt no connection to the university, seemed to find the institution more accessible to them after the visit. One senior-level administrator noted the large number of community members who came to see the former president and candidates, emphasizing that there were so many "Folks who had never been here before . . . there was standing room only" (personal communication, n.d.). ACME's provost also noted the impact on the community:

> Having Obama here was a signature and very visible event for the community. That was certainly a theme of that event. Our students were excited to have anyone of Clinton or Obama's visibility here. That was important for a lot of people in our community. I was happy that the university was willing to host such an event. It was packed . . . I think there were people here that had never set foot on this campus. (personal communication, n.d.)

ACME alums echoed the provost's sentiments in describing their excitement about the Clinton and Obama/Biden visits and their impact on the larger community. One former student leader described the visit this way:

> It made me proud to be a student at [ACME]. It brought the campus and the community together. To the Black community, who didn't go to the university, strangers came up and said they were proud of me . . . people I didn't even know. I can't wait to tell the stories to my kids. I was a part of history. (personal communication, n.d.)

In inadvertently fostering improvement in town–gown relations, ACME became a budding affirming organization. Especially Obama's visit to the campus made the local community feel ACME was much more welcoming than it had been in the past. This sense of welcome may have also led to improvements in the recruitment, retention, and promotion of members of groups historically denied access to, and opportunity at, the university.

Turnover in the University Presidency

Since the 2008 presidential campaign, not only has the ACME campus climate warmed, increasing diversity in the racial demographics of students, faculty, and staff suggests the campus has undergone systemic change as well. More change comes with the inauguration of a new president in the late spring of 2009, the creation of a special assistant to the president for diversity and inclusion position in 2010, and the approval of a new statement of diversity and community values in 2011. By the fall of 2011, students of color comprise 22 percent of the entering class (ACME, 2011, para. 7).

Specific to the selection of the new president, the Board of Visitors recognized that, imperative to the survival and growth of the institution, was someone with a vision for improving diversity across the campus. The presidential search process resulted in the appointment of ACME's first female president in its 100-year history. At the outset of her presidential tenure, ACME's new president outlined her mission, prompting development of a new strategic plan with explicit attention to diversity, including to many areas of diversity that had been overlooked for many years.

The Freedom Rides Reenacted

ACME has enjoyed the presence of the principle architect of the Freedom Rides as a faculty member for over 14 years. To pay homage to the Freedom Riders experience, ACME hosted a celebration of the 50th anniversary of the Freedom Rides in spring 2011. The celebration brought authors, scholars, and several well-known Freedom Riders to campus. Freedom Rider Congressman John Lewis was even the 2011 undergraduate commencement speaker and Freedom Rider Congressman Bob Filner was the 2011 graduate commencement speaker. ACME's provost stated:

> [The Freedom Rides Initiative] was an exceptionally well done set of initiatives. It had a number of wonderful components to it. It placed [our faculty Freedom Rider] directly, immediately, and physically on the campus. It was an opportunity for students to 'get on the bus.' It was superb that getting on the bus was understood as a matter of personal and social justice transformation which was absolutely in keeping with the legacy of [our faculty Freedom Rider]. I thought it was an excellent way to not only bring visibility to his legacy but its ongoing legacy to students, faculty, staff, and alumni . . . I loved the consistent emphasis on students understanding this not simply as a piece of history but

truly understanding this as an event in which people just like them . . . *students just like them*, made decisions on what was really important to them. (personal communication, n.d.)

Coincidentally, an ACME student (one of our alum interviewees) was one of 40 students chosen nationally to be a Student Rider or participant in an actual reenactment of the Freedom Rides sponsored by the PBS American Experience Project.

Diversity initiatives like the reenactment of the Freedom Rides emerged from and strengthened ACME's affirming organizational behavior. Other such initiatives followed. ACME's Student Transition Program, a summer bridge program for students of color, was expanded. A faculty handbook, out-lining equal opportunity and affirmative action policies and procedures, was developed and disseminated. The Division of Student Affairs' Multicultural Center was enhanced. The Office of Admissions received additional funding to support efforts to recruit students of color. The number and substance of these initiatives signals ACME's beginning transition from an affirming organization into a *redefining organization*.

Stage 5: The Redefining Organization

In the wake of the Freedom Rides celebration, ACME is attempting to *re-define* itself. Members of the ACME community are beginning to recognize the complexity in the consensual processes to define diversity, equity, and inclusion, as well as how much more complex it is to enact these definitions in daily campus life. One senior-level administrator noticed that campus pri-orities have shifted tremendously since the critical incident in the residence hall. "The president elevated diversity and inclusion into the discussion. We knew we needed the *language* to discuss it." To find such language, work-time was dedicated for staff to participate in mini-workshops, trainings, and leadership-led discussions. The goal of these sessions was to understand how diversity was being defined and operationalized across campus. One senior administrator noted, "Diversity for [the university president] meant African Americans" (personal communication, n.d.). Another senior administrator commented:

> But I still don't believe as an institution . . . that we have a deep understanding of what diversity is and why it is so intimately connected to the core mission of our institution and academic excellence. So in other words, I think [diversity] is a priority and a visible priority, but I don't think we've done enough work with the conversations we need to have and the experiences we need to have to bring

students, faculty, and staff to a deep, abiding understanding of what diversity is and why it's important. It's simply a manifestation of our core mission and directly related to our academic mission. (personal communication, n.d.)

Based on the perspectives shared in these development sessions, the university president's Strategic Plan for Diversity was crafted to include an aggressive recruitment and retention plan, an additional outreach program for students from underrepresented groups, an official declaration of the Dr. Martin Luther King, Jr. holiday, and mandatory diversity training for senior-level administrators. As a redefining organization, the campus began to invest itself in the ongoing work of diversity that characterizes an organization at this stage of MCOD.

Ally, Advocate, and Agent Strategies

A *multicultural organization* actively works to eliminate all forms of oppression at all organizational levels (Wall & Obear, 2008). An organizationally multicultural campus might think of itself as a community of social justice allies. However, in, "A Seat at the Table That I Set: Beyond Social Justice Allies," Jenkins (2009) suggests that campuses often overutilize the term *ally*, which she defines as "a person, group, or nation that is associated with others for some common cause or purpose," while overlooking other important solidarity roles (p. 1). Jenkins suggests multicultural organization stage campuses embrace three, equally important, partnership orientations: *ally*, *advocate*, and *agent*.

According to Jenkins (2009), allies are *relational* in that they are members (or composed of members) of a dominant group who actively support the struggles of target group members from outside the target group community. After catalytic organizational moments, like the residence-hall incident, disengaged segments of the campus community reengaged because the campus was beginning to be perceived as an ally to targeted groups. Likewise, celebration of the Freedom Rider legacy of one member of ACME's faculty may have encouraged members of the local community to engage with the campus.

Advocates are *vocal* about their responsibility to support social justice (Jenkins, 2009). Advocates argue, plead, support, and/or defend social justice ideals and causes. These individuals act as voices for change. Advocates may not identify with targeted groups, and they may or may not choose to take action beyond oral persuasion. After an awakening, several members of ACME's senior administration became advocates for campus change. They expressed support for: (a) continuing diversity initiatives, (b) increasing the number of minority students and faculty on campus, (c) increasing the number of Pell grant recipients accepted into the university, (d) increasing diverse students' access to financial aid, (e) reengaging the Freedom Rider faculty member as a visiting professor, as well as (f) improving recruitment, hiring, and retention of faculty of color. These initiatives were realized only after university leaders voiced the need for them on campus.

While justice-driven relationship builders and persuasive orators support MCOD, *action-oriented* individuals actually make things happen. Agency means having the power to act to create change (Jenkins, 2009). Agents work beyond empathetic relationships and vocal opposition, engaging in strategic action designed to bring about ongoing organizational improvement. Because ACME's warming climate is still a work in progress, agents are needed to initiate, support, and continue the work. One former student leader pointed out that, "The students pushed in the beginning. But in 2009, the university took charge of pushing diversity" (personal communication, n.d.).

ACME has much more work to do before it can claim to be a multicultural organization. The appointment of a special assistant to the president for diversity and inclusion, the anniversary celebration of the Freedom Rides, the establishment of an English-as-a-Second-Language program, and the creation of a postdoctoral fellowship in Civil Rights and Social Justice demonstrate the continuing and evolving work of the university. We anticipate that with ongoing agency from various quarters of the university, ACME will eventually become an all-encompassing multicultural organization.

10

The Unmet Promise

A Critical Race Theory Analysis of the Rise of an African American Studies Program

Michael E. Jennings

The Ebb and Flow of the Case

THE DISCIPLINARY HISTORY OF AFRICAN AMERICAN STUDIES is tied to struggle. The creation of the African American Studies (AAS) minor at University of ACME, Regional (UA, Regional) clearly reflects the reality of struggle and will serve as a case study for this chapter. From the beginning, university support for an AAS minor at the university was weak, although support from students and African American faculty was strong. The program faced several emerging obstacles and eventually faced declining enrollment and administrative support. However, a coalition of faculty, students, administrators, and community members emerged to help revitalize the minor and save it from ceasing to exist. The minor was eventually moved from one college within the university to another and was provided with the leadership and support that was necessary for it to thrive. The story of the creation, decline, and reemergence of an AAS program at UA, Regional serves as a strong example of how a diversity- and inclusion-focused academic program can come into being and overcome subsequent adversity in ways that unite campus and community stakeholders.

Overview of Institutional and Program Context

UA, Regional is a large, urban Hispanic Serving Institution (HSI) immersed in making the transition to become a tier one (i.e., research extensive) university. The past 12 years have seen the university grow tremendously, moving from being a mid-sized commuter campus to a large research university with a strong emphasis on recruiting full-time traditional undergraduate students. In short, UA, Regional is striving to change itself from a young, regionally known college into a large, traditional state university with a national reputation.

As the university has grown, its African American population has increased at a fast pace. By the end of 2011, the percentage of African American students was approximately 7 percent (UA, Regional, 2011a). Prior to this surge in enrollment, there were very few course offerings that addressed the African American experience in any academic discipline. The creation of an AAS minor was born of student demand, along with support from a handful of dedicated faculty members. The eventual decline of the program was largely the result of benign neglect on the part of university administrators who provided few resources and scant leadership to the minor. The reemergence of the program was similar to its initial organization in that it involved student activism emboldened by the work of a few committed faculty members. Additional factors, however, differentiated the reemergence of the minor: (a) strong support from a newly appointed interim provost, (b) the appointment of a full-time, tenure-track faculty member to promote and secure resources for the minor, and (c) strong and *vocal* support from the dean of the College of Education (COE).

The Problem

The demand for an AAS minor at UA, Regional created a dilemma revolving around issues of race, power, and pedagogy. Students who sought the creation of the minor often saw their request in terms of racial justice. They thought that having an AAS minor reflected the advancement of interests of African American students on a campus that seemed to have little concern for their needs. African American faculty saw the establishment of the minor as a way to challenge existing power relations within the university by recruiting and retaining more African American faculty, staff, and students. The university administration seemed to view the minor as an inconvenience to be tolerated, in the hope that it would soon go away. To complicate the situation further, during the minor's most problematic time, the chair of the department housing the minor displayed open hostility toward students and faculty who sought to strengthen the minor while it was under his control. This hostility eventually became public, and members of the larger, off-campus African American community became involved, demanding a meeting with

university administration. Quickly the situation became 'sticky,' reflecting
an increasing tension between the university administration and the African
American community, both on campus and across the city of ACME.

Theoretical Lens and Methodological Approach

In analyzing the race, power, and pedagogy dilemma surrounding the demand for the AAS minor, I utilize Critical Race Theory (CRT) as my primary
theoretical lens. CRT has evolved over the past 15 years as an important construct in the study of race in education because of its strong focus on *centering* the concept of race in education in a sociocultural context that challenges
dominant discourses (Ladson-Billings, 2005a). Additionally, CRT has become
an important component of the critical analysis of race in education because
of its development and use of critical research methodologies that challenge
mainstream ideas about the *subjectivity versus objectivity* binary around which
a great deal of educational research is structured (Delgado Bernal, 2002;
Parker & Lynn, 2002).

Central to CRT is the use of narrative and storytelling to challenge prevailing ideas and assumptions by "telling the stories of those people whose experiences are often not told" (Solórzano & Yosso, 2002a, p. 26). These stories
represent an important *counter story* that challenges the racist ideology used
to create, maintain, and justify the typical use of a *master narrative* in storytelling (Solórzano & Yosso, 2002a). Given the centrality of race in the race,
power, and pedagogy dilemma, the use of CRT's race-focused theoretical lens,
and, in counter story, a complimentary antiracist methodological approach,
fuller comprehension of the dilemma is realized.

The Entrance of Black Studies into the Academy

The first Black Studies department was institutionalized at San Francisco State
University as a degree-granting program in 1968. The process to establish the
program was long and arduous, reflecting the struggle of Black students and
local community members for self-determination, on and off campus (Rojas,
2007). This tradition of struggle for self-determination was not developed in
an historical vacuum. Rather, it was part of a broader intellectual-activist tradition existing for more than a century in the African American community
(Karenga, 1993). This tradition was also located in the larger turbulence of the
1960s, characterized by college student and community activism. Specifically,
the Civil Rights Movement, the Free Speech Movement, the Antiwar Move-

ment, and the Black Power Movement all influenced what was to become the Black Studies Movement in the mid-1960s (Karenga, 1993; Rojas, 2011).

The connection between the creation of the earliest Black Studies departments and the concept of "protest" was extremely strong. Rojas (forthcoming) points to the fact that "many programs, likely a majority, were created after rallies, student strikes, and sit-ins" (p. 10). Many of these protests called not just for Black Studies departments, but for Black Studies departments that specifically emphasized close connections with, and research related to, local African American communities (Rojas, 2007). Despite this focus on community concerns, many Black Studies departments found themselves being pushed to become part of the academic mainstream. As more Black Studies departments emerged, some took a mainstream approach by seeking to serve the university community in ways that were similar to existing traditional academic disciplines. These departments became less focused on nationalist agendas and local community involvement, and more concerned with providing traditional academic training, typified by interdisciplinarity and centering the Black experience.

Interestingly, Rooks (2006) notes that many universities sought to create Black Studies programs as a way to appease campus constituencies they regarded as radical. In doing so, some universities thought that Black Studies programs acted as a sort of 'insurance' against student unrest. Similarly, philanthropic entities like the Ford Foundation were willing to financially support Black Studies departments if they were not considered to be too radical, and if they appeared to fit into a specific integrationist model that eschewed politics, nationalism, and identity concerns (Rooks, 2006; Rojas, 2007).

The Entrance of African American Studies (AAS) at University of ACME, Regional

Prior to 2004, UA, Regional's history department housed the subfield of American studies. It was in this subfield that AAS found its genesis. The primary architect of the AAS minor was an Afro-Latina assistant professor who was serving as the director of the American studies department. She enlisted the help of a White male colleague in the English department to help begin the work of developing a minor in AAS in spring 2003. The chair of the history department at that time, however, was resistant to the idea of having an AAS minor in the history department. Sensing the presence of a roadblock, the two faculty members seeking to establish the minor turned to students for support and assistance.

A small group of undergraduate students at UA, Regional made a concerted effort to express their desire for such a program to the university's faculty and administration. Combined with advocacy on the part of the director of the

American studies program, the students' actions eventually pushed the university to support the creation of an AAS minor within the American studies program and housed in the history department. Although plans were approved to launch the minor, no financial support was offered, and no plans to bring in additional faculty were made. Only three minor-specific classes were created, the rest of the classes (and the bulk of them) coming from already-existing course offerings across the university.

Within a year, the faculty member who had spearheaded the founding of the minor left the university, perceiving a lack of support for her work from the dean of her college. With her departure, the AAS minor was moved to the Department of Political Science and Geography. This move occurred because the department was under the leadership of a chair who had previously been supportive of the minor, and who wanted to develop and sustain the minor as a valued part of the department. With this move, the minor enjoyed a period of relative stability and growth. But when a new chair was appointed to the department, a new era of resistance to the AAS minor emerged. The newly appointed chair was not sympathetic to the minor and had exceptionally poor relations with the previous chair and the faculty members who taught the majority of the classes in the minor, most of whom were adjuncts. The AAS minor began a period of rapid decline, characterized by fewer class offerings, low class enrollments, and limited visibility on campus and in the community.

During this time, at least one of the adjunct faculty members left the university, leaving most of the classes in the minor to be taught by a single adjunct faculty member. The adjunct faculty member who remained was well known and respected in the African American community and had a strong orientation towards radical politics and community organizing. But, the adjunct's social justice commitments caused considerable friction with the new chair, who clearly did not want any part of the AAS minor.

As a result of this friction, the adjunct faculty member rallied a number of students to the cause of the AAS minor. Together, they developed a larger organizing strategy to challenge the university on its treatment of the AAS minor. The students first sought to meet with the new chair, but their attempts were rebuffed. Similarly, the new chair's supervisor, the dean of the College of Liberal Arts (CLA), refused to meet with the students to discuss the minor's wane. In the midst of this upheaval, the adjunct faculty member resigned his position in protest. This put the minor in a difficult position, because there was no one else available to teach the minor's classes.

On their own now, the students once again rallied to support the minor, developing a more careful strategy that enlisted the help of members of ACME's African American community. A very public protest was held on campus by a small, but vocal, group of students. The protest drew a great deal of media attention, both locally and across the state, even reaching a few national outlets. The students also arranged a meeting with several local African American politicians who pledged to help pressure the university. A meeting was held with the interim provost where students and local community members demanded support for the AAS minor.

The friction seemed to have reached a critical juncture, and it was at this point that I became involved with the struggle to support the minor. At that time, I was an untenured assistant professor in an academic department located within the COE. Although I was not housed in the same college as the minor, I had a strong interest in AAS: It dovetailed with my research agenda and my previous teaching experience at another university. Additionally, I was founding president of a new campus group called the Black Faculty and Staff Association (BFSA). The newly formed BFSA was very concerned about the condition of the minor and vowed to make the maintenance and promotion of the minor one of its primary goals.

I discussed this matter at length with the dean of my college whom I knew was particularly supportive of issues surrounding students and faculty of color. We discussed the importance of having an AAS program on campus, and I raised the possibility of having the minor moved to the COE. The dean was very supportive of this idea and thought that the addition of the AAS minor to the COE's academic offerings would boost the college's capacity to recruit and train a more diverse group of teachers and educational leaders. We both realized that having an AAS minor in a COE was unprecedented. But in having this minor, we also both believed that we would reap numerous benefits for the college and the university. Accordingly, we agreed that she (my dean) would take the request to the Office of the Provost at the appropriate time. While this idea was under consideration by the provost, the AAS minor was still facing an immediate crisis.

During a meeting with the interim provost, I expressed concern about the state of the minor and told the provost that I feared the minor would cease to exist administratively, despite growing academic interest in it, if the university did not take immediate steps to ensure its survival. I suggested having the minor moved from the CLA to the COE on a temporary basis, while the university administration thought more about where an appropriate permanent location for it might be. The interim provost agreed, and the AAS minor was moved from the CLA to the COE on an interim basis beginning in January 2008.

This move faced opposition from some of the senior faculty in CLA who were disturbed that the dean of their college had not done more to nurture the AAS minor. They thought that the dean of the CLA should be held accountable for the decline of the minor and that the proper resources should be provided to the minor so that it could become a viable entity in the CLA. Others simply felt that AAS had "no business" in a COE and that the minor was being tossed around for political purposes. Within the COE, the minor was well received and most faculty members viewed it as a welcome addition to the college. But there were some COE faculty members who did not understand why the college would consider housing an AAS minor. Despite these misgivings, even these unconvinced faculty members did not raise any objections to the move. Once the temporary move was made permanent by the provost, the dean of COE asked me to serve as the Director of African American Studies. I readily accepted the position.

The most important first step in getting the minor back on track was securing the necessary resources to make the minor a success. I sat with the chair of my own department and discussed what types of resources would be necessary for this academic program to run smoothly. We drew up a detailed budget that included money for adjunct instructors, maintenance and operations, and professional development. The budget was approved by the dean of COE, and then by the interim provost.

With a decent budget in place, my initial goal was to stabilize the AAS minor by ensuring that courses were offered on a regular basis. Two experienced, adjunct faculty members were hired to offer the AAS classes on a consistently scheduled basis. Next, I actively sought opportunities to cross-list AAS classes with several other departments across the university. Although cross-listing was not new to the AAS minor, it seemed to be a very underutilized practice. Increasing the number of cross-listings raised the profile of the minor by extending the variety of AAS class offerings and affording students outside the minor the opportunity to explore the African American experience.

Finally, I made sure to engage key constituents across campus and in the community to help reestablish support for the newly revived minor. This involved meetings with student-affairs staff, advising-center staff, student leaders, faculty, and local community leaders. In discussions with each of these constituent groups, I emphasized my desire to increase the viability of the minor by increasing enrollment, adding a variety of class offerings, and connecting the minor with other entities, both on and off campus.

It is important to note, in retrospect, the political context that existed, both on campus and across the country, while the AAS minor underwent these changes. Then–Senator Barack Obama was in the midst of a bid to become the nominee of the Democratic Party in anticipation of the 2008 presidential election. His candidacy was not initially given much of a chance, but by the fall of 2008, he had outpaced other candidates and emerged as a leading contender for the nomination. Obama's campaign became a rallying point for African Americans who felt marginalized by the two-party political system. Beyond this political system, Obama's candidacy imbued a sense of hope and a belief that dominant discourses could be successfully challenged.

It was in this hopeful climate that the spirit of reform took on new life for the supporters of African American Studies at UA, Regional. Not surprisingly, since that time, the number of students participating in AAS courses has risen dramatically, from an average of 18 students per semester prior to spring 2008, to the fall 2011 average of 81 students per semester (UA, Regional, 2011b). The number of students choosing to declare an AAS minor has risen dramatically from an average of approximately three per semester prior to spring 2008, to the fall 2011 average of 12 students per semester (UA, Regional, 2011b).

A Critical Race Theory Analysis of African American Studies at University of ACME, Regional

Researchers in education have made extensive use of CRT in their analysis of the American educational system (Dixson & Rousseau, 2006; Ladson-Billings & Tate, 1995). These scholars have established several key features of CRT that give shape and emphasis to arguments about the nature of race in society. I will discuss two of these features and then reflect on how they give shape and emphasis to my experiences with AAS at UA, Regional.

First, CRT sees racism as being pervasive in the United States and representing "a normal fact of daily life in U.S. society" (Taylor, 2009, p. 5). Supporting this idea are the ideologies and assumptions of White supremacy that are ingrained in political, legal, and educational social structures in ways that make them almost unrecognizable (Delgado, 1995, as cited in Taylor, 2009). Second, CRT views White supremacy as having a profound effect on the world in that it is an "all-encompassing and omnipresent" system of privilege, power, and opportunities that are often invisible to its own beneficiaries (Taylor, 2009, p. 4).

Like many ethnic studies programs, AAS has faced an uphill fight from its very inception. Disinterested faculty, antagonistic administrators, apathetic students, and a host of other factors all played a role in this fight. But perhaps the most problematic issue facing AAS as a discipline is the threat of racism. Racist ideas about the inferiority of AAS are undergirded by the widespread, though often covert, culture of White supremacy that permeates campus environments (Swindell, 1997). Although White supremacy often conjures up images of hate groups like the Ku Klux Klan, in this analysis, White supremacy should be understood as a

> political, economic, and cultural system in which whites overwhelmingly control power and material resources, conscious and unconscious ideas of white superiority and entitlement are widespread, and relations of white dominance and non-white subordination are daily reenacted across a broad array of institutions and social settings. (Ansley, 1997, p. 592)

White supremacy has a very strong and defined presence within institutions of higher education (Swindell, 1997; Solórzano, Ceja, & Yosso, 2000).

The history and development of AAS reflects an ongoing attempt to combat White supremacy through the development of curricula and programs that reflect the African American experience. In discussing the history and purpose of AAS, Swindell (1997) asserts that "Africana Studies aims to overcome the system that oppresses it" (p. 20), while Cole (2004) sees the discipline as "a critique of educational institutions in American society and a set of proposals for beginning the long and difficult process of change in those institutions" (p. 23).

UA, Regional, although not a Predominantly White Institution (PWI), still reflects many of the White supremacist ideals that are pervasive in higher education. For example, some faculty and administrators were not supportive of the formation of the AAS minor because of their belief in the inherent inferiority of an academic discipline that focuses on the study of Black people. Further, until recently, the guardians of the AAS minor were among the least powerful in the institutional hierarchy: untenured assistant professors, adjunct faculty, and students of color.

Moreover, this lack of support indicates a covert form of privilege and power on campus that rendered itself nearly unrecognizable. Some of this privilege can still be seen in the unwelcoming institutional climate for Black faculty members who do research in AAS. Those faculty members who approach AAS research utilizing alternative epistemologies that challenge the status quo and advocate a radical departure from mainstream scholarly research are under particular pressure (Conyers, 1997). Such oppositional scholarship has been a hallmark of both CRT and of AAS since its inception (Rooks, 2006). Although AAS has grown to encompass scholars and scholarship that also reflects mainstream research and ideologies, the discipline of AAS, by and large, still reflects a critical tone that challenges mainstream research in the academy.

The critical tone embodied by AAS in its development at UA, Regional is not merely critical for the sake of being critical, or critical for the sake of becoming a part of what Cole (2004) calls the "intellectual establishment" (p. 26). Instead, the development of AAS at UA, Regional has embodied a sort of critical participatory intellectualism that advocates radical scholarship, encourages community participation, and critiques the liberal tradition within the academy. In doing so, the AAS minor at UA, Regional embraces the idea of social justice, while rejecting values and practices that reify White supremacy, patriarchy, homophobia, and a host of other ideologies that serve to perpetuate the oppressive status quo.

Conclusion

The case presented in this chapter goes beyond the traditional struggle over change in university-level curriculum. Instead, the case illuminates deeper issues of race, power, and pedagogy that play out in a specific university context. If these issues resonate with the lived experiences of faculty, staff, students, and off-campus stakeholders elsewhere, then this case achieves Case Study Method validity (Stake, 1995).

The enormous changes that occurred to the AAS minor in early 2008 parallel broader changes in the African American political context nationwide. A sense of urgency developed from the emergence of then–Senator Barack Obama's presidential candidacy in the final months of 2007, but it was not until early 2008 that he seemed to emerge as a strong contender for the Democratic nomination. Likewise, at UA, Regional, African American students took to the streets and made an effort to link the issue of curriculum change with the concept of social justice. In doing so, they challenged established norms and forced the university power structure to address their concerns. At one time, this change, like Obama's presidency, seemed impossible. However, a varied constituency of campus leaders and faculty members came together with the local community to help initiate change. As the spring 2008 semester moved forward, Obama's candidacy pervaded the African American community on campus and interest in the AAS minor soared to new heights.

Since the events discussed in this chapter, the university has made great strides toward institutionalizing diversity in its curriculum by establishing a single administrative unit to bring together the various ethnic studies programs, along with the women's studies program, into one university-wide administrative unit. This unit was created to promote interdisciplinary teaching, scholarship, and community engagement in ways that move beyond traditional disciplinary boundaries.

The creation of this unit was strongly supported by the university president who issued an official proclamation of its establishment at a campus event that was well attended by senior university officials, faculty, students, and the local news media. The unit was placed under the direction of the COE with the hopes that the dean of the COE would make the new unit an integral part of her college, thereby helping it to grow and flourish.

Although it is still too early to discern the long-term success of this new unit, its very presence has become a strong force for the affirmation of diversity on the UA, Regional campus. The unit is also becoming a recognized entity in the local community. Resultantly, the unit is helping the university to fulfill its mission to realize institutional equity.

Stories from the *Faculty* Frontlines

Bailey W. Jackson

THE CASE STUDIES IN THIS THIRD SECTION FOCUS on the role of faculty and teaching graduate students in teacher education and/or in the teaching of diversity-focused content, as well as on the role of the affirmative action officer charged with diversifying faculty hires across disciplines. The researcher-activists who author these cases present cutting-edge analyses of what diversifying the curriculum and the faculty in higher education truly entails.

With respect to diversity in higher education, faculty may have campus-wide responsibility (e.g., for African American Studies or a campus diversity course requirement) or its members' efforts may focus only on their discipline (for recruiting students of color into teacher education, teaching a departmental diversity course requirement, etc.). Typically, they have a 'view from the side'—looking from their disciplinary location, department, and/or college or school 'outward' to varying extents. Despite commitment to diversity, faculty may still tend to view university hierarchy through the lens of tenure status, tenure-track appointment (versus clinical faculty), full-time status (versus adjunct), and graduate-student status (as teaching or research assistants), and, therefore, its members are sometimes perceived to fail in 'walking the talk' of their diversity knowledge in their interactions with colleagues, students, and staff, and/or to be 'out of touch' with the 'real world' of diversity even in their areas of expertise (e.g., the distance between theory and practice).

Because of the graduate-teaching-assistant-to-tenured-full-professor caste system, how "faculty" is defined and its members' corresponding experiences can vary significantly from one institution to the next. Accordingly, a faculty member's connection to his or her institution, college, or department; relationship with colleagues and students; and commitment to an equity, diversity, and/or social-justice agenda can appear very different at each step in the faculty hierarchy. Generally, faculty members who are committed to social justice not only teach about issues of social injustice that individuals and groups experience it in the world, they also testify to social injustice that they, as faculty members, experience in the academy. Faculty experiences of injustice are typically focused on its members' relationships with campus administrators (at all levels), their campus colleagues (broadly defined, but typically other faculty members), and their relationships with the students that they teach and advise. Because faculty members rely on 'collegiality,' it is often difficult to get to the social-justice issues that reside within their unique experience. This is made more difficult because the faculty is intimately involved in the admission and hiring of future 'colleagues'; thus, faculty members have a strong tendency to admit and hire 'their own.' As a result, it can be difficult, if not sometimes impossible, to cultivate faculty critical self-reflection and self-critique about pedagogical approach, course-content transformation, student empowerment, junior-colleague mentorship, and departmental governance.

While justice-seeking faculty members can be instructors, researchers, as well as campus and community activists, faculty-initiated efforts to enact social justice in the academy are typically focused on classroom activities. Regardless of how "classroom" is defined—the learning derived in a room in a campus building, during a community-based activity, and/or from an 'aha' moment that emerges in dialogue between students sitting at a bus stop—faculty goals remain constant: advancing student knowledge about, and dispositions for, varied manifestations of social change, social liberation, and social inclusion.

Faculty members working in an institution in the earlier stages of Multicultural Organization Development (MCOD) (Exclusionary and White Male Club) often encounter little encouragement, support, or reward for teaching to, researching about, and acting on justice interests; often the best that they can hope for is tolerance of their justice agendas. Faculty members working in an institution in the middle stages of MCOD (Equal Opportunity Compliance and Affirmative Action) typically find their justice commitments viewed as 'nice things to do' *in addition to* their 'real' instructional, inquiry, and service assignments. Faculty members working in an institution in the later stages of MCOD (Redefining and Multicultural) more commonly have their educational, scholarly, and practical justice pursuits considered part of their core responsibilities. But the process of MCOD can progress differentially within the same institution. Accordingly, some departments in some colleges within a single institution may operate in the earlier stages of MCOD, while others simultaneously function in the later stages. Case 12 describes this phenomenon well. Likewise, some equity, diversity, or even social-justice issues may be engaged within an institution with the limited or reluctant understanding that characterizes the earlier stages of MCOD (e.g., heroes and holidays approaches to curricular change efforts), while other issues will be embraced with the more advanced consciousness representative of the later stages (e.g., race-conscious admissions practices). Case 13 illustrates this dynamic vis-à-vis race and gender. Cases 11, 14, and 15 demonstrate what happens when there is institutional ambiguity about commitment to equity, diversity, and social justice—generally manifest as a gap between rhetoric and reality—even on the part of faculty members who are ardent advocates for social justice. With these cases, the complexity of MCOD in everyday campus life is revealed—equity, diversity, and social justice do not progress monolithically and coherently from one stage of MCOD to the next, rather they progress in multifarious fashion.

11

"Just (Don't) Do It!"

Tensions between Articulated Commitments and Action at The ACME State University

Kenneth J. Fasching-Varner and Vanessa Dodo Seriki

Constructing the Case

This chapter undertakes a critical exploration of the institutional *problematics* of race that manifest at The ACME State University (The ASU), a large research extensive university in the Midwest (Fasching-Varner, 2009). Our analysis draws on Critical Race Theory (CRT) to interrogate the workings of The ASU's preservice teacher-education program. Educational scholars have used CRT as a mechanism for understanding how race impacts educational opportunities and outcomes (Delgado Bernal & Villalpando, 2002; Duncan, 2002; Ladson-Billings & Tate, 1995; Morris, 2001; Solórzano & Yosso, 2002a; Tate, 1994; Taylor, 2000). Specifically, our analysis draws upon the CRT elements of counterstorytelling and Whiteness as property (Chapman, 2006; DeCuir & Dixson, 2004; Delgado, 1989; Dixson & Rousseau, 2005; Fasching-Varner, 2009; Ladson-Billings, 1996, 1999, 2001, 2005b, 2006; Ladson-Billings & Tate, 1995; Lawrence, 1995; Solórzano & Yosso, 2002a).

After telling our counterstory, we *unpack* it so as to provide context to the experiences embedded within it (Dixson & Rousseau, 2005); we do this in a manner consistent with this volume's focus on the study of the case (Merriam, 1998; Stake, 1995; Yin, 2009). What occurs at The ASU with regard to the institutional workings of race(ism) and the lack of commitment to issues of diversity is consistent with what occurs in other higher-education institutions, including many of those at focus in the other cases in this volume.

Our examination is situated within the Obama-era context, a context that has exacerbated the erroneous notion that, as a nation, we have moved beyond the ills of race and racism. Not only do we firmly reject neoliberal and right-leaning arguments that the Obama era represents a postracial society, our experiences at The ASU suggest that higher-educational institutions generally, and those charged with preparing future teachers specifically, continue to have significant struggles with race in this era.

Pressing the Core: A Counterstory

Mr. Bigg was elected president of Cap City in part for his professed love of the people, supported by his articulated commitment to what he called a Social and Academic Mobility Plan (SAAMP). When he ran for president, Mr. Bigg promised strengthened educational outcomes for all of the nation's children, and an end to social inequity through SAAMP.

Once elected, Mr. Bigg's first order of business was to select a cabinet and press secretaries. Mr. Bigg first hired Addy Jones as his general press secretary; Addy's experience was as an educational scholar and expert in ending inequity in schooling systems. Addy had a keen understanding of how identity dimensions, like race, gender, and class, factored into educational outcomes. Addy was told to recruit two undersecretaries who would apprentice her in these knowledge bases, and also serve as spokespeople on SAAMP to the press core and to viewers of the various media outlets influenced by the press core. Addy hired Buddy Whitespoon as well as Ebony Brown to be her undersecretaries. Addy and her undersecretaries were responsible for communicating the overall message of SAAMP to the public at large. This meant that they worked with the press core and their media interns, specifically focusing attention on helping these interns learn to become full-fledged members of the press core. Addy, Buddy, and Ebony also put together a plan for spreading the word about, and facilitating implementation of, the SAAMP. Mr. Bigg hired other press secretaries as well, including Holly Greensmooth whose expertise centered on promoting the English language.

Addy and her team made visits to all the local media outlets. During these visits, they looked to see how the press core and interns were talking about and implementing Mr. Bigg's SAAMP. Addy, Buddy, and Ebony all began to notice that understanding of SAAMP was articulated, but that it was rarely being implemented. Having each been members of the press core prior to working in Mr. Bigg's administration, the team began to offer workshops designed to get the press core and interns, and the local media outlets for whom they worked/interned, to move from talk to action with respect to SAAMP.

During the workshops, Buddy also began to notice that the media interns of color were often neglected in conversations with their press core mentors and that, outside the presence of the interns of color, members of the press core and White interns discussed the interns of color negatively. Buddy shared his observation with Mr. Bigg and Holly in a series of SAAMP meetings. In particular, Buddy expressed concerns about what he saw as the highly racialized ways SAAMP was playing out, especially the disparity in treatment and quality of mentorship for media interns of color.

Similarly, Ebony had concerns about her interactions with media interns from the dominant group. One example was Ebony's interactions with a White, male media intern named Ned. In discussion with Ebony one day, Ned asserted, "I don't like covering stories in the cities, the whole music and way of life is just something I don't agree with." Ned was unmoved by Ebony's efforts to help him understand those city stories differently. So, Ebony began to document Ned's reactions and related attitudes toward covering city stories. She took this documentation to Ned first to see whether he would be motivated to begin thinking differently about city stories when faced with a body of his own statements. Instead, Ned became very angry. He argued that SAAMP was a waste of time, as was his media internship to the extent that it required him to cover city stories. Next Ebony took her concerns about Ned to Mr. Bigg and his other press secretaries. But despite some sympathetic initial interactions, Mr. Bigg and most of the other press secretaries feared being sued by Ned. For that reason, Mr. Bigg decided to have Holly work with Ned on his city stories, even though Holly had no prior media experience, and no experience living or working in urban communities. Ebony would still "technically" supervise Ned, but Holly would be the one to give Ned feedback on his city stories, with an eye toward "nurturing" his learning about the people on whom these stories focused. Mr. Bigg felt this would be the best way to "negotiate the conflict" between Ned and Ebony. When Ebony asked Mr. Bigg why he was not requiring Ned, as a media intern, to "negotiate the conflict" directly with her, as one of the city-story specific press secretaries in the manner SAAMP described, Mr. Bigg suggested that Ebony could do better things with her time than worry about that.

Before long, Addy, Buddy, and Ebony began to hear complaints about their work with the media. Various media interns complained to the press core, and other press secretaries, especially Holly, that what Addy's team was saying and doing in relationship to SAAMP made them feel uncomfortable. While they agreed with the theory of SAAMP, they could not reconcile it with what Addy, Buddy, and Ebony were asking them to do to enact SAAMP. They wanted relief from Addy and her team's insistence that they be held accountable for living the principles of SAAMP. Holly went to Mr. Bigg with these complaints and suggested that if he simply got rid of Addy and her troublemaking team, Holly and the other press secretaries could take on the overall promotion of SAAMP, and do so in a manner that would make all the media stakeholders happy.

Mr. Bigg told Addy that her team's work to align the theory and practice of SAAMP went too far. He asked Addy to focus on the rhetoric of SAAMP and to let go of the praxis of it, since that was what was making the media uncomfortable. Addy reminded Mr. Bigg that her team was only doing what he himself had laid out in SAAMP for them to do.

Mr. Bigg eventually gave in to the complaints. He dismissed Addy from her work as press secretary and transferred her to a technical role in the Office of Social Awareness that precluded her from having any further interaction with the media interns, the press core, and the larger media outlets. Ebony and Buddy were also reassigned.

Eventually Addy was selected to be the press secretary for a different government agency, leaving her work with Mr. Bigg altogether. Ebony and Buddy completed their undersecretary training in Mr. Bigg's administration, and then went on to obtain press secretary jobs of their own, also with other governmental agencies. Addy, Buddy, and Ebony all hoped that once outside of Cap City and Mr. Bigg's influence, they would be able to walk the talk of SAAMP in their new press secretary roles.

Critical Race Theory (CRT) Exploration

Unpacking the Counterstory

Unpacking our counterstory is the requisite next step in this CRT analysis so that the nature and operationalization of racism in our (real-life) story can be made transparent and explicit (Dixson & Rousseau, 2005; Lawrence, 1995; Solórzano & Yosso, 2002a). Table 11.1 reveals the counterstory by contrasting the (actual) story elements in our—Kenny and Vanessa's—real experience at The ASU, with our—Buddy and Ebony's—fictionalized experience in Mr. Bigg's administration. In analyzing our real experience, we will use our real names, but retain the fictionalized names of the other players.

Whiteness as Property

Harris (1995) has suggested that Whiteness be understood as property. Acknowledging the inalienability of Whiteness creates an absoluteness about Whiteness that affords people perceived to be White rights that operate in society in the same way that property rights do. According to Harris (1995), a paradox exists whereby Whiteness is infinitely absolute. In other words, one drop of White blood never makes one White, yet one drop of Black blood inherently excludes one from Whiteness, ultimately decreasing one's value. Thus, Whiteness, purely located at the level of phenotype, represents an absolute that garners higher value as property (Hall, 1997; Montagu, 1997;

Table 11.1.
Counterstory Elements Unpacked

Story Element	Actual Representation
The ACME State University (The ASU)	A large midwestern research extensive university where Addy was an associate professor and Ebony (Vanessa) and Buddy (Kenny) were doctoral students.
Cap City	The city where The ASU is located.
Mr. Bigg	Specifically represents the faculty director of The ASU's preservice teacher-education program; generally represents The ASU's College of Education Leadership (including the section head, dean, associate deans, etc.).
SAAMP	The conflicting vision about diversity and engagement, particularly around race inequity, articulated at The ASU that lived in articulation but not in action.
Press Core	The majority White, female, in-service teachers throughout the nation generally; in particular those who host, as cooperating teachers, preservice candidates from The ASU.
Media Interns	The majority White, female, preservice teacher candidates in education programs throughout the nation; in particular the candidates at The ASU.
Media Viewers	The students and families that are recipients of public education at the hands of the Press Core (in-service teachers) and Media Interns (preservice teachers).
Addy Jones	Associate professor of color with expertise in diversity and equity education, and graduate student advisor to Buddy and Ebony.
Buddy Whitespoon	A privileged, White, male, doctoral student and Media Intern (preservice teacher) supervisor at The ASU. Currently an assistant professor of education.
Ebony Brown	A Black, female, doctoral student and Media Intern (preservice teacher) supervisor at The ASU. Currently an assistant professor of education.
Holly Greensmooth	Generally represents the majority White and female professoriate in PK–12 teacher education throughout the nation and at The ASU; specifically represents several actual faculty members who worked to undermine efforts taken by Addy, Buddy, and Ebony.
Ned	A White, male, preservice teacher-education student at The ASU who expressed frustration and anger about having to have urban school placements during his preservice teacher education program.
Office of Representation (OR)	An office in the College of Education at The ASU that provided equity and diversity outreach.

Winant, 2000). Harris (1995) argues that Whites capitalize on the value of Whiteness for a variety of purposes, including enjoyment, suggesting that inherent in Whiteness is also a reputational value (i.e., promoting a specific White image amplifies the reputational value of Whiteness).

Whiteness also excludes insofar as Whites never make explicit what Whiteness is, but rather explain, at length, what Whiteness is not. Allowing the definition of Whiteness to fluctuate, as markets do, enables the tight control of positive valuation of Whiteness (Harris, 1995). While Whiteness as property is theoretically complex in the CRT literature, for the purposes of our analysis, the following guiding principles are most important to consider: (a) ultimately, White academics experience a sense of value to what they believe their Whiteness represents literally and metaphorically; (b) because this value has meaning for White academics, they go to great lengths to protect the value of their Whiteness; (c) in protecting the value of their own Whiteness, White academics leverage academics of color, when convenient or opportune, as a mechanism to shield themselves from the negative consequence of meaningfully engaging White students in discourse and action centered on race; and finally, (d) White academics make decisions about how to evaluate the value of other White academics' Whiteness when those academics demonstrate commitments and actions beyond a threshold where the White majority is comfortable.

Whiteness as Property and Our Unpacked Story

While our counterstory describes events in a fictitious setting, it shares both metaphorical and literal connections with our real experiences at The ASU. We use the idea of Whiteness as property to explain and analyze these connections in order to reveal the larger institutional realities they represent.

Unpacking Addy and Ebony (Vanessa)

Addy was supposedly hired to promote diversity in The ASU's teacher-education unit and the local schools with whom this unit works. As a young professor and scholar of color with diversity-related teaching and research expertise, The ASU was eager to position Addy's hire as one that would bring needed racial diversity to the faculty as well as to the preservice teachers in her courses. However, The ASU was less eager to support Addy in authentically pursuing this work. In fact, the manner in which Addy engaged in her work was problematic to The ASU, because it was far more action-based than the institution was willing to support. Once Addy demonstrated resistance to only speaking diversity, as opposed to also engaging in diversity action, Mr. Bigg and Holly Greensmooth quickly cast Addy as an "angry Black woman."

As The ASU's sole expert on diversity, Addy unfairly bore the responsibility for raising issues of equity and diversity with pre- and in-service teachers. Because Addy was assigned to deal with these issues, faculty members, like Holly, could then ignore these issues, at least until Addy's engagement of the issues caused discomfort to her predominantly White students. As this discomfort grew, Holly and other faculty complained about Addy to program directors, assistant deans, and deans in an attempt to have Addy obey the unspoken rule at The ASU to "speak diversity, just don't do it."

Similarly, Vanessa experienced a sense of disconnection with The ASU pre-service teachers and faculty in relationship to her race. Vanessa was aware that her role as a doctoral student served a technical function for the institution—the supervision of preservice teacher interns, while her role as a *Black* doctoral student served a political function for the institution—her diversity was manipulated and leveraged as evidence of institutional progress. While Vanessa was at The ASU, there were no other faculty members or doctoral students of color in her teaching field, science education, within the College of Education. When issues of race came up, often masked by code words like 'culture' or 'urban,' Vanessa was the "go-to" Black face in the room (Delgado & Stefancic, 1992). Recognizing the lack of diversity in the teacher-preparation program and the significant diversity of the schools in which preservice teachers were placed, Vanessa probed into and pushed teacher-education students' thinking around race, particularly around their privileged racial position, in ways that The ASU faculty and administrators felt were less than ideal.

The preservice teacher interns, Holly, and other faculty members enact Whiteness to control Blackness; here, controlling Blackness means ensuring that Blackness maintains its relative (lesser) value to Whiteness, and that Addy and Vanessa maintain their corresponding relative (lower) property value to The ASU. Addy's and Vanessa's Blackness is valued to the extent that it furthers The ASU's goal of *appearing* to be committed to equity and social justice. Black faculty members like Addy and Black graduate students like Vanessa can "speak for them, and not be one of them" where "them" are issues of diversity and diverse populations (Ladson-Billings, 2005b, p. 232). The ASU capitalizes on Addy's and Vanessa's Blackness to protect the value of Whiteness in so far as their presence and roles absolve other faculty members, like Holly, from even having to deal with uncomfortable conversations about race. At the same time, Addy and Vanessa are punished for enacting racialized epistemologies in the preparation of urban teachers, in essence highlighting that their Blackness has less value than their colleagues' Whiteness, even though Addy was expressly hired because of her expertise in diversity, and

Vanessa was specifically recruited as a graduate student of color to be *the* diversity in science education at The ASU.

The ASU faculty and staff value diversity as a primarily White interest when it is merely articulated, but not when it is actually enacted. If other professors were to teach the diversity courses or formally engage with equity and diversity in their other courses, they may run the risk of being critiqued as promoting a Black agenda, potentially damaging their property value as Whites. But as long as faculty and graduate students of color, like Addy and Vanessa, are around, the property value of The ASU's White faculty and graduate students remains high. Since Addy's and Vanessa's Blackness is not valued, it can be leveraged when convenient to preserve the property value of White faculty. So, when undergraduate students complain that they are uncomfortable with Addy's course content or Vanessa's supervision of their urban teaching placements, the White faculty's response is always to coddle the undergraduates, never to support their faculty and graduate-student colleagues in pushing undergraduates, especially those undergraduates from dominant identity groups, to further examine their discomfort with issues of diversity.

Addy and Vanessa also represent many images that conflict with how White colleagues at The ASU have cast Blackness. Addy has a PhD and Vanessa, at that time, had a master's degree and was pursuing a PhD. They are clearly intelligent, knowledgeable, scholarly, industrious, and responsible; they are also middle class, law-abiding, and sophisticated. At The ASU, these qualities are perceived to be the property of White faculty and students, and consequently, give value only to Whiteness, not Blackness. As such, Crenshaw (1995) argues that the use of these qualities are expected to be for the sole enjoyment of Whites, not also people of color, especially those who do not conform to the expectations of Whites and Whiteness. So, when these qualities are attached to people of color like Addy and Vanessa, identity confusion is created for their White colleagues (Crenshaw, 1995). "'Black images' such as lazy, unintelligent . . . ignorant, criminal, shiftless, and lascivious" represent Blackness to White people (Crenshaw, 1995, p. 115). Thus, there is a disconnect between what Addy and Vanessa are and what Addy and Vanessa are cast to be. This disconnect places Addy's and Vanessa's value at a great distance (and far below) that of their White counterparts.

Unpacking Buddy (Kenny)

Kenny also struggled with The ASU's White expectations, though as a White male and, therefore, part of the dominant group, his struggle is different. Kenny was one of Addy's doctoral students in the preservice teacher-preparation program. Kenny's White race consciousness and antiracist disposition, as well as his positive relationship with Addy, led to him being questioned about, and admonished for, his interactions around race and racism. Kenny's commitment to walk his race talk meant challenging Mr. Bigg, Holly, and other program faculty members and graduate students in a series of program meetings in his second year at The ASU. Kenny questioned the pattern he observed in the disparate treatment of undergraduate students of color in the program. He wanted to know why these preservice teachers of color seemed to be subjected to hostile learning environments in their university courses, while being supported in the field by their graduate student supervisors (Kenny and Vanessa's peers). In response to Kenny's questioning, Mr. Bigg and Holly met privately with Kenny to try and understand why he was so concerned about race. Given that he was a White male, his racial concerns seemed skewed to Mr. Bigg and Holly, because these concerns did not appear to represent Kenny's racial self-interest. As Mr. Bigg put it, "It would be better for your career if you stopped talking about race so much, it's not like it [race] affects you." Holly even started a campaign among the faculty in The ASU's College of Education to frame Kenny as overly concerned with *Addy's interests* and, therefore, unable to see how the discomfort his conversations about race were damaging the educational and professional experiences of others. Kenny's commitments to what Holly perceived to be a Black and Brown agenda enabled Holly to devalue Kenny's Whiteness, making it inabsolute, unlike the Whiteness of the faculty and other White graduate students. Holly's utter inability to conceive of Kenny's racial posture as anything other than pathological even caused her to suggest Kenny see a neurologist stating, "I'm worried you might have a brain tumor or something wrong."

Interestingly, Addy never suggested to Kenny that he challenge Mr. Bigg or Holly—there was no racial confrontation conspiracy, despite Mr. Bigg's and Holly's perception to the contrary. Kenny's mere affiliation with Addy led Mr. Bigg, Holly, and the rest of the faculty to perceive that Kenny and Addy shared a hostile racial agenda. Consequently, Kenny's value as a White person was reduced within The ASU context, because his personal and political values did not align with the institution's primarily White interests. Rather than exploring with Kenny the origins of his values, Mr. Bigg and Holly simply ascribed them to the narrative they had already constructed about Addy and her race-focused work. Not surprisingly, Kenny's graduate-assistant duties, like Addy's teaching ones, were reassigned.

Mr. Bigg and Holly cited their need to have preservice teacher supervisors who were, in Mr. Bigg's words, "fair and objective" as the reason for Kenny's reassignment. Inherent in Mr. Bigg's comments is his belief that no conversation about race, particularly one in which institutional norms are challenged, could ever be fair or objective. Consequently privileged positions and perspectives become the default basis for considering fairness and objectivity, particularly in the pursuit of maintaining the property value of Whiteness. Mr. Bigg was unwilling (or unable) to acknowledge that in framing fair and objective as he did, he revealed his own subjectivity as well as his self-interest in maintaining the property value of Whiteness (Peshkin, 1988).

Kenny's critical engagement with Whiteness, problematizing of race, and refusal to play by the White rules of the race norm game led faculty members in the teacher-education program to not want to work with him. As a result, Kenny is framed as less-than, less "industrious, intelligent, moral, responsible," and the value of his White privilege at The ASU is diminished (Harris, 1995, p. 113). The challenge for Kenny and others in similar situations is to continue to resist institutional norms and related positions of privilege, in spite of the personal loss of institutional privilege and the related devaluation of their Whiteness. While what Kenny experienced at The ASU is unique for White people, it is the everyday experience of people of color, whether they are inside or outside higher education. Thus, if Kenny is committed to continuing his proactive work around race, he has to expect that he will have many more experiences like the ones he had at The ASU. At the same time, Kenny has to remember that he remains White, even if other Whites at The ASU do not value his Whiteness. Further, outside the ASU context, Kenny's White privilege in society remains fully intact, unless he continues to act against that privilege day in and day out. When White academics experience a loss of value to Whiteness caused by committing themselves to the right thing over the White thing, they must understand that contextually they still experience a great deal of racial privilege, both in the academy and society at large. Challenging racist and other discriminatory postures, in spite of potential loss of White identity value, is part and parcel of the work of White equity and diversity workers. This is especially the reality when articulated institutional commitments are not seriously undertaken.

Unpacking Ned

During one quarter in the teacher-education program, preservice teacher-education student Ned decided to push back against what he perceived as an expressed value for racial diversity in the program being expressed by Vanessa. He pushed back professing emphatically that he did not understand, like, or condone urban culture and did not want to work with urban students. Vanessa was not immediately certain how Ned was using the word "urban." But after reviewing the demographics of Ned's previous quarters' teaching placements, she realized that Ned had only interned in suburban schools with predominantly White student populations. It then became clear to Vanessa that Ned was using the word "urban" as code for "Black." She pressed Ned to lay out his beliefs about *urban* culture and students. Ned indicated that he just did not like the music, stating, "You know the gangster rap that's full of violence, and the unmotivated students."

Ned's picture of urban conjures up stereotypical images of Blackness as *immoral, lazy, and unintelligent* (Crenshaw, 1995). Ned's mental image of Black people suggests that he believes Black students have no rights to the property value of the education that he and other White students receive. To maintain his own racial property value, Ned could not be caught extending his White privilege (and the corresponding White value of this privilege) to Black students. Yet, if his teacher-education program required a placement in a racially diverse urban school, he would have no choice but to do so. Once placed in such a school, Ned continued to enact his Whiteness in ways that connoted his valuing of Whiteness over Blackness. His tone of voice and demeanor when engaging with Black students, or White students who behaved in ways that represented Blackness to him, was condescending at best, and often hostile. Ned rarely addressed his Black or "Black-acting" students directly unless he had to; and when he had to, he addressed them differently—his remarks were short, curt, and unfriendly, causing many students to stop speaking to him altogether.

Ned's posture in conversations with Vanessa was no better. He rarely made eye contact with her and responded only defensively to all of her feedback. Ned blamed the lack of student engagement in his classroom on the students themselves, claiming they were lazy and/or lacked intellectual capacity. Vanessa pressed Ned to engage in critical self-reflection and consider the role of his racial identity in the classroom, especially its impact on his teaching action or inaction with different students. Annoyed by Vanessa's persistence, Ned complained about Vanessa to Mr. Bigg. While Vanessa documented Ned's racism, thinking it might become a concern for the program, Mr. Bigg began documenting Ned's complaints about Vanessa. Soon, Vanessa, like Addy and Kenny, was called in for a *sit down* with Mr. Bigg. After Mr. Bigg laid out Ned's complaints about Vanessa, Vanessa provided Mr. Bigg with her documentation illustrating that Ned did not possess the requisite dispositions needed to work with all students. Vanessa suggested that the institution should not endorse an intern with Ned's dispositions, because he was likely to cause significant harm to students. While Mr. Bigg was initially sympathetic to Vanessa's position, particularly considering the vast amount of documentation she had, and the valiant effort she had made to engage Ned in critical self-reflection, he ultimately sided with Ned by arguing that Ned should be allowed to continue in the program simply because, "We really do not want a lawsuit, and anyway this is the first time there has been a problem."

Ned's enactment of his Whiteness resurfaced at the end of the term when, after there had been no change in his disposition, his final grade from Vanessa reflected that he lacked the prerequisite dispositions for meeting the needs of all students. Enraged that he had not gotten "an A," Ned contacted Mr. Bigg, demanding to know why he received a lower grade. Being given a copy of the grading rubric did not alleviate Ned's anger. He successfully appealed his grade by arguing that it was based on the fact that he was a White male who did not want to be in an urban setting, and not on his performance as a teacher.

In seeking to understand why her supervisory authority had not been institutionally supported, Vanessa contacted Mr. Bigg. Mr. Bigg told Vanessa that it was probably not a great use of her time to challenge students like Ned. Ultimately, Mr. Bigg's actions communicated to Vanessa that when the value of Whiteness (supporting Ned) is juxtaposed against the value of Blackness (supporting Vanessa), the administration chooses to support Whiteness. In so doing, The ASU consciously backed off its stated commitment to live in action what it articulated as a value. In these actions, we see that The ASU's College of Education essentially supported the idea that diversity *is* worth talking about, but it *is not* worth doing anything about, if it means jeopardizing the value of any White person's Whiteness.

Concluding Thoughts

White academics engage in discriminatory warfare, often without consciously recognizing it. The counterstory presented herein serves to illustrate the nature of this warfare in teacher education at The ASU. Through analysis, we see that preservice teacher-preparation programs fail to close the PK–12 performance gap between White students and students of color, despite their claim that doing so is their top priority. Interestingly, practices that further widen the gap between White and Black students in K–12 settings are reinforced, reinscribed, and made acceptable to future educators, who mostly represent White, middle-class, female interests. Further, by breeding and then reifying racist educational practices, teacher-training efforts actually extend the education debt that disproportionately accrues against students of color (Ladson-Billings, 2006).

These operating practices in teacher education, like those at The ASU, give further credence to Bell's (1995b) notion of *racial realism,* which asserts that racism and discrimination are normative and pervasive in mainstream society. Consequently, any suggestion that racism and discrimination do not, or no longer, exist in society must be challenged. Only when racism and discrimination are accepted as real, can we work to imagine and build a different reality.

The incremental and conditional accommodation of diversity seen in Mr. Bigg's SAAMP program, and in The ASU's expressed-but-not-lived commitment to diversity, will fail students, scholars, and citizens of color until serious action is institutionally embraced.

But even this case and its analysis are limited by partiality and perspective. Lived experiences, whether presented through story and/or critical inquiry, are subjective. While an analytical framework, like that of Whiteness as property, compliments the counterstory telling aspect of CRT by enabling a substantive race examination, no social change will occur unless our stories and analyses bring forward a change in praxis for both us (as authors) and our readers. Toward that end we must ask ourselves: *To what extent do our very own behaviors create or exacerbate discriminatory warfare at an institution like The ASU? Given the institutional roadblocks to diversity present in many higher-education institutions, how do we take action against this warfare? To what extent are we willing to realize that our very presence as diversity and equity workers is likely the result of institutional struggle to match, in action, to that which they verbally commit?*

As educators, we have an obligation to proactively examine the ways in which we structure course syllabi, participate in shared governance and other institutional service, and undertake scholarly endeavors that challenge the status quo of racial privilege. Through this examination, we must resist the academy's seductive interest in turning us into thinkers and talkers, but not doers; into people satisfied with words over actions (at worst), or confused about how to approach these institutional commitments differently (at best).

Consciousness does not necessarily "create a unified, coherent self . . . [but the] . . . unconscious certainly cannot" (St. Pierre, 2000, p. 501). Similarly, "A large part of the behavior that produces racial discrimination is influenced by unconscious racial motivation" (Lawrence 1995, p. 237). Accordingly, we close this chapter with a call to stay vigilant. The work to end racial discrimination in education and to bring about educational equity never ends. When we choose to enter into equity and diversity work, we must do so aware of the complex and contradictory limits imposed on this work by dominant interests. Even attempting to redistribute the property value of Whiteness to all individuals and groups within an institutional context is not enough. Instead, we must seek to establish diversity as community property through which we all share currency.

Anyone wishing to join in the collaborative work for social justice must also be willing to undertake the personal work of developing an antidiscriminatory disposition. Social justice is made more urgent by individual transgressions. Work to close the gaps and repay the debts leveraged against underrepresented populations by our educational system is the most significant work our society can undertake in the 21st century. With urgency, we ask readers to think about how racism and discrimination exacerbate these gaps and debts, and how both individual and collective equity and diversity work can reconcile them.

12

Déjà Vu

Dynamism of Racism in Policies and Practices Aimed at Alleviating Discrimination

Shirley Mthethwa-Sommers

Rhetoric and Reality

HIGHER-EDUCATION INSTITUTIONS IN THE UNITED STATES have made tremendous strides toward embracing and cultivating environments receptive to racial diversity. Many colleges and universities have been deliberate in implementing affirmative-action policies to recruit students and faculty members of color. Often, today's institutional mission statements indicate commitment to support and respect diversity (Henderson, 2011). Despite having affirmative-action policies in place, mission statements declaring support for diversity, and even academic programs dedicated to diverse epistemologies, racial equity, and social justice are still elusive in many higher-education institutions. Faculty members of color in these institutions often report lukewarm reception at best, and hostility at worst (Dixson & Dingus, 2007; Ladson-Billings, 2005b; Muñoz, Ordoñez Jasis, Young, & McLaren, 2004).

The historic election of then–Senator Obama as president of the United States raised hope for racial acceptance and related change for many faculty of color, especially because, as a presidential candidate, Obama made a commitment to educational equity. As a senator, Obama expressed cognizance of inequities engendered by social class, gender, and racial disparities and their corrosive impact on education in general (Darling-Hammond, 2009). As soon as President Obama took office, however, it was clear that his prior commitment to educational equity and cognizance of how social class, race, and gender privilege and marginalize people would be overshadowed by his neoliberal, race-neutral, and market-based approach to education policy. The rhetoric of social justice proffered by presidential candidate Obama did not align with the policies of President Obama.

It is of note that President Obama, while an individual, is also a representative of his administration and the larger executive branch of the U.S. government. Critique of President Obama in this chapter is not primarily a critique of him as an individual, but a critique of him as the leader of his administration and of the manner in which he wields his executive powers. As Martin (1992) points out, institutions are composed of individuals who determine policies and practices of institutions.

The disconnect between rhetoric and policies evident in Obama's transition from senator to president is also apparent in higher-education institutions vis-à-vis their diversity efforts. On one hand, these institutions profess acceptance of diversity and social justice. On the other hand, they implement policies and practices that sabotage diversity and social-justice initiatives.

Using vignettes, this chapter presents two case studies that provide glimpses of the rhetoric–policy disconnect in the higher-education context through the eyes of those the disconnect directly impacts. These vignettes serve as exemplars of how, in spite of good intentions, institutions continue to uphold what hooks (2000) calls *White supremacist practices* that undermine their own missions and goals relating to cultivating and embracing racial diversity. The chapter contributes to the "few works [that] have examined the context for [social justice oriented] faculty in teacher education" (Muñoz, et al., 2004, p. 170).

Theoretical Framework

Critical Race Theory (CRT) originated from legal studies (Bell, 1992) but has been applied to educational contexts (Ladson-Billings, 2005b). The fundamental idea in CRT is that racism is entrenched in the "psychology, memory, society, and culture of the modern world" (Bell, 1992, p. xiv). In this chapter, I focus on two tenets of CRT, namely, an examination of how institutional structures, practices, and policies reinforce race-based privileges (Delgado & Stefancic, 2000) and *counter storytelling*, which seeks to allow voices that are often muted to be heard (Delgado, 1999; Solórzano & Yosso, 2002b).

Institutions and Reinforcement of Race-Based Inequalities

It is irrefutable that the United States has made tremendous progress toward racial equality. Despite this progress, Bell (1995c) contends that many institutions covertly or overtly perpetuate race-based inequalities through policies and practices. Higher-education institutions, similar to other institutions, have policies and practices anchored in the notion of colorblindness, which serves to sustain and normalize White privilege. Colorblindness normalizes White privilege and racism by pretending to ignore (render invisible) differences (of color, race, caste, etc.) upon which racial disparities are predicated (Bonilla-Silva, 1997). In refusing to acknowledge racial differences, people cannot claim discriminatory treatment on the basis of color (Delgado, 1999).

Counter Storytelling

Counter storytelling is salient to CRT as it "allows us to examine the interconnectivity of race, racism, and gendered racism in higher education" (Smith, Yosso, & Solórzano, 2006, p. 564). Counter storytelling "challenges the experiences of whites as the normative standard and grounds its conceptual framework in the distinctive experience of people of color" (Taylor, 1998, p. 122). These stories are meant to unveil the micro-level impact of consciously or unconsciously perpetuated institutional racism (Solórzano, 1997). Additionally, counter storytelling "exposes the contradictions inherent in the dominant storyline" of higher-education institutions whose mission statements include goals of embracing diversity and commitments to racial social justice, but whose policies and practices simultaneously sabotage attempts to realize these goals (Zamudio, Russell, Rios, & Bridgeman, 2011, p. ix).

Methodology

Counter storytelling is employed in this chapter through two case studies. The case study method accurately captures real-life situations and provides an opportunity for an in-depth understanding of a phenomenon (Noor, 2008; Yin, 1993). One case focuses on the policy and practice of requiring one diversity course for teacher-education students; the other case focuses on the policy and practice of using student evaluations in tenure and promotion decision making. These two case studies provide a complex view of one institution's attempt to meet its social-justice-oriented mission.

Vignettes for the case study are collected by recording the stories of two faculty of color at a large Midwestern public institution, hereafter referred to as University of ACME City (UAC). UAC is located in an urban area that was once economically thriving with many car- and clothing-manufacturing factories; most of these factories have moved overseas. UAC is vital to the area's economic survival. UAC is a historically and predominantly White public institution and serves thousands of students from all over the nation. Its mission statement asserts that the institution respects and honors all forms of diversity and is opposed to any form of discrimination on the basis of race, color, religion, gender, sexual orientation, and nationality.

Participants in the case study are the only two African American women in the College of Education (COE) at UAC, where both have been at the institution for four years. Ruth works in the department housing the only diversity course, and Dora works in the Department of Special Education. In conversation, Ruth and Dora share their stories of being the only faculty of color at UAC, particularly how their work as social-justice-oriented educators has presented challenges, and how they have attempted to address these challenges. The vignettes unveil a racist dynamic with overt connections to Jim Crow laws, as well as covert exclusion of people of color through the privileging of Whiteness (Bonilla-Silva, 1997).

Vignette # 1: Neutrality

Two faculty members of color at UAC's COE, Dora and Ruth, have decided to meet in between their classes for a quick cup of coffee in the cafeteria. Dora looks dejected, so Ruth decides to ask her why she appears down:

"Are you alright, Dora?"

Dora responds, "I just came out of a meeting with the chair of my department. Apparently some students have complained that I spend a lot of time discussing the overrepresentation of African American boys in special education, and suggest I am not covering relevant material. The chair recommends that I leave that topic to you guys, the folks who teach the diversity course and focus on the material relevant to *all* special-education students."

"What did you say?" Ruth interjects.

Dora continues, "I explained that we were discussing the social construction of ability and disability and how it intersects with social constructions of racial capability, etc. [The chair] did not want to hear it. She said she is only interested in me doing well as a professor in this institution. She wants me to succeed here."

"And?" Ruth interposes again.

Dora reacts, "What else could I say? That was the end of the meeting."

"You should say something," Ruth says in a low voice. "You should send her an e-mail, you know, at least about the legitimacy of what you were teaching. I'm sorry you are going through this."

Dora laments, "What's worse is that I have a class right now, and I had prepared to examine behavioral styles that contribute to the disproportionate representation of African American boys in special education."

The brief exchange between Dora and Ruth illuminates: (a) roadblocks to social-justice-oriented education, (b) the assumed neutrality of special education based on the notion of colorblindness, and (c) how a well-meaning White administrator can end up protecting Whiteness.

Roadblocks to Social-Justice-Oriented Education

Social-justice education is defined as education that unveils and seeks to transform oppressive structures and practices within schools and society (Mthethwa-Sommers, 2001). Dora's story above reveals that she was engaging in social-justice education when she unveiled the social construction of ability and its corresponding intersections of race and culturally based notions of who is perceived to be 'normal.' In other words, she was exposing the oppressive ideologies that undergird the disproportionate overrepresentation of African American boys in nongifted special-education classes.

The main roadblock toward social-justice education at UAC is imposed by the policy that requires students to take one course in diversity; this limits discussions of social-justice issues to the designated class. While the policy may be an improvement on the past, when many institutions and accreditation bodies did not require prospective and in-service teachers to take even one such course, the policy only exists because it serves *interest convergence.* Interest convergence theory argues that social-justice gains for people of color must also be beneficial to the White dominant group to even be partially achieved (Bell, 1995c). With increasingly diverse student demographics in public schools, *some* knowledge about diversity is deemed necessary for the predominantly White teaching force. The one-diversity-course policy, while potentially beneficial to future PK–12 students of color, also serves the current academic and future professional needs of the White students who constitute the majority of the preservice teaching force. Supposedly, the diversity course is designed to prepare teachers to effectively reach and teach students who are racially and culturally different from themselves, yet course content foci and delivery methods are often designed in manners that undermine this goal. Thus, the one-diversity-course policy is really aimed at ensuring employment for teachers from the dominant group: If these teachers have taken this course, then they are "competent" to teach culturally diverse students, so they can be hired in lieu of teachers of color. In this way, the one-diversity-course policy leads to the preservation of teaching jobs for teachers from the dominant group, in the same way that legislation following *Brown v. Board of Education* (1954) created teaching jobs for White teachers in Black schools, while preserving White schools, and the teaching jobs in them, for White teachers as well.

The Assumed Neutrality of Special Education

When Dora is told to focus on special education and leave diversity-related material to people who teach the diversity course, the implicit message is that special education is race/neutral and colorblind and, therefore, does not involve diversity. Portraying special education as colorblind masks the fact that it engages issues in the field in a way that is only pertinent to the dominant group. Invocation of colorblindness or racial neutrality has, thus, a corresponding assertion of Whiteness (Bonilla-Silva, 1997; Lewis, 2001). When Dora's department chair calls for race neutrality, she is embracing and perpetuating the status quo and rendering ineffectual the institution's mission and the COE's goals of social justice.

Asserting the value of Whiteness in the cloak of colorblindness results in the further exclusion of other groups. By advising Dora to abdicate teaching diversity to teachers of the diversity course, the chair essentially advocates for the purposeful exclusion of any discussion of the realities PK–12 students of color face in special education. Such subtle, yet impactful, exclusion demonstrates the vitality of institutional racism from the loud *de jure* Jim Crow exclusion of the 19th century, to the quiet *de facto* curricular practices that fly in the face of the institution's proclamation of inclusion and social justice in the 21st century.

Well-Meaning Administrator Acting as Guard of the Status Quo

The vignette suggests that Dora's chair cares about students and the faculty. She listens to White students' complaints about Dora's focus on African American males in special-education classes, and responds to the complaint by advising Dora to refrain from teaching about diversity issues. To justify the injunction, the chair suggests that avoiding diversity in the special-education courses will improve Dora's professional trajectory at UAC. In many ways, she is providing Dora with the political ins-and-outs of how to succeed in the academy.

While Dora's chair's actions were meant to express care for Dora personally, they also reveal that the chair does not understand the racialized context in which society operates, and what DiAngelo (2011) calls *White fragility*:

a state in which even a minimum amount of racial stress becomes intolerable, triggering a range of defensive moves. These moves include the outward display of emotions such as anger, fear, and guilt, and behaviors such as argumentation, silence, and leaving the stress-inducing situation. These behaviors, in turn, function to reinstate white racial equilibrium. (p. 57)

The students who complained about Dora are textbook examples of White fragility. By responding to the students the way she did, the chair protected the value of Whiteness; in this case, the protection necessitates the exclusion of people of color's experiences in special education (Harris, 1993). She used her power as chair to guard and protect Whiteness, and its concomitant privileges, by allowing the White students to exert their racial power in the curriculum, thereby silencing Dora. When the chair advises Dora to desist teaching about diversity in her course, Dora is being encouraged to accept the status quo and uphold Whiteness disguised as neutrality. As an individual in a position of authority, Dora's chair represents the institution; consequently, a critique of her actions is also a critique of the institution that places people in positions of power who, in turn, undermine its mission.

Vignette # 2: The Myth of Objectivity in Student Evaluations

Ruth and Dora decide to meet off campus in a nearby restaurant for lunch. For the last two years at UAC, Ruth, who teaches the required diversity course in education, has been receiving unfavorable student evaluations:

> "I had a chat with the chair of my department about my evaluations," Ruth said beginning the discussion.
> "Who initiated the meeting?" Dora asked.
> Ruth continues, "The chair did. She was very supportive and said she is aware of the scholarship on faculty of color in the academy. I really appreciated that. She has observed me teach several times and tells me that my teaching style is very similar to others in my department; yet, they get better evaluations than me."
> "It is good to have someone in your corner," says Dora.
> "Yes, but she is concerned that the tenure committee might not see it that way. She is willing to write a letter explaining the scholarship on faculty of color's disparate evaluation," Ruth said.
> "What does she suggest you do?" Dora asked.
> Ruth responds, "She gave me some directions on how to write my self-evaluation in relationship to the difficulty of the course material for students, especially when it is presented by a person who is perceived to be partial. She will then support my letter by providing her letter with the scholarship on these issues."
> "Can we swap departmental chairs?" Dora joked.

There are three salient interrelated issues that can be extracted from the vignette above: (a) student evaluations are not objective; (b) even with administrators who are supportive, tenure and promotion policies that rely heavily on student evaluations can be a barrier to advancement of faculty diversity; and (c) the solidarity shown by Ruth's departmental chair and Dora are important.

Student Evaluations as an "Objective" and Customer Service-Based Tool

The academy is a place that should push students out of their comfort zones in order to have them see the world from another vantage point (Rose-Redwood, 2010). It should provide students with opportunities to unsettle and disturb their normalized epistemologies, cause cognitive dissonance, and interrogate injustices (Giroux, 1998). This is precisely the aim of Ruth's diversity course. When some White students are pushed out of their comfort zones and are unsettled by a faculty member of color, however, they are likely to react defensively by poorly scoring that faculty member on class evaluations. As a result, student evaluations are not objective; instead, they offer another opportunity to resist the content of a course. Anderson and Smith (2005) report that student evaluations of faculty of color are consistently lower than their White counterparts, just as in Ruth's case. Reliance upon student evaluations for career advancement in the academy defeats the institution's espoused values of diversity and social justice. This occurs because these evaluations are informed and shaped by the value ascribed to Whiteness, maleness, and other forms of dominance.

Reliance on student evaluations is also anchored in neo-liberal perceptions of education as a business or what Giroux (2010) calls *casino capitalism*-based approaches to education where "market-based values . . . undermine democratic values" (p. 342). Additionally, student evaluations are embedded in the business or market-based approach to customer service. If the customer is not satisfied, for whatever reason, then the customer has the right to complain, and the institution has the authority to remove the source of customer dissatisfaction. In this case, a professor's identities and curriculum cause student discontent. Giroux (2010), citing Frémaux (2010), reminds us that the market-based approach "does not constitute a social project. It is . . . the site where inequalities that will persist throughout social existence are born" (p. 348). In other words, the implementation of market-based customer service ideology, such as student evaluations at the UAC, reinforces race/gender privilege and disadvantage under the guise of colorblindness and race neutrality. Crenshaw (1997) asserts that the principle of colorblindness simultaneously veils, and implicitly asserts, the power of race, because invocation of colorblindness is used to mask and disregard racial differences while asserting Whiteness. Morrison (1995) argues that an "act of racelessness . . . is itself a racial act" (p. 46). Higher education's deployment of colorblind policies and practices, therefore, serves to "protect the status quo" and reinforces race-based inequities (Lewis, 2001, p. 801).

Importance of Solidarity

In addition to revealing subtle forms of racism and sexism at UAC, Dora's and Ruth's stories also illuminate the significance of solidarity for psychological and emotional wellbeing. Women faculty members of color constitute a low percentage of faculty nationally; Native Americans constitute 0.6 percent, Latinas comprise 4 percent, Asian Americans make up 6.7 percent, and African Americans compose 7 percent (Turner, González, & Wong Lau, 2011, p. 199). Such low numbers of women faculty members of color in the academy tends to lead to isolation and injury as a result of daily, "innocuous" interactions "characterized by white put-downs, done in automatic, pre-conscious, or unconscious fashion" (Pierce, 1974, p. 515). Solidarity among women faculty members of color who are social-justice-oriented becomes salient for their very survival. Dora and Ruth had biweekly meetings where they commiserated and shared their stories. Some of the meetings, as presented in Vignette #1, were unplanned, occurring between classes, but critical in the face of structures that undermined their epistemologies, professional work, and their psyches as African American women.

The support Ruth's chair provided is also essential. Ruth's chair is an example of an ally who understands the risks of teaching social-justice education (Muñoz, et al., 2004). Such understanding from a dominant group member is critical for faculty members of color who often feel isolated and misunderstood, the way Dora felt. Ruth's departmental chair showed solidarity with her through her willingness to 'speak truth to power' about the lack of objectivity in student evaluations, indicating that it was a practice that undercut UAC's mission to embrace and cultivate diversity. People like Ruth's chair illuminate the necessity of having people in leadership positions, academic and administrative, who value social justice, especially if the institution, like UAC, purports to embrace diversity and social justice. Such people become the true implementers of the institutional mission.

Conclusion and Implications

Alger (1998) points out that the presence of faculty members of color is an indicator of an institution's commitment to diversity and social justice. Dora and Ruth's presence at the University of ACME City does point to the institution's commitment to diversity and social justice. Such commitment, however, is enervated by institutional policies and practices. Through two vignettes of African American women faculty members and a CRT framework, the chapter has shown how everyday lives of these faculty members are shaped by the valuation of Whiteness and colorblindness. This chapter illustrates how maintenance of the status quo excludes people of color in the curriculum, and erects barriers to the actual attainment of diversity as espoused in the institution's mission statement.

The chapter has three main implications for higher-education institutions. First, teacher-education programs should require social-justice issues to be infused in all courses taught in the program. Having one course that deals with diversity and social-justice issues marginalizes these issues and further asserts the value of Whiteness (Fasching-Varner & Dodo Seriki, 2012; Harris, 1993). Second, administrators should serve as stewards of, not impediments to, the institution's diversity mission. To function in this capacity requires an understanding that classrooms are contested, racialized spaces (Dixson & Dingus, 2007). Consequently, student complaints about faculty of color should be understood in that context. As CRT theorists point out, students are also human beings who live in a society undergirded by White supremacist and sexist belief systems (Zamudio, et al., 2011). Third, higher-education institutions need to align their mission statements with tools for faculty evaluations. Dependence on student evaluations for ascertaining teacher efficacy in the tenure and promotion process implicitly embraces false notions of objectivity and colorblindness. Bonilla-Silva (1997) reminds us that "colorblindness" and "objectivity" are code words for the negation of diversity and preservation of the status quo. Institutions need to ask critical questions such as: *Who benefits from, and is marginalized by, student evaluations? What are student evaluations actually measuring? How do student evaluations actually contribute toward meeting the diversity goals of an institution? What alternative forms of evaluation can be implemented?* Responding to these questions might be a pertinent next step toward actualizing the diversity mission statements espoused in higher education.

Postscript

Dora has since left UAC and academia altogether; she started an afterschool tutoring company in a high-needs area of ACME City. She also serves as a special-education consultant for the local public-school district. Ruth received tenure last year and remains at UAC. It is especially important to point out that both Dora and Ruth expected to be met with resistance, and at times acrimony, when doing social-justice work. Yet, they also anticipated the institution, vis-à-vis chairpersons and deans, to be supportive of their work, given that this work is aligned with the institution's stated mission. In Dora's case, lack of support made her departure all but inevitable because she was characterized as incompetent in her teaching, while the context in which she taught remained uninterrogated. In Ruth's case, the presence of support made her success much more likely. In doing social-justice work, institutional affirmation made her decide to continue, albeit still expecting, and at times experiencing, resistance.

13

"Isn't Affirmative Action Illegal?"

Eugene Oropeza Fujimoto

Race and Representation

MANY ASPECTS OF DIVERSITY HAVE RECEIVED INADVERTENT ATTENTION in higher education over at least the last 10 years. One area that stands out for its lack of progress is the racial and ethnic diversity of faculty. In all four-year public colleges and universities in the United States from 2008–2009, faculty members of color made up 19 percent of the total faculty, with African American faculty stagnating at 5 percent for at least the previous decade (ICAS, 2011; Wilds, 2000). Meanwhile, during the 2008–2009 academic year, students of color comprised nearly 30 percent of all students in these same four-year institutions (ICAS, 2011). The consequences of this continued underrepresentation of faculty of color range from isolation for faculty members of color and fewer role models for the increasing number of students of color, to more narrow cultural perspectives in curricular and pedagogical offerings. *Why is underrepresentation occurring at a time when campuses across the country increasingly profess a commitment to diversity?*

This chapter utilizes a Critical Race Theory (CRT) analysis in presenting a *counterstory* (Delgado, 1989) to the often-stated majoritarian reasons for the lack of progress in hiring faculty of color. Stories that counter the generally accepted reality

> can open new windows into reality, showing us that there are possibilities for life other than the ones we live. They enrich imagination and teach that by combining elements from the story and current reality, we may construct a new world richer than either alone. (Delgado, 1989, pp. 2414–2415)

This chapter presents a counterstory developed from a composite of diversity hiring efforts on several actual campuses, collectively referred to as ACME University. It reveals collusion between administrators and faculty members that result in the de facto dismantling of policy intended to ensure affirmative-action compliance. As a composite tale, this chapter operates loosely as both and simultaneously a single-case and a cross-case study (Denzin, 1984).

Background

Studies have attempted to explain the lack of faculty diversity from numerous perspectives: the *leaky* pipeline to the professoriate; the at least unconscious *racial bias* of hiring committees (Fraser & Hunt, 2011); the need to *interrupt the usual* in hiring practices (Smith, Turner, Osei-Kofi, & Richards, 2004); the *chilly climate* for faculty members of color (Turner, Myers, & Creswell, 1999); and, the *privilege* of particular social identities as they are enacted on campuses (Maher & Tetrault, 2007). One of the most vexing aspects of this problem that has received less attention is the role of leaders as they influence, and are influenced by, the campus culture, and how aspects of that culture manifest in policies and practices.

Recent external influences on institutional culture include the increasing prevalence of colorblind ideologies, along with legal attacks on affirmative action (Bonilla-Silva, 2006). *How do such antidiversity influences prevail, often despite apparent broad commitment to diversity as an idea and value? Why do efforts by diversity coordinators and affirmative-action officers often remain stalled and/or thwarted, while the rhetoric of diversity appears stronger and more embedded than ever?*

Legal challenges to affirmative action have made diversity-related decision making more complex. The degree to which these external challenges influence the institutional culture and internal decision making, however, is frequently determined by the leadership. The culture of higher education is often symbolic in nature, more so than in other types of organizations (Scott, 1998; Williams, Berger, & McClendon, 2005). Relevant characteristics of colleges and universities include: ambiguous and unclear goals, departments and divisions that are *loosely coupled* (Birnbaum, 1992; Weick, 1983), and *garbage can* decision-making processes with little predictability and/or accountability (March & Olsen, 1976). These characteristics leave much of what occurs on campus subject to interpretation. How individuals choose to interpret situations is highly influenced by organizational symbols or stories, and the capacity of leaders to help people make sense of their environment (Gioia & Thomas, 1996; Smircich & Morgan, 1982; Weick, 2006).

Majoritarian Hiring Stories

The stories that explain the lack of progress in faculty diversity are largely examples of a single *majoritarian* story (Delgado, 1989, p. 2412); a shared, but unacknowledged, story told by those with institutionalized influence or power. Such a story usually includes some or all of the following elements:

1. There are not enough minorities in the pool of candidates;
2. Minorities in the pool have many offers from which to choose, so they do not choose us;
3. If a minority accepts our offer, she/he will likely use our position as a stepping stone, and we need more stability for our students;
4. We are committed to diversity, but not at the expense of lowering our academic standards;
5. We do get minority candidates who have strong credentials, but often they are not in the specific area in which we have a need; hopefully, they will apply next year when we may have a position in that area; and/or,
6. Some minority candidates have strong qualifications, but do not appear to be a good fit for our department; the person would likely not be happy here, and we would be setting her/him up for failure.

By and large, research shows these explanations are either exaggerated or outright myth (Smith, et al., 2004). But the power of the majoritarian story remains dominant, in spite of the facts. *What options exist for alternative realities to counter this prevailing point of view?* CRT's conception of counterstories provides one such alternative.

Counterstories: The "Facts" versus the "Truth"

Williams (1995) discusses the important role and responsibility that storytellers play in American Indian culture. This includes maintaining the integral community connections of *kinship and blood, marriage and friendship, alliance and solidarity through stories.* The Storytellers:

> who are most listened to and trusted in the tribe, will always use their imagination to make the story fit the occasion. Whether the story gets the "facts" right is really not all that important. An Indian Storyteller is much more interested in the "truth" contained in a story. And a great Storyteller always makes that "truth" in the story fit the needs of the moment. (pp. xi–xii)

What is meant by the difference between the "facts" and the "truth"? Are these one and the same? Or are they even related? And if they are, how are they related?

Facts of a situation may be indisputable by most. The candidate and members of the hiring committee, for example, are all present the day of the interview. Committee members took an African American candidate out for dinner that evening. These are facts. One of the professors on the committee made a comment to a candidate that is construed by some committee members as racist in nature. Others disagree. The truth of what occurred and its impact on a candidate and an interview is a very different matter. There are likely as many versions of why a candidate decided to withdraw from the search following an interview as there are people who were in the room during an incident. Determining the truth of an incident is often not easy, not only because different people have different perceptions, although that is certainly the reality, but because, "We are what we imagine," and "our very existence consists in our imagination of ourselves" (Delgado, 1995b, p. xii). This very conception of truth, our imagination of ourselves, and the actions that go on around us is integral to, but perhaps is all we have of, how we envision ourselves and our beings.

Given how important stories are at revealing truth, and that the storytellers "always make that 'truth' in the story fit the needs of the moment" (Delgado, 1995b, pp. xi–xii), *what are the needs of this moment, at this particular time in our collective history?* Obviously, we have many needs in the 21st century, especially in the current Obama era. Primary among these needs continues to be our willingness to understand race, racism, and its deleterious effects on social and economic inequality. In this light, this chapter reveals one story of our continuing struggle to racially diversify our faculty ranks in higher education.

A Counterstory of Leadership and Hiring Diversity

Beginnings: Preparing for a Journey Full of Hope and Promise

It was a clear, sunny, April morning, and the snow was finally gone. It was the kind of Midwest day that made one grateful for 50-degree weather, and hopeful that the long, frigid winter was over. The walk from the parking lot to the administration building was not as long on such days, and I was looking forward to my meeting with the vice president, a strong and able supporter of diversity efforts on campus, later that day.

I had been hired only a few months back as the campus affirmative-action officer. My hire brought a promise of change to ACME University, a mid-sized, regional, public campus. Diversity work had been my career for many years. I relished the challenge of doing this work in an environment that appeared to have substantial support for diversity efforts from the president and vice president. Diversifying the faculty was one of their, and my, primary goals.

"Good morning, Henry!" said ACME University Provost and Vice President of Academic Affairs Kennedy, as I entered his office. "Looks like a good day to travel! Do you have your recruiting team together?"

"Good morning, Norm. Not quite yet, but I am close to getting a commitment from Dr. Garrett, whom I think would be a great team member. She is an alumna of Howard University and has a number of contacts at the other campuses we will visit. I hope to hear from her today."

Faculty member Cora Garrett and I would form the core team on our inaugural recruiting visit to several Historically Black Colleges and Universities (HBCUs). We were interested in developing relationships with schools with high percentages of students of color in their doctoral programs. We had identified several such schools and would be visiting them soon. Provost Kennedy had identified which departments would be getting new faculty positions in the fall, for which we could begin to recruit during our visits.

"Will anyone else be joining you and Cora? It would be great to have faculty from some of the departments that will be recruiting candidates go with you. Any luck on that?" asked Kennedy.

"Yes, Dr. Emily Young in Biological Science said she is interested in joining us. And two of the HBCUs we are visiting have doctoral programs in her area," I said.

"Great. The funding is in place. Make it happen," Provost Kennedy replied.

As one of the steps in our strategic plan was to diversify the faculty, the possible immediate outcome of recruiting African American graduate students in fields where we would have openings, such as biological science, was exciting. Developing relationships that could create a pipeline for these graduate students to join us regularly was an important lockstep in our long-term development in this area. Garrett and Young made the commitment to join me on the recruitment trip; we would confirm our travel plans during the end of semester by the end of the week.

The Journey Takes a Turn . . . Keeping Our Eyes on the Prize

May was winding down, and our trip was scheduled for the following week. Emily Young's email caught me by surprise that day. Young said she had impending project deadlines that were taking longer than expected, and she would be unable to make the trip. With such little notice, it would be unlikely we could find a replacement. Cora Garrett and I would proceed without her, but it was quite a disappointment to not have Young joining us. It would also prove to be an omen of more disappointment to come.

The recruiting trip was largely a successful venture. Although there were many other schools in the process of recruiting from these HBCUs, the reception we received from our hosts on each campus made us feel welcome, and the contacts we made with particular departments appeared to hold much promise. As it turned out, the biological science department at one campus had a recent graduate, Dr. Monique Hunter, an African American woman in her 30s, who was in a postdoctorate position and seeking a tenure-track opening. We had lunch with Monique. She had not heard of our university or about our biological science vacancy, but she had family in a city neighboring our campus. She was affable, engaging, and appeared genuinely interested in our position.

"We are so pleased to have met you. We will be in touch as soon as the position is announced," said Garrett.

"Yes, I look forward to hearing from you. It looks like it could be a good match for my interests," replied Hunter.

"Great. Thank you for sharing your vita. I will be passing it on to the department," I said.

Her interest in teaching undergraduates matched well with our university's focus, and her area of research appeared applicable to the department's needs as well. We left with a mutual sense of excitement and possibility.

Waiting at the airport for our flight home, Garrett and I were effusive about our potential to grow relationships with the HBCUs we visited, and the potential immediate payback of our first such efforts in this regard in Monique Hunter, a strong candidate for one of our open faculty positions. Our excitement was short lived.

"Oh my . . ." said Garrett, as she checked her email on her laptop.

"Everything okay?" I asked.

"I cannot believe it." Garrett was now holding her head as if a migraine had struck.

"What on earth is going on?" I said.

Garrett handed me her laptop. It was a campus-wide message from our university system chancellor. Provost Kennedy was selected to be an interim vice chancellor at the system office, overseeing the academic affairs of all campuses in the system. It was a two-year appointment, and just long enough to kill our campus momentum. Garrett and I looked at each other, thinking the same thing. While the message said he planned to return to the campus, we knew Kennedy would not be back.

"I need a drink," said Garrett.

I followed her to the bar as we commiserated over what this all meant. Administrators such as Kennedy, with the commitment and courage to act on diversity initiatives, had been few and far between in our experience. Kennedy's likely replacement was the associate provost, Helen Browning, a White woman who had made some admirable decisions in hiring people of color. But she was nowhere near Kennedy's equal as a leader, an astute judge of how to move an institution forward, or an advocate for diversity. We knew our diversity efforts were in serious jeopardy, and we had to act fast.

We got out our phones. My calls were directed at stalling the appointment of Browning. Garrett contacted people who might also be considered viable internal replacements for Kennedy. An Asian American colleague, chair of the English department, appeared interested in the provost position. She had made several forays into administration, and had great respect from the faculty. Our efforts on both fronts continued upon our return to campus. I met with President Notting and Provost Kennedy, imploring them to consider candidates other than Browning. We mobilized interest groups on campus who were politically positioned to influence the decision by the president and provost on this matter. A flurry of meetings, emails, memos, and late night discussions ensued. In the end, the efforts were in vain. The president had made up his mind, perhaps from the outset. He had grown close to Browning (their families socialized), and he felt her qualifications were strong enough to warrant the appointment. Further, he could satisfy *some* diversity advocates by arguing that having a woman as interim provost was a positive step.

The day Browning's hiring was announced, there was a pall of dejection hanging over the heads of many diversity advocates on campus. Garrett and I headed for a local diner to have lunch.

"Well, here we go again. One step forward, two steps back. Bell's (1992) notion of *interest convergence* strikes again," said Garrett.

"It is discouraging, but what do you mean by interest convergence?" I asked.

"You know, Whites will generally not make decisions to benefit people of color unless they benefit as well. President Notting had a chance to move interested, qualified people of color, who were also race conscious, into administration. These positions do not come up very often. Instead he took the 'safe' route, hiring a White woman with a mediocre record on diversity, who he knows personally, and who will be unlikely to challenge him," said Cora.

"I see what you are saying. I guess it might have been better for us to have taken an approach with the president that illustrated how he and his career could have benefited by moving the diversity agenda forward by appointing someone else," I said.

"That may have been a better approach. White folks generally are not going to do this just because it is the right thing to do. Even Kennedy's motives are, I believe, a function of his understanding of the interconnectedness of his leadership, career, and progress on campus diversity efforts," said Garrett.

"At the same time, it seems to me that trying to ensure the convergence of interests can be a slippery slope toward denying that race and racism need to be more directly addressed by policy. Wilson (1987) tried to walk that line in his scholarship, and he got slammed for his book, *The Declining Significance of Race,*" I said.

"No question about it, but he came back a few years later and wrote about the need for developing social policy beyond race to get at the (admittedly racialized) 'underclass,' while simultaneously maintaining policies that specifically address racial discrimination (Wilson, 1987, p. 120). But I agree," said Cora, "it can be a politically fine line to walk!"

"It is a tightrope on which we may need to be better at balancing. But, there are more immediate things that we can still do right now. With all the faculty openings we have, there continue to be possibilities for meaningful change at this moment," I said.

The Dismantling of an Equity Effort . . .

Soon, the summer was gone; the leaves began to change color. It was a beautiful sight for a Californian like me, when there is frost in the morning. The signs of the approaching winter were still unfamiliar, but I appreciated them.

My relationships with President Notting and Interim Vice President Browning were now professional and cordial, but strained as a result of the past summer's political wrangling that nevertheless resulted in Browning's hire. Yet, I was hopeful about capitalizing on our recruitment efforts. I checked on the applicant pools for the open searches and found no racial diversity in the biological science faculty candidate pool, not even Monique Hunter. Alarmed, I called Department Chair Emily Young.

"Good afternoon, Emily. How is the semester going for you?" I inquired.

"Well, busier than usual with the search going on. How are things with you?" asked Emily.

"Not bad. In fact, I wanted to ask about the search. I just took a look at your pool's demographics. It is lacking in racial diversity. And I did not even see Monique Hunter's name in it. Did you get a chance to contact her? Remember, I left her information for you after our recruiting trip," I said.

"Oh, you know, I do not think I did. But I am sure if she is still interested, she will be checking our website," said Emily.

"But, Emily, it is precisely this kind of follow-through that can make all the difference. We need to get on this right away!" I exclaimed.

"Well, okay, but she has the same opportunity as anybody else to see the position announcement. I will contact her today. She did seem to have a strong background," said Emily.

"Thank you," I said, exasperated by the casual nature of Emily's responses.

Eventually, Hunter did apply for the position. She was interviewed by phone, but did not make it to the finalist pool, nor did any person of color. I examined the vitas of all of the finalists carefully, particularly in comparison to Hunter's vita and the position announcement. Hunter appeared as strong as the others in most all of the major categories that were scored. I sought Vice President Browning's support in adding Hunter to the final interview pool.

"Given that we are underutilizing people of color in this academic area, I think we are justified in ensuring that diverse finalists are brought into the pool," I asserted.

Browning said, "Well, this is really the faculty purview, but I can see your point. Go ahead."

"Okay, I appreciate that. Can we send a joint message to the department on this?" I asked.

"I am heading for a conference this afternoon, and I am swamped until then. Go ahead and send the message yourself, and tell them that I support the idea," said Browning.

I took a deep breath. "Alright. I will do my best. See you when you return."

Then, 'all hell broke loose.' I found out later that once I took the initiative to add Hunter to the on-campus interview pool, several biological science department faculty members went directly to the president and claimed I had overstepped my bounds as an affirmative-action officer. They insisted that Hunter not be added to the finalists' pool, and that we revisit the hiring procedures and my role in them.

President Notting formed a taskforce to review the faculty-hiring procedures. He hand-picked faculty members to join the taskforce. Seven were White, one was African American, and I was an ex-officio member. When I reviewed who would be serving on the taskforce, I knew I was in trouble. Every member, including the African American, could be categorized as either knowing very little about, or being actively opposed to, affirmative action in hiring. In response, I asked faculty colleagues who were supportive of affirmative action to show up to the meetings. Those who did were informed by the president that they were welcome, but they were not allowed to speak during the proceedings.

The committee had four meetings. My arguments for maintaining affirmative-action checkpoints in the process were not successful. The hiring procedures, including those that fundamentally maintained my role as an affirmative-action officer, would be eviscerated. I appealed to the university system legal office. This office responded to my appeal stating that these checkpoints could, in fact, *not* be removed. Yet somehow this detail was lost in the chain of command and communication from the system's legal office to the president. The campus's legal compliance with equal opportunity and affirmative-action law and policy fell by the wayside. Then came the notice that the biological science department had hired a White woman faculty member.

The Struggle Continues:
The Significance of Race and Why Leadership Matters

It was December, and a steady snow was falling. My office door, usually open, was closed. A knock came unexpectedly. Cora Garrett had stopped by. I offered her a cup of tea, and we spent the afternoon together.

"Well, friend, how you doing?" Garrett inquired.

"I have seen better days, that is for sure. If it were not for folks like you, it would be easy to hang it up," I said.

"Maybe Bell (1992) was right. You know, the *permanence of racism*. I always thought that this was an extreme position. But when I see how our institutions hold so firmly to the White status quo and the notion of Whiteness as normative, it is difficult to come to any other logical conclusion," Garrett opined.

"Yes, and I was thinking about the 'colorblind' narrative that has also pervaded campus thinking. Every person on that taskforce has been brainwashed into believing that if we just treat everyone—if it were even possible to do so—'the same,' equity will eventually be achieved. One taskforce member even said—with smugness—'Isn't affirmative action illegal anyway?' Everyone else on the taskforce seemed to nod in agreement, ignorant of the fact that any institution receiving federal funds, like ours, needs to file an affirmative-action plan annually, subject to Presidential Executive Order 10925 signed in 1961. Once this exchange took place, I knew the taskforce's decision was a foregone conclusion," I said.

"And what happened to the statement from the system's legal counsel; I thought we had their support on this?" Garret asked.

"So did I. But it is not easy to challenge a sitting president who has, and wants to keep, the support of the faculty senate. There are so many layers of politics we have to penetrate, and you know as well as I do that even legal interpretations can be influenced by politics. Look at *Bush v. Gore* in 2000," I said.

"Oh, please do not remind me. You know, this does make me think about Bell again, as well as Lipsitz's (2006) work on *the possessive investment in Whiteness*. They both talk about *Brown v. Board of Education* (1954) and how while this "landmark" legislation may have ruled segregation illegal, it did little to nothing to assist in dismantling structures of racist oppression in our schools," said Garrett.

"Well, yes. And we still get caught up in seeing racism as a *personal* prejudice, rather than a *systematic* way through which inequality is reproduced. As a result, the concept of White privilege can get confounded with intentionality. In reality, the way privilege is enacted has more to do with impact, than intent," I said, getting worked up.

"This feeds the notion that when we talk about an investment in Whiteness, it is difficult for some to see that this talk is less about White people, and more about a system of oppression. Ironically, the system that we just started to challenge here on campus through the new hiring procedures and recruitment we were doing was dedicated to eroding this system. But now even that small progress has been shut down," Garrett said, slamming her fist on the desk.

We were both silent for a time, watching the snow falling outside.

"I wonder what Kennedy might have done?" said Garrett.

"Well, I can tell you. Kennedy understood how this institution works. He had developed the kinds of relationships with the faculty that are needed to keep things moving in the right direction. He and I would have been working more closely on the searches, and he would have done work in public and behind the scenes to head off any faculty members from going directly to the president if concerns about our efforts had emerged. And Kennedy would have made it clear that there would be a cost to pay for noncompliance—a cost most faculty members and departments would not be willing to pay. Browning may have the potential to learn this; but to do so, she has to develop a deep sense of understanding and commitment to the cause of equity. It is a rare quality, particularly for presidents and provosts," I said.

"Rare indeed," said Garrett.

"How about we go for dinner; I'll buy," I said.

"Well, that is a rare offer in itself that I cannot pass up," said Garrett.

We set out for the parking lot. A couple of inches of snow had fallen. There was a quietness that only comes with new fallen snow. It was good to have a colleague in the struggle.

14

Equity at the Fringes

The Continuing Peripheral Enactment of Equity and Diversity in the Preparation of PK–12 Teachers

Roderick L. Carey and Laura S. Yee

Institutional Context Setting

The University of ACME, Flagship (ACME) has approximately 37,000 students enrolled in more than 125 undergraduate and 110 graduate degree programs (ACME, 2011a, sect. 1, para. 1). Students from various states and countries enroll at this highly selective university. Attracted by top education, criminology, business, architecture, engineering, performing arts, and journalism programs, students also come to this suburban campus for the 27 Division 1 NCAA sports teams, and the cornucopia of clubs, musical groups, and Greek-letter organizations, all of which create its active and engaged student body (ACME, 2011a, sect. 6, para. 1).

Though more than 34 percent of the current undergraduate population is composed of students of color, the university has a troubling past with regard to establishing meaningful policies and practices of integration and inclusion that truly support diversity and equity for the campus as a whole (ACME, 2011b, p. 1). Between 1935 and 1954, during the height of the campus's early growth, the university was led by a segregationist president who vehemently opposed Black integration (ACME, 2011c, para. 5–8). As a result of rigid exclusionary admission policies, the university found itself involved in various widely publicized legal battles for integration.

Since that time, ACME has dramatically shifted its culture through the increased recruitment and enrollment of students of color, and through the implementation of programs geared to support students from diverse backgrounds. The university has made significant strides in diversifying the student body, and, to a lesser extent faculty, while also offering programs to foster the academic and social success of traditionally underserved students of color. Despite these efforts, we see evidence of the need for greater cross-cultural dialogue among all ACME students.

We are two PhD students of color who teach disciplinary content-focused and diversity/equity-focused undergraduate and graduate courses to teacher candidates in ACME's College of Education (COE). This chapter presents the challenges we face at ACME in attempting to prepare PK–12 classroom teachers in an environment where the rhetoric of diversity and equity is laudable, but the institutional commitment to these goals is dubious. The questions driving our investigation are: *How do our experiences as instructors of color, working with predominantly White, middle-class, and monolingual students, illustrate the institutional commitment, or lack thereof, to diversity and equity? And how does the institutional context in which we work shape our roles as teacher educators who support diversity and equity?*

We acknowledge our belief that preparing future teachers to best serve increasingly ethnically, culturally, racially, and linguistically diverse PK–12 students is one of the most significant jobs of teacher educators (Hollins & Guzman, 2005; Howard, 2010; Melnick & Zeichner, 1997, 1998; Milner, 2010; Villegas & Lucas, 2002). The work of preparing future teachers involves many challenges, the most notable being the large discrepancy between teacher-candidate demographics and the demographics of the students whom they will eventually teach. Obama-era projections show that this gap will continue to widen; that is, the majority of teachers will likely continue to be White and monolingual, while the majority of PK–12 students will increasingly be from groups that are more culturally, racially, linguistically, and socioeconomically diverse (Howard, 2010; Melnick & Zeichner, 1998; Milner, 2010). Adding to the complexity of preparing teachers for this demographic reality are the *postracial* and *colorblind* discourses ushered in by the Obama era (Bonilla-Silva, 2009). These discourses serve as a barrier to honest and open discussions about the central role of race in teaching and learning.

While we suggest that ACME attempts to support and embrace racial and ethnic diversity on campus, we posit that these practices largely constitute *peripheral*, rather than *central*, enactment of diversity and equity. This institutional dilemma impacts our courses and, subsequently, our students' approaches to their work with diverse students in two ways:

1. Our teacher-education students have little significant experience engaging in dialogue about issues of difference with diverse peers; this leaves them with steep learning curves when it comes to understanding the diversity of their future PK–12 students; and
2. There is an absence of commitment to the central enactment of equity and diversity throughout the teacher-preparation program coursework.

Both of these factors delay or prevent crucial diversity discussions that teacher candidates need to have. This problem is exacerbated by relying solely on particular individual instructors to raise these issues in specific diversity-related courses. Our analysis is framed primarily by this dilemma; though, we recognize there are other dilemmas to consider.

We focus our attention on this dilemma by discussing two facets of Critical Race Theory (CRT) that inform our analysis, and then by reflecting on our classroom experiences. By combining our stories, we simultaneously offer two single-case and one collective-case study (Denzin, 1984). This study design enables us to compare and contrast moments of tension in our respective classrooms. We then suggest practices, informed by CRT, to improve classroom interactions among students. Through fostering informed dialogue in their classrooms, we believe that teacher educators support existing institutional commitments to diversity and equity by bringing them from the periphery to the center.

Critical Approaches to Classroom Case Narratives

We use a critical approach to analyze our experiences, highlighting how the complexity of unacknowledged *racialized* language in our classrooms provides evidence of the lack of centrally enacted institutional diversity and equity at our university (Chapman, 2007; Omi & Winant, 1994). According to critical race scholars, CRT contains focuses on the *intercentricity of race and racism with other forms of subordination* and *the challenge to dominant ideology* (Ladson-Billings, 1998; Ladson-Billings & Tate, 1995; Lynn, Yosso, Solórzano, & Parker, 2002; Solórzano, 1997, 1998; Solórzano & Delgado Bernal, 2001; Solórzano & Yosso, 2002a). The first focus highlights race as a permanent, endemic, and central, rather than marginal, factor in defining an individual's experiences, that also considers their intersecting subordination based on class, race, immigration status, phenotype, and sexuality, among others. The second focus objects to "traditional claims educational institutions make toward objectivity, meritocracy, colorblindness, race neutrality, and equal opportunity" (Solórzano & Yosso, 2002a, p. 26).

While we do not specifically emphasize it in our case analysis, we use a third concept of CRT—*the centrality of experiential knowledge*—as a legitimate basis for examining our classroom experiences through personal narratives (Solórzano & Yosso, 2002a). We recognize that our narratives represent two specific lenses that inform our positionality and interpretation of these cases: that of a Black male and of a Chinese female (Guba & Lincoln, 1994). Finally, these CRT concepts allow us to identify *majoritarian narratives* that surface within our classroom discourses, for example, those narratives that convey the perspective and, thus, norm the social location of an historically privileged group of people, such as White, male, middle and/or upper class, and heterosexual (Chapman, 2007; Solórzano & Yosso, 2002a).

We present two interwoven vignettes to illuminate our institutional analysis of how our students either present *race language*, front and center, or conceal it (Nieto, 2000). We then engage each other through written dialogue to facilitate deeper reflection on our respective experiences (Stake, 1995).

Classroom Encounters

Laura's Encounter

My coinstructor and I wait while students enter the lecture hall. Faces in the room are predominantly White and female, with the exception of two male students (one of whom is Indian), three Black female students, and a handful of mostly Korean students. The Asian students always sit together, as do the Black students. While there is no visible tension among students, the visible separation is obvious.

This was Book Club day, when students would discuss their thoughts and reactions to a book of their choice, one of the choices being Kozol's (1991) *Savage Inequalities.* After students shared reflections on their books in small groups, discussion of the books is opened up to the whole class. What began with students sharing their reactions to the school climate in the under-resourced schools described by Kozol morphed into a critique of the local school system, widely understood to underserve its mostly African American and Latina/Latino student population.

Laura: *This talk about the school system further perpetuates historic, majoritarian narratives painting this community as containing "bad" neighborhoods with "violent" people.*

Students began sharing things they had heard about this school system: "Those kids were so bad."

"They're so violent."

"It's so sad."

"Their families don't have time."

"Parents don't spend enough time with them."

Before long, there was a constant flow of more comments like this focusing on what they suspected occurs in these schools.

Laura: *Yet, students never mentioned race, even though it is well known that the community served by the school system is predominantly African American. Race is a central component of all social interactions. Truly seeing and acknowledging its central role, however, requires deconstructing the illusions of meritocracy, colorblindness, and equal opportunity that permeate students' understandings within this institution. My students' inability to fully acknowledge race as an issue bothered me, but I listened, waiting to see whether counter narratives or alternative perspectives would emerge.*

Rod: *While I wonder why students didn't choose to sit with those outside of their own racial group, what immediately shook me was the language used to describe children, especially Black children. The terms "they" and "their" intentionally creates distance. In addition, the word "violent" is harsh, and carries a strong sense of determinism, as if "they," the Black children, always have and always will be violent, based on the assumption that they must come from violent families. It also appears that students did not consider how their descriptions of Black children were steeped in the unacknowledged intersections of race and class. Student assertions leave no space for critiquing the larger society's racialized oppression from which these Black students come.*

It was then that I saw one of my three Black students, Jessica, in my peripheral vision, quietly listening to her peers' comments, as she always did.

Laura: *I made a special effort to reach out to Jessica and the two other Black students in my class that semester. Like Dixson and Dingus (2007), I find building relationships with my minority students to be particularly important, since students of color are noticeably outnumbered, outvoiced, and outrepresented by their White peers in the College of Education. During one-on-one interactions, Jessica was verbose and open about her opinions. Was her silence during the class at all related to the presence of a historically dominant ideology and majoritarian narrative within our classroom and our institution? I wish I had asked.*

Rod: *Could it be that her habit of remaining silent in class is informed by her prior and present classroom experiences?*

Neither she, nor others, changed the tone of the discussion. Thus, I felt obligated to chime in and interrupt the cycle of deficit comments.

Rod: *Through the lens of the centricity of race, as a Black male, regardless of how much education I receive, I carry around stigmas of being labeled bad, violent, or from a family that does not care. When many people see me, they assume they know my story before they even talk to me. Without acknowledging race as central to social interactions, these teacher candidates may unintentionally further marginalize their future Black students by assuming things that are not true. I wonder what occurred in these White teacher candidates' lives, or what was missing in their prior experiences, that allowed them to think it is okay to speak of young people, particularly Black students, as violent and bad.*

After reminding the class that some urban schools are very successful at graduating students who go on to many successful endeavors, I saw Jessica nodding.

Laura: *I reaffirmed her own lived experience, even if she did not speak. I cannot help wondering whether another instructor would have done so.*
There were no comments after I spoke. Time was up, and students departed for their next class.

Rod: *I continually worry about whether students from overrepresented identity groups ever consider how their words, or even their presences, influence how students like Jessica feel when comments are made regarding Blacks. While the White students limited what they said to their own current understandings, these casually delivered comments are problematic in these class discussions. Letting these comments go without intervention leaves our White students unprepared for their future roles as teachers of diverse students. I wonder how many of our students have ever engaged in sustained and informed cross-cultural dialogue? How many of our White teacher candidates see the development of cross-cultural understanding and the unpacking of their own racial privilege as important in their teaching practice? Is there anything that ACME could do to ensure that students would not graduate harboring similar sentiments, essentially graduating from the institution unchanged?*

Rod's Encounter

Along the classroom wall, I displayed a multitude of questions/statements related to diversity and equity like:
"Students' success in school depends primarily on how hard they work."

"Economically disadvantaged students have more to gain, because they have less to bring to the classroom."

"An important part of learning to be a teacher involves examining one's own attitudes and beliefs about race, class, gender, disability, religion, and sexual orientation."

For each question/statement, students responded by walking to one of four corners in the room labeled Strongly Agree, Agree, Disagree, or Strongly Disagree. Once gathered in these corners, students discussed the rationales underlying their opinion on the question/statement with the goal of identifying, through consensus, the most compelling rationale. Once each corner found the consensus rationale, they shared it with the whole class to try and encourage or convince other students to come into 'their corner.'

Rod: *As students shared individual responses on the questions/comments, I chimed in to push their thinking and clarity. I was cognizant of how I used language in my feedback. I did not want to silence any voices, nor make anyone to feel marginalized because of someone else's response.*

Laura: *While these students were used to each other's presence, were they comfortable with discussions of difference? How did you perceive various identity markers (e.g., race, class, gender, sexual orientation) to affect their social interactions during, and/or to influence how they responded to, this exercise? These markers might have encouraged them to choose a less "risky" response. If so, what does that say about the institutionalization of diversity and equity work at our university?*

Brent, a White male, noted that he could not understand why "people like Al Sharpton make such a big deal of race." He then made disparaging comments about Al Sharpton, and continued, "I mean, we have Obama in the White House, and he's Black! But people like Al Sharpton still have these marches, and I just don't understand what the big deal is!"

Rod: *While his sentiment bothered me, his tone actually made me mad. Brent was referencing a recent march in which I had participated. While I felt dismayed and offended at his comment, I closely monitored my response so as not to silence him and others from freely expressing their beliefs. That Brent felt it was okay to approach racial issues in such a cavalier and dismissive manner, despite spending four years at our relatively diverse university, troubled me. Within a diversity course, Brent was boldly asserting that he could not understand what the "big deal is" with race. The implication was that if he could not understand* *the purpose of the march, the march had no purpose. The colorblind lens Brent used to critique Al Sharpton also informed Brent's usage of Obama's election as evidence for why race did not matter anymore. Through skillful intervention into these 'teachable moments,' Brent eventually became one of the most engaged and transformed students in the class. In addition, he and his classmates made tremendous strides toward becoming better positioned to work in diverse classrooms. I can only imagine how much further they could have developed with more (earlier or later) classroom opportunities for dialogue on race, class, gender, sexual orientation, and other differences.*

Challenges in Teaching for Diversity and Equity

While the cavalier language often used by White students in diversity dialogue threatens to silence the voices of students of color, it also serves as evidence that ACME's enactment of diversity and equity is peripheral, rather than central; this is particularly the reality in ACME's COE. While we acknowledge that students' language usage alone may not fully characterize peripheral enactment, this language usage, coupled with the absence of critical pedagogy in most classes, suggests that majoritarian narratives likely operate on campus, especially in the COE, in ways that perpetuate dominant ideologies and possibly silence nondominant voices. By paying and calling attention to these dynamics in our teaching, we help develop our students' own critical lenses as they prepare to teach equitably in their future diverse classrooms.

Despite an absence of widespread institutional structures that stimulate cross-cultural dialogues about difference at ACME, we assert that strides have been made to move diversity and equity from the fringes to a more central location within the teacher education program in the COE. For example, collaborative teams of instructors (including tenure-track professors, teacher-certification program leaders, and graduate students) work diligently to create anchor syllabi for diversity- and equity-centered courses. Though many of our students adhere to postracial and colorblind ideologies (Bonilla-Silva, 2009), we critically address these ideologies over two-to-three class sessions through readings, reflection activities, and discussion on issues like *White privilege* (Howard, 2006). Accordingly, we believe we have made progress in centering marginalized perspectives in our courses. While other strides, initiated by cohorts of individuals on the ground level, have been made as well, more still needs to occur institutionally to ensure the central enactment of diversity and equity. This central enactment is what is most needed in today's increasingly diverse Obama era.

Moving Diversity from the Fringes to the Center

Our narratives in this chapter reveal and represent our shared sense of ACME's *peripheral*, rather than *central*, enactment of diversity and equity work, particularly as evidenced through the colorblind and uncritical discourses in our COE classrooms. The institution certainly enrolls students of color, hires faculty members of color, hires/appoints people of color into administrative roles, and implements programming to support diverse students. Yet, without the infusion of diversity and equity work into everyday curriculum, discourse, and institutional culture, ACME relegates diversity and equity to the periphery. It remains *at the fringes*, resting on the efforts of committed, but isolated, individuals.

To ensure socially just outcomes at ACME, issues of race, power, injustice, and marginalization need to be foregrounded in all classroom discussions, not relegated solely to diversity classes (Nieto, 2000). Further, we believe that a critical lens is necessary not only to elucidate the kind of issues we have discussed herein, but bring about their resolution; that is, we need to 'talk the talk' *and* 'walk the walk.' We posit that university scholars and practitioners need to re/commit themselves to incorporating critical lenses in their research, in interactions with students and colleagues, and in their classroom curriculum and pedagogy. Moving an institution's diversity and equity efforts from the periphery to the center requires all stakeholders in this effort to think critically about every aspect of the institution from, for example, macro-level hiring, to programming, to admissions policies, to micro-level instruction, to advising, among others. The nature of discourse use across institutional aspects must also be critically considered. Critical thinking and consideration in these veins is not new, but in the Obama-era context, their importance is amplified. The time is now for every quarter of every higher-education institution, particularly ACME's COE, to take seriously the responsibility for teaching our nation's diverse youth well. *Can we risk not doing so?*

15

On the Battlefield for Social Justice in the Education of Teachers

The Dangers and Dangerousness of Challenging Whiteness in Predominantly White Institutions and Teacher-Preparation Programs

Brenda G. Juárez and Cleveland Hayes

The Problem of Good

IN THIS CHAPTER, WE ARE CONCERNED WITH THE PROBLEM of good and the continuing inadequacy of teacher preparation in the United States. Good, as a problem, is exemplified by the actions of the eight White clergymen in Alabama who openly opposed, and actively worked against, Dr. Martin Luther King, Jr. during the Birmingham street demonstrations of 1963, all the while enunciating ideals of common brotherhood, community, and understanding (Carpenter, Durick, Grafman, Hardin, Harmon, Murray, Ramage, & Stallings, 1963). When individuals and groups who profess commitment to goodwill and the democratic ideals of social justice, yet simultaneously do everything within their power to ensure that such commitment and ideals are never realized, the problem of good becomes visible.

We define the problem of good as the insidious paternalism embedded within White liberalism, its privileging of the collective histories, characteristics, and interests of Whites, and its emphasis "on the individual to the exclusion of the group, on liberty instead of equality, [and] on gradual rather than precipitous changes" (Bennett, 1964, p. 84). In the context of public higher education, the problem of good can be easily seen in the preparation of future teachers. Despite consensus that teachers need multicultural preparation, the reality is that "teacher preparation programs continue to graduate and credential educators who are not prepared to effectively teach students of color" (Blanchett, 2006, p. 27).

As authors—Brenda and Cleveland—one of us identifies as White and female and the other as Black and male. We are teacher educators who have spent our professional lives in predominantly White teacher-education programs that have all officially expressed strong commitments to social justice in their mission statements. In these environments, we have both been tasked with teaching required multicultural education and social foundations of education courses. When teaching these courses, we have both run up against the problem of good and faced similar challenges in attempting to resolve the problem, despite taking somewhat different resolution approaches correlated to our different race and gender positionalities.

In this chapter, we explore how the problem of good in teacher education often subverts and derails the democratic aims of equity, diversity, inclusion, and social justice, despite claiming to support these aims. Goodness in teacher education subverts and derails democratic aims by: (a) relying on institutional decision-making authority, and (b) guiding interactions in manners that reinforce the existing racial hierarchy. We support our exploration of goodness with a critical analysis of Brenda's experience in an effort to understand how our actions failed in seeking to resolve the problem of good.

We use (auto)ethnographic case study methods and a Critical Race Theory (CRT) framework to delineate our case. Our exploration of the problem of good is rooted in both Brenda's and Cleveland's perspectives as teacher educators. In this exploration, we highlight the mechanisms operating in the problem of good and the trials and tribulations associated with seeking to resolve the problem (which requires challenging goodness). The experience Brenda relates takes place at the University of Regional ACME (Regional ACME), located in the Deep South region of the United States. By illuminating the inherent discord between goodness and social justice in teacher education, and the disappointing reality contained with the discord, we hope to help realize more robustly democratic and just educational experiences for all students.

Critical Race Theory (CRT) Framework

CRT is a useful tool for complexly examining all forms of oppression, particularly oppression based on race (Dixson & Rousseau, 2006). CRT provides a platform for voices typically silenced within mainstream discourses to be heard; to name their own realities through the use of *narrative, chronicle, story, parable,* and *counterstory* (Dudziak, 1988; Ladson-Billings, 1998). By focusing on covert discourses, CRT can help reveal the daily workings of Whiteness and the problem of good in teacher education.

While Cleveland is typically treated as a member of a specific hybrid group (i.e., Black men) in his daily life, Brenda's Whiteness enables her to function in her life as an individual (as opposed to a White individual). While being a woman can have the effect of undermining the individualizing effect of Brenda's Whiteness (if she is perceived to challenge patriarchal norms), it can also have the effect of augmenting this effect (if, as a woman, her challenges to patriarchy are not taken seriously). Because Whiteness is privileged in the United States, even if Brenda chooses to challenge this privilege by, for example, challenging racism and/or attempting to expose the contrived transparency of Whiteness by calling attention to its existence, she is still treated as an individual, because she is White. CRT names this double standard so that the problem of good can be explored uninterrupted by the privileged, White, individualism that maintains the existing racial hierarchy (Bennett, 1964; Leonardo, 2005; Merryfield, 2000; Stanley, 2006b).

Case Study Approach

Case study research focuses on examining the lived experiences of individuals or groups in a specific context or setting, often conveyed through their life stories, for the purpose of interrogating the experiential knowledge and related meaning construction that they generate within the boundaries of their context (Creswell, 2011; Stake, 2005). To that end, Brenda's story examines the systems and structures operating around her as a teacher-education faculty member as she experiences "patterns of unanticipated as well as expected relationships" with respect to her efforts to promote social justice (Stake, 1995, p. 41).

Brenda's Story: I Do Not Hate White People

People often find me to be a walking contradiction. Being a White female with long blonde hair, blue eyes, and a soft voice, others often assume that I will be very passive, easygoing, and quiet with little to say or do beyond accessorizing my wardrobe. One of my students said I was 'kindergarten sweet,' but the readily visible Malcolm X tattoo on my upper left arm juxtaposed with my easy movement in six-inch stiletto heels left her puzzled. She did not know how to make sense of me as a teacher-education faculty member.

With my students and others, I am never colorblind. In my classes, I often use words that name and unpack difficult, often volatile, issues of race and racism in the classroom; these words are often considered profane and impolite, especially in the Bible Belt of the American South. As a result of this pedagogical approach, in course evaluations, students have described my teaching as employing "shock and awe" techniques. But as a teacher educator, I feel I must get through to them, which sometimes requires a 'wake up call.' For example, on the first day of class at the outset of a semester, I have been known to take time to look over the faces of my new students and then firmly and directly ask them, "Why is it that in a city where the population is over half African American that there are so many White people in this room?" My students are going to be teachers, so I want, and expect, them to be able to give me answers to difficult questions like this one.

Given that most of my students will be teachers in the community surrounding Regional ACME, I use the short amount of time and influence I have to prepare them, as effectively and efficiently as I can, for the realities of teaching they will face at some point during their careers. I choose not to be soft or 'velvet-gloved' with my students, because: (a) I do not want them to enter their PK–12 classrooms like most teachers do, unprepared to teach most, if not all, students; and (b) I do not want their teaching actions to exacerbate the growing, incredibly disturbing, school-to-prison pipeline. Instead, I push my students to recognize the ways structural racism negatively impacts an individual's life chances so that, as teachers, they will engage students in ways that mitigate or altogether eliminate these impacts. To help students understand how structural racism operates in schools, I use a swear word in class that, when used on a school bus by a seven-year-old African American boy, got him suspended. This real-life example is further informed by class readings on the overrepresentation of African American and Latino male students in severe disciplinary-action and expulsion statistics. My students react to the use of swear words (by the seven-year-old as well as by me) in ways that are meant to imply that they have never responded so inappropriately in any situation in their lives.

Because of my teaching approach, I have earned a reputation in the community surrounding Regional ACME, as well as in digital communities, like Facebook (www.facebook.com), as either a loved or hated White professor, a professor who apparently hates her own race, and as a professor who is "a Nazi" against White people. Some students have digitally tagged me as a "raving lunatic" in warning other students to get out of my class as quickly as possible or stay away from my classes altogether. Perhaps in response to this tag, a young White man in my class got right up in my face, coming very close to physically hitting me, before he turned around, packed his things, and left the class permanently. In another instance, a young, Black woman circulated a petition to have me fired; apparently, she obtained a fair number of signatures. Not long ago, on his way home from work, my partner stopped for a cup coffee at a local shop. The shop owner commented to him that her daughter had just completed a wonderful semester at Regional ACME, despite having had a "White woman [professor] who hates other White people." Although I had never met this coffee shop owner, my partner (and later I) knew immediately that she was referring to me; this was not the first time this had happened, either.

I recognize that some of my teaching methods may be considered eccentric or quirky, and that some Regional ACME students and local community members have not appreciated my approach. I can live with these reactions. However, my concern about these reactions is their negative effect on my ability to earn a living because of how they facilitated faculty colleagues' and department and college administrators' efforts to silence me, as well as to preclude me from maintaining employment. The following informal and formal conversational context vignettes will serve to illustrate this reality.

I posit that we, as teacher educators, do not teach our students how to be effective teachers to all students. Thus, at Regional ACME, I consistently refused to back down from speaking out about how the Whiteness of our teacher curriculum and instructional practices operated to compromise the educational outcomes of the student populations in the public schools who hired our graduates. This is where the problem of good had very real and serious consequences for me, both personally and professionally. Despite my desire to improve my program's capacity to effectively prepare all teachers to effectively teach all students, Whiteness asserted itself to prevent this from happening. Here, Whiteness manifests as the refusal of Regional ACME teacher education faculty and education college administrators to meaningfully address race-based inequities embedded within the department's and college's daily educational and administrative practices.

Informal Conversations in the Hallways

Conversation 1

White, male, untenured, assistant professor: "Brenda, here is the article you forgot on the printer."

Brenda: "Oh, thanks. How did you know it was mine?"

White, male, untenured, assistant professor: [*Laughing*] "Who else around here would copy an article on the recruitment and retention of minority teacher candidates?"

Brenda: "I see your point."

Conversation 2

Brenda: "I'm really concerned that so many of the students and faculty here, both Black and White, have no idea who wrote the famous American novel, *Black Boy*, written in 1945. The author, Richard Wright, was from the South, someone from here, where we live, and someone famous, not some obscure person. Given the racial demographics of this region and our public schools, we should require a course on the history of Black education."

White, male, college administrator: "The program is already full. We don't have any room for another class."

Conversation 3

Brenda: [*Speaking to a group of students enrolling in a foundations of education course*] "Try not to get too worked up about it when you hear things like that about me. It used to bother me, too, but students will talk among themselves and make negative comments about professors."

White female student 1: "Dr. J, this was no student. This was a professor who was standing in front of a class in this building telling us not to take your class."

White female student 2: "Yeah. I wasn't in that class, but I have a paper from advising where the advisor wrote right on it: 'Not Juárez.' I can show you the paper."

Arab-descent male student: "When I came here, I went on a university tour. When someone asked about the professors, the guide said, 'everyone is great, except one named Juárez.' I think the guide was talking about all the homework you give, though."

Brenda: [*Laughing*] "Did I not say that I don't win a lot of love or popularity contests for calling out White supremacy in education? I rest my case."

Formal Conversations in Meetings

Conversation 1

White, female, tenured professor: "We need more placement venues for our student teachers for their state licensure requirements. We should think about a diversity of placement possibilities. Is it possible to place student teachers outside of the state?"

White, male, college administrator: "We can place them in Vietnam, if we want."

White, female, tenured professor: "Great. That should take care of our diversity requirement."

Brenda: "Maybe it's not simply about placing our student teachers in culturally diverse places, but also about 'unpacking' what happens in those places. After all, research suggests that simply placing student teachers in culturally diverse environments sometimes just reaffirms negative stereotypes that they already have in their minds about the people in those environments."

[*Long moment of silence.*]

White, male, college administrator: [*As if there has been no break in the conversation, and as if Brenda has not spoken*] "We can work out the logistics of placing students in Mexico, too. It's just a matter of planning and working out the details."

Conversation 2

White, male, tenured professor: "Democratic education is based on the ideals espoused by Thomas Jefferson and other founding fathers. Students have to know about these ideas."

Brenda: "Yes. And they should also be discussing the ways Jefferson and the other founding fathers embodied contradictions between their articulated ideals about equality and their practice of race-based exclusion."

White, male, tenured professor: "I get so sick of people disrespecting the founding fathers and playing the gender card, the race card, and every other card. We are long past the problems we used to have, and the people who keep bringing them up again and again are the ones who keep the problems of the past alive today. My grandfather came from Czechoslovakia, had no shoes, and was hungry all the time, too."

Conversation 3

White, male, college administrator: "We have to integrate technology into our courses."

While, male, full professor: "I use Skype (www.skype.com) and webchat sites in my classes."

Brenda: "I agree. Integrating technology is important, especially since we know that access to technology tends to be differentially distributed along race and class lines. I think we also need to think about why we are using technology—to what end? Technology can very effectively teach my child how not to be Latina and my neighbor's child how not to be Black."

[*Long silent pause. None of the 12 faculty members seated around the long conference table moves or makes a sound. The college administrator at the table looks coldly and directly at Brenda, locking eyes with her for a period of time that seems endless. Everyone seems uncomfortable.*]

Postscript

Not long after formal Conversation 3 took place, I was given official notification that I had pushed concerns about Whiteness too far, one too many times. The notification summoned me to the main administration office on a specific date and at a specified time. When I responded to the summons, two White male administrators stood side-by-side while one handed me a letter informing me that my employment contract would not be renewed. As I look back on formal Conversation 3, I see that my comments in it were 'the straw that broke the camel's back.' Still, I cannot help but wonder whether being softer or gentler in my approach in surfacing Whiteness and the problem of good in teacher education would have led to a different outcome.

That said, I still think I made a couple of mistakes. My first mistake was not maintaining an open mind and, in so doing, becoming just like the people with whom I was in disagreement. They were not willing to hear what I had to say, but I did not want to hear what they had to say either. Unfortunately, the people who are most affected by this stalemate are our teacher-education students and the future PK–12 students. My second mistake was that I do not believe I leveraged my White privilege properly. If my ultimate goal was to meaningfully empower students from underrepresented groups, particularly students of color, then silencing White or White-identified students, colleagues, and administrators, or creating an environment in which they felt silenced, was not the best approach to realize that goal. Still, as a White person, I feel I do have a special responsibility to engage and challenge other Whites, especially about race and Whiteness, lest I contribute to the *permanence of racism* (Bell, 1992). *So, how do I uphold this responsibility in realizing my ultimate goal without being silenced or silencing others?*

Seeking to Resolve the Problem of Good

The preceding informal and formal conversational context vignettes illustrate Brenda's experience as an individual. Her Whiteness became visible in the criticism she incurred, only because she was perceived to be acting against her racial self-interest and, therefore, aberrantly.

These vignettes also serve as an exemplar of why democratic ideals and social justice are still sorely needed in teacher education in the Obama era. We recognize that the problem of good is complex, thus not easily located in "them" or "us" as the source of the problem, but rather more a function of "them v. us" or "us v. them," or an antidialogic posture on all of our parts in avoiding or facing the problem. Because of this complexity, and in also seeking to answer Brenda's question, we explore three potential dispositions that we believe we can adopt to more effectively engage colleagues in seeking to resolve the problem of good. These dispositions involve: (a) scaffolding understandings of systemic racism *with* colleagues, (b) assuming colleagues have an internal logic for their attitudes and behaviors, and (c) being sincere in engaging colleagues in dialogue.

Scaffolding

Though we subscribe to CRT's assertion that racism is an endemic part of American society, we often erroneously presume that *either* our colleagues also subscribe to this assertion (thus, that they understand, and will support, our antiracist interventions), *or* that they do not recognize the subtleties of racism, namely, those behaviors that are far more covert than what many people call to mind when thinking about racism as a primarily Jim Crow-era phenomenon (thus, that we have to "educate" them). Though *scaffolding* is a common pedagogical technique used and taught in teacher education, we believe the potential benefits of also employing scaffolding in intracollegial engagement of concerns about racism in teacher education are overlooked (Sleeter, Torres, & Laughlin, 2004). For example, had Brenda taken the time to work *with* her Regional ACME colleagues to scaffold a genuine understanding of the more subtle forms of racism found in education, including in educational technology and distance education, she might have gained more traction in seeking to resolve the problem of good. Further, she might have learned things about what her colleagues *actually* knew and/or believed about racism that could have helped her to identify potential allies, as well as focus scaffolding efforts in areas where racial understanding was the most lacking. Clearly, one 'take-away' from Brenda's experience is that working with colleagues to recognize the limits of our collective racism (whether, for example, internalized in people of color, contested in progressive White people, or still-unacknowledged in all people) must happen on terms that take into account the different places along the recognition continuum at which we each sit. How we name (or not) the contours of racism will correspond to our location on the continuum. Most important to remember is that these locations can and do change, and the manner of our scaffolding can impact how that change occurs (in what direction, how quickly, etc.) (Bergerson, 2003; Dei, Karumanchery, & Karumanchery-Luik, 2007; Gillborn, 2005).

Internal Logic

To be generous, it is likely that many of our well-meaning colleagues in higher education are steeped in a generational discourse where colorblindness is a valued ideal, believed to promote equality. Brenda assumed that her Regional ACME colleagues understood that colorblindness is not only unpracticeable, but that it is also not an appropriate ideal for social justice. Hence, the source of Brenda's troubled interactions with her colleagues may lie in the following, albeit faulty, logic: If someone sincerely believes that colorblindness promotes equality, while they might view antiracist behavior as positive in theory, they might also view the practice of antiracist behavior (e.g., conversation about race or racism) as undermining their efforts to promote equality. If Brenda's Regional ACME colleagues subscribed to this logic, they would perceive Brenda's attitudes and behaviors around race and racism to be dissonant. On the one hand, they would see her as articulating the same antiracist values they do. But on the other hand, they would see her continuing to bring race and racism into conversation, thereby preventing racism the necessary opportunity to 'die a natural death.' While we vehemently disagree with the so-called logic of colorblindness and argue that it does not, and cannot, actually work in the real world, we can reasonably imagine how someone who lacked deeper understandings, or avoided facing deeper realities of race or racism, could buy into this logic. In seeking to resolve the problem of good with our colleagues, we must make it clear to them that we recognize and appreciate their articulation of antiracist values, at the same time that we articulate that claiming opposition to racism does preclude people, especially White people, from expressing racist attitudes and demonstrating racist behaviors. But we must go one step further: if ending racism is rooted in words *and* actions, then we must not only articulate this but enact it. Because we want to be *effective* antiracist educators, we have to walk our talk by both challenging and supporting each other (antiracist educator to antiracist educator), as well as our colleagues, no matter where they are in their current antiracist development. In this way, we all come to see ourselves as people who reject racism but who nevertheless may still embody White supremacist values (Bergerson, 2003; Gillborn, 2005; hooks, 1989).

Sincere Dialogue

As social-justice educators, we sometimes do not take the time to engage in sincere dialogue with our colleagues, especially about our respective life experiences and the corresponding roots of our personal (not ideological) commitments to social justice. Brenda did not acknowledge that her Regional ACME colleagues' life experiences were legitimate and, further, critical to their understanding of equity, diversity, and inclusion. By reducing her colleagues' life experiences to ones of privilege imbued by racism, Brenda lost ground in seeking to resolve the problem of good. If she had instead engaged her colleagues with dialogic questions about their own experiences of race, she could have built the relationship foundation necessary to begin to unpack goodness.

We Continue to Struggle, Albeit Not Alone

Many scholars before us have delivered emotionally demanding, intellectually insightful critiques of the challenges associated with working against the Whiteness in teacher education and society at large. With this chapter, we seek to illustrate how working against Whiteness operates as the problem of good, as well as how this problem can begin to be resolved with self-awareness, humility, and integrity. Unfortunately, this chapter also reaffirms the persistence of White supremacy in teacher education, higher education, and society despite the ever-changing ways that it manifests. While diversifying the faculty and student ranks in teacher education would not resolve the problem of good in the field, because teacher education is such a White world, the problem of good within in it persists, largely unfettered. We refuse to excuse or justify this (Juárez & Hayes, 2010).

In the interstices between our naming of racism, exploration and analysis of the problem of good, and critical self-reflection on both, we hope this chapter illustrates that all engaged parties, in this case, all teacher educators, must be willing to listen to each other to glean mutual understanding, as all perspectives provide insight into how the problem of good will eventually be resolved. Though some social-justice advocates choose to disengage from the oppressor, whether the oppressor is understood to be located in themselves or in others, we believe that such disengagement continues to give the oppressor power, particularly the power to exclude. Instead, we choose to engage the oppressor by asking: *How do we work together for 'the good' against 'goodness?'* Through Brenda's story, in particular, we have come to recognize that what is most crucial about this question is that it does not frame White people as good or bad. Rather, it seeks ways to 'speak truth to power,' particularly when those in power imagine themselves to be committed to goodwill and the democratic ideals of social justice, but act in ways that continue to undermine the good.

So What? Who Cares? And What's Our Point about Diversity?

Margaret-Mary Sulentic Dowell

Context Setting

FRENCH NOVELIST ALPHONSE KARR (1808–1890) IS CREDITED with penning the well-known phrase, "*Plus ça change, plus c'est la même chose*" (1849, n. p.). Translated into English, it reads, "The more things change, the more they stay the same." Having gained proverb-like status, the phrase suggests that change, especially that considered tumultuous and restless, does not ultimately deeply alter reality; rather, it strengthens and fortifies the existing state of affairs. As we consider the influence, impact, and effect of racism in public higher education, Karr's phrase takes on significant meaning.

My charge in writing this piece was to read each of the 15 cases presented in this volume and fashion a summation chapter capturing the essence of the cases in order to present a succinct snapshot of what, in sum, they reveal about diversity work in public higher education in the Obama era. Both excited and awed at my directive, I immersed myself in reading and rereading seminal Critical Race Theory (CRT) manuscripts, including Bell's *Faces at the Bottom of the Well: The Permanence of Racism* (1992) and "Racial Realism— After We're Gone: Prudent Speculations on America in a Post-Racial Epoch" (1995a), as well as Ladson-Billings and Tate's foundational piece, "Towards a Critical Race Theory of Education" (1995), often considered the CRT bridge from Law to Education. I armed myself with Bell's assertion that, "racism is entrenched in the psychology, memory, society, and culture of the modern world" (1992, p. xiv), as well as his claim that institutions perpetuate racial inequality through institutional practices and policy implementation. I also called to conscious attention Ladson-Billings and Tate's observation regarding the profound influential role race has assumed in fashioning U.S. history. I then read and reflected upon each case chapter selected for inclusion. As an odd and unplanned but coincidental bit of fortuity, in the interlude between receiving chapters, I found myself rereading Brown's pivotal manuscript, *Bury My Heart at Wounded Knee: An Indian History of the American West* (1971). It is a provocative narrative that tells the story of the American West through the voices of members of the Dakota, Ute, Sioux, and Cheyenne nations. It is also an unforgettable, powerful, moving, and thoroughly documented account of the systematic destruction of the American Indian people during the second half of the nineteenth century. Against this backdrop, I continued reading this volume's case chapters, attempting to distill a main point from each to use in crafting this précis.

An intellectual medley of the chapters began to emerge in my mind so I created a table to assist me in harmonizing my thoughts. In Table R1, I list each case's unit or units of study, type of public institution, institutional geographic location, and the CRT (and other) elements used to delineate it. The contents of Table R1 offer a commentary of sorts on the depth and breadth of equity/diversity workers who responded to the call for chapters and whose chapters were ultimately selected for inclusion. Interestingly, cases presented highlight that over half (nine) of the public institutions studied are located somewhere in the southern region (Southeast, South, Southwest) of the United States; four are Midwest institutions; one public institution from the West is included, and two were situated in the Mid-Atlantic region of the United States. No institutions from the northern tier of the United States, from the Pacific Northwest, Alaska, or Hawai'i were examined as part of the cases included in this volume. Neither were any that situated their cases in Historically Black Colleges and Universities (HBCUs), Tribal Colleges, or Asian American and Native American Pacific Islander Serving Institutions (AANAPISIs); while two cases are located in Hispanic-Serving Institutions (HSIs), in most instances the institutions at focus herein are Historically and/or Predominantly White Institutions (HWIs/PWIs). Readers should draw their own conclusions about areas of the United States and institutional types that are both included and not included in this volume; but these omissions also suggest areas for future research. Overwhelmingly, the cases in this volume engaged a vast array of narrative forms both from CRT and other theoretical and conceptual orientations. The cases also included attention to myriad CRT elements and employed several other organizational frameworks. From these accounts, an intricate tapestry that chronicles the complex realities of equity/diversity work in public higher education emerges.

Table R1.
Demographic Case Information

Case	Institution	Locale	CRT and Other Elements
1	University, Local Area	Southwest	Narrative, interest convergence, Whiteness as property, expansive versus restrictive policy
2	State University	South	Voice/counternarrative, colorblindness, Black Feminist Thought, Critical Whiteness Studies, imposition, Whiteness, interest convergence
3	State University	Midwest	Voice/counternarrative, colorblindness, hegemony
4	Flagship	Southwest	Narrative, interest convergence, permanence of racism, racial symbols, cultural subordination, CDO organizational archetypes, Multi-Contextual Model for Diverse Learning Environments
5	Flagship A Flagship B	Appalachia Appalachia	Voice/counternarrative, intersectionality
6	Flagship	Mid-Atlantic	Counterstory, Sociology of Knowledge, informational knowledge, imperial scholarship, dilemmas of serving two masters, interest convergence, permanence of racism
7	University, Regional	Midwest	Voice/counternarrative, Critical Multiculturalism and Cultural Studies Theory, Critical Theory
8	University, Regional (HSI)	Gulf Coast	Narrative, Critical Pedagogy, Critical Theory, localized critique, inscription of Whiteness and "non-Whiteness," research typology process, arts-based inquiry
9	Liberal Arts University	South	Narrative, Criticalist, Emancipatory, power relations, campus climate dimensions, Multicultural Organizational Development
10	University, Regional (HSI)	Southwest	Counterstory/masternarrative, race, power, and pedagogy dilemma, subjectivity versus objectivity
11	Flagship	Midwest	Counterstory, unpacking, problematics, Whiteness as property
12	City University	Midwest	Counterstory, White supremacist practices, colorblindness
13	State University	West	Counterstory, majoritarianism
14	Flagship	Mid-Atlantic	Voice/counternarrative, intercentricity of race and racism, challenge to dominant ideology, centrality of experiential knowledge
15	University, Southern Regional	South	Voice/counternarrative, problem of good/ness

So What?

What emerge in all the cases in this volume are powerful metaphors of struggle and battle. In some of the cases presented, important instances of camaraderie, fellowship, and solidarity also emerge. While the issues and settings differ across cases, through the voices and experiences of the equity/diversity workers who contributed to this volume, clearly, in every case, there is an expressed need for constant vigilance to protect, sustain, elevate, and amplify the positions, offices, departments, and divisions from which they engage 'the work.' Themes based on the metaphors of struggle and battle permeate all 15 cases, evidenced in myriad dichotomous terms/concepts that the authors invoke/construct in describing the 'frontlines' of their work. Table R2 highlights these themes.

Historically, faculty, staff, and student members of university communities fought, especially through grassroots activism, to establish departments and degree programs in, for example, Ethnic Studies, Women Studies, and Queer Studies, as well as to create divisional and campus-wide equity and diversity offices, and other Safe Zones. In this book we see that current equity/diversity workers find themselves fighting for these same things today; fighting for their existence, acceptance, and funding support even in the Obama era. At the same time this book also presents stories of success: A major research

Table R2.
Struggle and Battle Themes

Struggle	*Battle*
Underprivileged	Privileged
Strange	Normal
Subordinate	Dominate
Marginalized	Legitimized
Oppressed	Oppressor
Peripheral	Central
Alternative	Mainstream
Inaccessibility	Accessibility
Fringe	Core
Exclusion	Inclusion
Resistance	Cooptation
Incoherence	Coherence
Counternarratives	Masternarratives
Underrepresented	Overrepresented
Margins	Center
Acculturation	Assimilation
Liberatory	Majoritarian
Counterhegemonic	Hegemonic

university that restructured vice presidential portfolios across campus to put
equity/diversity affairs on par with student, academic, and administrative affairs, and a small liberal arts college whose climate has warmed from resisting
desegregation to honoring past Freedom Riders.

In Case 2, Albert and Barker discussed higher education's slow movement
toward increasing minority access. Many illustrations of this reality emerge
in the "Stories from the *Chief Diversity Officer* Frontlines" section of this volume. A Chief Diversity Officer (CDO) position is created at one large, public
state institution in the 1990s, but only as a response to and a result of federally
mandated integration directives; another university does not even establish
its first CDO until 2009, but relationally demotes it by 2011. Also highlighting the slowness of change in the "Stories from the *Mid-Level Administrator*
Frontlines" section, readers learned about a Special Assistant to the President
for Diversity and Inclusion that was finally created (but never filled) at a public institution of higher education in 2010, a full 45 years, nearly half a century, after the Voting Rights Act of 1965. In Case 7, Lea, Teuber, Jones, and
Wolfgram shared concern over the slow pace of change in discussing institutional history being a drag on change, at the same time that current national
and regional politics rapidly reverse change that took generations to achieve.

What these cases also made clear is the persistent need for equity/diversity
work/ers in public higher education despite the presence of these workers/
this work in the academy for more than 30 years. In Case 6, Brimhall-Vargas
engaged this dilemma in analyzing the distance between rhetoric and reality
in relationship to the responsibilities given to equity/diversity workers, but
the lack of corresponding authority vested in them to carry those responsibilities out. In Case 11, Fasching-Varner and Dodo Seriki contended with the
rhetoric–reality gap in examining how diverse people and diversity people
are simultaneously exploited to promote stated institutional commitments
to diversity, and punished when they seek to live those commitments in their
campus work. Increasingly, campuses want to talk the talk of diversity, just
not walk the walk of equity. In the same vein, in Case 13, Fujimoto questioned why the efforts of diversity coordinators and equity officers stall or get
thwarted while the rhetoric of diversity gets stronger and more embedded in
the fabric of academic life.

Indeed, while equity/diversity work in higher education can be a counterhegemonic force, hegemony is an elusive and otherwise difficult beast to slay.
In Case 8, Loveless and Griffith used visual typology (an image) to illustrate
the complex dynamics with which they wrestled in examining individual and
group identities, experiences, and ideas in relationship to institutional power
and subordination. Backlash against multiculturalism can also manifest as
imagery, and sometimes such backlash can become a flash point for periods of

more rapid change. In Case 9, Gold and Cox recounted how a racist "comic" posted in a resident hall bathroom became a catalyst for cultivating justice-driven relationships, vocal advocacy, and progressive action. Yes, the struggle continues because the battle is still being waged.

Who Cares?

So, is this simply another book devoted to and aimed at scholars in the academy? Is this merely a gown not town concern? Or, is this body of work larger in scope and emblematic of much bigger issues in society? Racism is indeed a raging elephant in the classroom, on campus, and in communities at large. The ultimate goal of the cases in this volume is to promote and advocate for the *counter*stories, narratives, views, and perspectives of people on campus and in the streets who remain peripheral. Unless every voice is used, heard, and affirmed, the democratic/dialogic fabric of United States society will continue to fray. At some point that fraying will arrive at the center, the mainstream, the powerful, and the dominant, revealing that social justice is in everyone's interest—indeed it is where all interests truly converge. In Case 3, Anderson described how informal relationship building between a core group of faculty members led to broader relationship building with members of the local community surrounding the campus, which, over time, led to the establishment of a permanent CDO position. In sharing a reality—that equity/diversity are worth fighting for—relationships were defined, giving rise to meaningful events. We should all care about the cases in this volume because they reflect the reality of the larger societal issues with which we all must contend, lest we all—100 percent of us—lose.

We should all care about and be moved to action against the market-driven mentality undermining democratic (small 'd') principles not just in the United States, but the world over. We should all care that the privatization and corporatization of American society has not simply infiltrated, but is already coopting, public education. As Giroux (2011b) so aptly terms it, *casino capitalism*-based approaches to schooling threaten the fundamental promises of public education. In Case 1, Clark echoes Giroux in discussing the notion of diversity becoming soul-less and being put up 'for sale.' Neoliberal frameworks, language, and strategies are dangerous. They reduce the value of public higher education to SAT scores, 'FTEs' (Full-Time Enrollment), graduation rates, research funding, and the sole alignment of teaching and learning to workforce demands. Accordingly, notions of public higher education as a place and space to expand all students' social, cultural, and intellectual horizons through critical thought and action are being withered away.

Against the backdrop of colleges and universities discussed in this book, we see the composite institutional response to racism as too often isolated into *an* initiative, compartmentalized into *one* position, existing in name but without true power, leadership, or action. In Case 14, Carey and Yee posited that when discussions of diversity are left to the discretion of individual instructors in specific diversity-related courses, those most hurt are the ones already at greatest peril: PK–12 students in our nation's persistently failing urban public schools. In addressing teacher education, many of the cases in the "Stories from the *Faculty* Frontlines" section of this volume speak to this tendency toward the compartmentalization of diversity. *Diversity?* It's taught in the multicultural class. *Disability rights?* We deal with those in special-education coursework. *Minority concerns?* They're covered in another department altogether. A powerful illustration of this tendency is found in Case 12, wherein Mthethwa-Sommers delineated how well-meaning administrators act as guards of the status quo by watering down issues related to equity and inclusion to make them palatable to White, middle-class students and then relegating them to 'their rightful (White-full) place,' the one required diversity course. Similarly, in Case 15, Juárez and Hayes revealed that the notion of 'goodness,' while individually well-intentioned, subverts and derails the democratic aims of social justice in teacher-preparation programs.

What's Our Point about Diversity in Higher Education?

It is as if higher education has stopped its development on diversity at the awareness stage, assigning the responsibility for diversity to an entry level position in Student Affairs, establishing a separate (but never equal) office for it in Human Resources, or creating a Multicultural Center in the basement of a residence hall. *So why do we bother to continue with our efforts? What can be done differently to get equity/diversity work/ers in higher education from the margins to the center once and for all?* In Case 5, Anders, DeVita, and Oliver postulated that identity is never one-dimensional, rather it is intersectional. So too are equity and diversity. Engaging intersectionality as a response to the permanence of racism and other "isms" not only promises, but delivers, transformative results. As Vincent, Sanders, and Ferguson articulated in Case 4, when senior campus leaders have robust understandings of the depth and breadth of diversity in all its dimensions, its centrality to the mission of public higher education becomes crystal clear. When this happens, the entire campus infrastructure shifts so that the positional authority and resource allocation necessary to realize equity and live diversity can be established. Leadership surfaces as central to the struggle for equity, and essential for the cause of equity.

So, just how important is diversity work in higher education? It's really, really, really important because *our* point *about* diversity is *the* point *of* diversity: all for one, one for all. As issues of race and racism continue to permeate our society, unity through diversity should permeate our words and deeds. Many threads make a cloth strong, and all colors make a rainbow. Only in valuing all histories, respecting all cultures, appreciating all experiences, cherishing all voices, and treasuring all stories, will public higher education and the greater public emerge as strong and vibrant. As Jennings recommended in Case 10, the goal of higher education should be to bring about critical participatory intellectualism—an orientation to academic inquiry that encourages community participation, critiques liberal traditions within the academy, and cultivates radical scholarship that also engages communities beyond the ivory tower.

Carta al lector

Una Llamada para Ocupar

Kenneth J. Fasching-Varner,
Christine Clark, y Mark Brimhall-Vargas

25 de enero de 2012

Estimados colegas universitarios de asuntos de equidad y diversidad:

Como el primer periodo de gobierno de la época de Obama ya se está acabando, parece lógico evaluar el panorama político, social y educativo de los Estados Unidos y del extranjero. Especialmente debido a que la administración de Obama no se jacta de sus logros y méritos, ni tampoco se detiene para lamentar los desafíos que se le presentan. Entonces, ¿ *Dónde nos encontramos actualmente?*

En lo que respecta a los logros, hemos visto, aunque de forma moderada y lenta, una tasa positiva de crecimiento económico, en parte debido a que el gobierno tomó posesión de la compañía General Motors, lo cual resultó en salvaguardar 1.4 millones de empleos. Además, hemos visto reformas relacionadas con Wall Street, con las prácticas de las operaciones de tarjetas de crédito y con los préstamos estudiantiles. Hemos visto el trámite y la aprobación de un proyecto de ley sobre los pagos de estímulo económico, la ley de Lilly Ledbetter Fair Pay Act (pago justo para las mujeres), y la nueva ley del GI Bill (para los veteranos de las guerras). También hemos visto la reforma sobre el sistema de salud, la aprobación de ley sobre seguridad y modernización alimenticia, las nuevas regulaciones del tabaco, la aprobación de la ley de Matthew Shepard en contra de los crímenes de odio, y el fin oficial de la política militar de "Don't Ask, Don't Tell" (No Pregunte, No Diga). Como último punto, la ocupación militar de nuestras tropas en Irak ha terminado. También, las tropas en Afganistán se están preparando para salir de ese país.

Veinticinco de los terroristas más peligrosos han sido encarcelados o asesinados (aunque nosotros no estamos de acuerdo, ni creemos que la muerte de nadie es motivo de *celebración*).

Al mismo tiempo, con respecto a los desafíos, el sistema público de educación desde el jardín de niños hasta el doceavo grado, sigue sufriendo segregación por raza y clase socioeconómica, sobre todo en escuelas que sirven y educan a poblaciones que históricamente no han sido representadas como debe ser. Estas escuelas están severamente comprometidas estructuralmente y no reciben financiamiento a la altura de las demás. Del mismo modo, los colegios y las universidades públicas se encuentran en reducción presupuestal permanente, lo cual ha dado como resultado un aumento en las colegiaturas, alejando cada vez más, y más, a estas instituciones de su misión pública.

No podemos ignorar la relación entre estos problemas y el estancamiento político en el Congreso. De una manera que va muy en contra de la postura de diálogo que nosotros promovemos al publicarse este libro, muchos de nuestros líderes nacionales han decidido que es más importante promover sus intereses personales, políticos y económicos, que el bienestar de las personas que los eligieron y a las cuales deben representar. Aunque estos líderes dicen tener como intenciones 'corregir' las cosas, (con un regreso a la postura ideológica de derecha), lo que afirman que el Presidente Obama ha hecho mal, revela cada vez más la retórica que Robin DiAngelo llamaría la *fragilidad del blanco*, que se describe de varias maneras en este volumen. También, al mismo tiempo, su retórica actúa como una forma de *liderazgo imperial*, relacionado con la *erudición imperial* presentada por Richard Delgado, tal como se refiere en otros contextos en este volumen. También, como se plantea en este volumen, su planteamiento oral de representación no coincide con las acciones que ellos toman.

Al entrar en el ciclo electoral del 2012, nosotros todavía no estamos seguros quién de entre los republicanos, y/o de otros partidos políticos, se postulará en contra del Presidente Obama. Actualmente, la lista está llèna de republicanos conservadores y neo-conservadores, candidatos religiosos evangélicos que han, irónicamente, promovido la idea de que la época de Obama es la época "post-racial" de forma deliberada en formas raciales y racistas. Aunque muchos de los ataques que ha enfrentado en su contra el Presidente Obama no han sido distintos de los que fueron emitidos contra sus predecesores, el nivel de la virulencia de otros ataques en contra de su persona no tienen paralelo en la historia de la crítica política y la crítica de candidatos presidenciales en los Estados Unidos. Aunque sería fácil únicamente ubicar la crítica racial sobre el Presidente Obama en la postura ideológica de derecha, la realidad es que el racismo y los prejuicios raciales viven en todos nosotros. Al terminar este libro, está por verse si, como nación, nosotros podremos desplazarnos a través y más allá de esta crítica contra el Presidente Obama, hacia un liderazgo que sea realmente bipartidario, colaborativo y representativo.

Este libro también relata logros y desafíos; y, además, trata el tema de un movimiento hacia un nuevo ciclo en el que aún quedan preguntas por contestar a las que necesitamos respuestas. Sin embargo, tenemos obstáculos que debemos superar y resolver, y así, a través de esta carta dirigida al lector, hacemos un llamado para que ustedes hagan frente a estas interrogantes y a estos obstáculos, como los verán, en esta obra. Al contestar al llamado, les pedimos que pasen del diálogo a los hechos, como lo hemos visto en las protestas públicas que se conocen como Occupy W/All Street/s. En resumen, estamos pidiendo que desplacen estas protestas, a través del trabajo de equidad y diversidad, para que, de forma consciente y deliverada, *Ocupemos la Academia (Occupy the Academy)*. Al hacerlo, les pedimos que consideren el futuro, pasado y el presente del trabajo de equidad y diversidad universitaria de la siguiente manera:

1. *Reflexionen sobre sus experiencias y compártanlas* con sus colegas en esta misma rama laboral y generosamente hagan un intercambio social, cultural y de capital político existente en 'el trabajo';
2. *Desafíen* al 'status quo' neo-liberal y neo-conservador que impregna gran parte de la equidad/diversidad en el panorama de la educación universitaria; y
3. *Edifiquen y registren* su(s) caso(s) de equidad/diversidad para poder continuar informando sobre la obra didáctica.

Conforme pasa el tiempo, las situaciones cambian, pero como vemos en los relatos presentados en este libro, las situaciones no cambian tan rápidamente, ni lo suficiente en un sentido amplio. De este modo, congelando estos y otros relatos en su momento, no solo en este volumen, sino también al progresar hacia delante, somos testigos de las experiencias que estos representan, especialmente de las cicatrices que han quedado como testigos de estas luchas que han combatido no solo los trabajadores de equidad/diversidad, sino también las personas que tienen interés en la obra. En consecuencia, estos relatos sirven como guía para que los trabajadores puedan concentrar sus esfuerzos y para dirigir los siguientes pasos: el futuro de ayer se convierte en la actualidad y en el pasado del mañana.

Para dar acceso a este trabajo colectivo hemos creado una página en Facebook que se puede encontrar buscando "Occupy the Academy." Los animamos a participar y a utilizar este espacio creado en Facebook para compartir sus retos y también sus éxitos con respecto a este tema (www.facebook.com). Así podremos encontrar la afirmación y la crítica radical de sus esfuerzos.

Lo hacemos con el fin de que exista un intercambio de ideas y recursos. Al mismo tiempo, debemos apreciar el valor de esta época digital en el más puro espíritu del diálogo y de la acción dialógica . Les pedimos, más aun, que encuentren nuevas oportunidades para que se desconecten por un momento de sus aparatos electrónicos y en cambio se conécten con nuestra comunidad en forma personal, de corazón a corazón.

En solidaridad,

Kenneth J. Fasching-Varner

Christine Clark

Mark Brimhall-Vargas

An Open Letter

A Call to Occupy

Kenneth J. Fasching-Varner, Christine Clark,
and Mark Brimhall-Vargas

January 25, 2012

Dear Higher-Education Equity and Diversity Worker Colleagues,

As the first term of the Obama era is beginning to wind down, it seems logical to take stock of the political, social, and educational landscape in the United States and abroad. This is especially the case since the Obama administration does not brag much about accomplishments, nor dwell on challenges. *So, where are we?*

On the accomplishments side, we have seen, albeit small and slow, a positive economic growth rate, in part due to the government takeover of General Motors, which resulted in the saving of 1.4 million jobs. Additionally we have seen reforms to Wall Street, credit card practices, and student loan programs. We have experienced the passage of economic stimulus packages, the Lilly Ledbetter Fair Pay Act for Women, and a new GI Bill. We have also seen healthcare reform, passage of a Food Safety Modernization Act, new tobacco regulations, passage of the Matthew Shepard Hate Crimes Prevention Act, and the official end of the Don't Ask, Don't Tell policy. More recently, the formal military occupation of Iraq ended, troops are being drawn down in Afghanistan, and at least 25 key terrorists have been imprisoned or assassinated (not that we believe anyone's death should be *celebrated*).

At the same time, on the challenges side, public PK–12 schools throughout the nation face continuing resegregation by race and class, with schools that serve historically underrepresented populations being the most severely underfunded and structurally compromised. Likewise, public colleges and universities find themselves in perpetual budget retrenchment, the effect of which has meant significant increases in tuition leading these institutions further and further away from their public mission.

We cannot ignore the relationship between these challenges and the political logjam that has become Capitol Hill. In a manner most opposed to the dialogic posture we promote at the outset of this volume, many of our national leaders have decided that it is more important to promote their personal, political, and economic interests than the wellbeing of the people they were elected by and to represent. While these leaders purport to want to 'right,' literally and figuratively (i.e., turn to the Right), what they claim President Obama has done wrong, increasingly their rhetoric reveals what Robin DiAngelo would call their *White fragility*, described in various manners in this volume. At the same time this rhetoric also acts as a form of *imperial leadership* in the vein of Richard Delgado's *imperial scholarship* as discussed in other contexts in this volume. Also as engaged in this volume, their talk of representation is not matched in their walk.

As we enter into the 2012 election cycle we are yet unsure who from the Republican and/or third party ranks will run against President Obama. Presently the Republican slate is filled with conservative and neoconservative religious evangelical candidates who have, ironically, promoted the notion of the Obama era as postracial in deliberately racial and racist ways. While many of the attacks President Obama has faced are not unlike those of previous presidents, the level of vitriol in other attacks on him is unparalleled in the history of political and presidential candidate critique in the United States. While it would be easy to only locate the racialized critique of President Obama on the Right, the reality is that it lives in all of us. As we finish this book it remains to be seen whether or not we, as a nation, will be able to move through and past this particular critique of President Obama toward truly bipartisan, collaborative, and representative leadership.

This book also speaks of accomplishments and challenges; and, it also speaks of movement into a next cycle in which there remain yet unanswered questions for which we need answers, and yet unresolved obstacles to overcome. And so, through this open letter we call you to take up these questions and obstacles—as you see them—in this work. In taking them up, we ask you to move them from dialogue into dialogic action, like what we see in the Occupy W/All Street/s protests. In short, we are asking you to move those protests, through equity and diversity work, to—consciously and deliberately—*Occupy the Academy*. In so doing we ask you to consider the past, present, and future of equity and diversity work in public higher education in the following manner:

1. *Reflect upon and share* your experiences in equity/diversity work with other equity/diversity workers—generously exchange the social, cultural, and political capital of 'the work';
2. *Challenge* the neoliberal and neoconservative status quo that permeates much of the current equity/diversity landscape in public higher education; and
3. *Build and record* your equity/diversity case(s) to so as to continue to inform the work.

As time passes situations change, but as we see in the narratives presented in this volume, situations do not change quickly, enough, and/or in expansive directions. Thus, by locking these and other narratives in time, not just in this volume but also moving forward, we bear witness to the experiences they represent, especially the battle scars they have caused to not only equity/diversity workers but also to stakeholders in the work. Accordingly, these narratives provide a roadmap for where workers need to concentrate efforts and for where the work needs to go next: Yesterday's future becomes today's moment and tomorrow's past.

To facilitate this collective work, we have created a Facebook page that can be found by searching "Occupy the Academy" on Facebook (www.facebook.com). We encourage you to join and use this page space to share your challenges and successes; to find affirmation for, and radical critique of, your efforts; and, to exchange ideas and resources. At the same time that we see the value of digital occupation, in the purest spirit of dialogue and dialogic action, we urge you, even more so, to find opportunities to disconnect from your devices, and instead plug into our community face-to-face, hand-in-hand, heart-to-heart.

In Solidarity,

Kenneth J. Fasching-Varner

Christine Clark

Mark Brimhall-Vargas

Afterword

Damon A. Williams

The Strategic Diversity Leadership Era

EVERY DIVERSITY ERA HAS A THEME. The 1960s and 1970s are still thought of as the *years of true affirmative action,* when federal legislation and landmark court decisions fueled the diversification of colleges and universities at unprecedented levels; the 1990s were the *retrenchment years,* when a rising anti-affirmative-action sentiment led to shifts in the court's interpretations of diversity and a much weaker diversity policy environment (Zamani-Gallaher, O'Neil Green, Brown, & Stoval, 2009). The changes in our economy, our demographic, and the need for colleges and universities to prepare global citizens have inspired a new era:

1. An era in which diversity work must be emboldened;
2. An era in which our ability to achieve our institutional diversity goals is of vital importance to remaining globally competitive and accomplishing the educational attainment agenda set forth by President Barack Obama and others;
3. An era calling for colleges and universities to educate students at all levels of society, not simply those at the top of the privilege pyramid;
4. An era in which diversity is defined not only in terms of race, ethnicity, and gender, but in ways that embrace the needs and agendas of groups who are diverse in terms of sexual orientation, nationality, religion, and economic background, among other prominent aspects that must be part of the twenty-first-century diversity conversation;

5. An era in which our diversity efforts must be viewed not only as an *end* in terms of *increasing the numbers* of diverse students, faculty, and staff, but also as an essential ingredient or *means* of enhancing student learning and development, research, scholarship, and institutional excellence: an era of *strategic diversity leadership*.

This new millennial model of change gravitates toward strategic diversity leaders—that is, leaders who constantly look to evolve the system by making it more diverse, equitable, and inclusive for others (Williams & Wade-Golden, 2012a, 2012b). Becoming a strategic diversity leader requires reading the external and internal environment, navigating often treacherous organizational politics, leveraging the best of what we know about diversity-themed change as both art and science, and engaging others in the process of shifting the cultures of colleges and universities that are legendarily complex and resistant to movement.

As this volume illustrates, in the current era, we do not have to guess at how to diversify our faculty applicant pools, infuse diversity into the curriculum, create powerful intergroup dialogue platforms, eliminate educational achievement gaps, establish diversity plans that work, or assess the educational benefits of diversity. For nearly 30 years, scholars have dedicated their lives to creating an evidence-based understanding of how to do strategic diversity leadership work in the academy (Allen, Epps, & Haniff, 1991; Bauman, Bustillos, Bensimon, Brown, & Bartee, 2005; Bensimon, 2004; Bolman & Deal, 2003; Bowen & Bok, 1998; Chang, Witt, Jones, & Hakuta, 2003; Clayton-Pederson, Parker, Smith, Moreno, & Teraguch, 2007; Garcia, Hudgins, McTighe-Musil, Nettles, Sedlacek, & Smith, 2001; Gurin, Lehman, & Lewis, 2007; Harper, 2008; Hurtado, 2001; Hurtado, Milem, Clayton-Pedersen, & Allen, 1999; Jackson, 2007; Jackson & Hardiman, 1994; Jackson & Holvino, 1988; Kezar, 2001, 2011; Milem, Chang, & Antonio, 2005; Milem & Hakuta, 2000; Sedlacek, 2004; Smith, 1996; Smith, Gerbrick, Figueroa, Harris Watkins, Levitan, Cradoc Moore, Merchant, Dov Beliak, & Figueroa, 1997; Smith, Wolf, & Levitan, 1994; Tierney, 1992, 1993; Williams, Berger, & McClendon, 2005; Williams & Wade-Golden, 2012a, 2012b).

The Challenge of Strategic Diversity Leaders

The diversity *workers* whose stories are showcased in this book are also diversity *leaders* who understand the struggle and fight against the grain of tradition, racism, and exclusion, using strategic planning, multicultural organizational redesign efforts, diversity admissions and hiring initiatives, community engagement efforts, and other tools to spark new possibilities in pursuit of four key strategic diversity leadership goals: (a) increasing access and equity for historically underrepresented groups; (b) creating a multicultural and inclusive campus environment for every student, faculty, and staff member; (c) instating curricular and cocurricular initiatives to prepare students for a diverse and global world; and (d) advancing diversity-themed scholarship and research to drive understanding of diversity, equity, and inclusion issues at the domestic and global levels (Williams & Wade-Golden, 2012a, 2012b).

Diversity is no longer an issue that can be swept under the table, under-funded, or ignored until a crisis occurs. On the contrary, diversity in its myriad forms must be engaged daily and, from an institutional perspective, strategically. At its best, our system of higher education continues to set the standard for excellence that remains the envy of the world. However, the way that this system prioritizes racial, economic, gender, LGBTQ (lesbian, gay, bisexual, transgender, queer), and other forms of diversity remains ineffec-tive, particularly in light of powerful environmental forces that are reshaping the strategic context of the academy, as well as the values that drive its hiring practices, pedagogy, and budgeting priorities.

As this book emphasizes, our ability to inspire change and transforma-tion is less connected to the election of the nation's first African American president, and more to the day-to-day leadership of dedicated and resilient diversity professionals who can harness the power of a changing strategic landscape, elevating the diversity conversation in ways both new and historic. The Critical Race Theory analyses reveal the difficulty and personal cost as-sociated with strategic diversity leadership and in attempting to transform institutions that are deeply resistant to organizational change.

This volume illustrates that material commitment to action must be put into place daily if college and university diversity efforts are to be more than simply high-profile window dressing. As the late Frank Hale Jr., vice provost emeritus of Ohio State University, was known for saying, "Commitment without currency is counterfeit, and don't let anyone tell you differently!"

Until the values, leadership practices, pedagogies, and other priorities of our institutions are permeated by diversity enterprise flush with capital and endowed with real authority, the responsibility for moving our campus di-versity efforts forward will remain only on the shoulders of the chief diversity officers, diversity and equity professionals, and campus diversity champions occupying academia. As occupiers, we must remain vigilant in our efforts to dismantle a system that was not created to accommodate diversity, but that must evolve to face and embrace the reality of this new era where our issues—diversity issues—are paramount to the survival and prosperity of the world in which we live today.

References

ACME Department of Administration (ADA) [sic]. (2011). 2011–2013 executive budget. Retrieved from nevadabudget.org/index.php/publications/executivebudget/318-2011-2013-executive-budget

ACME State University (ACME State) [sic]. (2011). College portrait. Retrieved from http://www.collegeportraits.org/MO/MSU/characteristics

ACME State University (ASU) [sic]. (2011a). College portrait. Retrieved from http://www.collegeportraits.org/LA/LSU/characteristics

ACME State University (ASU) [sic]. (2011b). Demographics. Retrieved from http://www.lsusports.net/ViewArticle.dbml?DB_OEM_ID=5200&ATCLID=177345

Aguirre, A. (2000). *Women and minority faculty in the academic workplace: Recruitment, retention, and academic culture.* San Francisco, CA: Jossey-Bass.

Alexander, M. (2010, February 8). The new Jim Crow. *The Huffington Post.* Retrieved from http://www.huffingtonpost.com/michelle-alexander/the-new-jim-crow_b_454469.html

Alger, J. (1998). Minority faculty and measuring merit: Start by playing fair. *Academe,* 74(4), 65–94.

Allen, W., Epps, E., & Haniff, N. (Eds.). (1991). *College in black and white: African American students in predominantly white and in historically black public universities.* Albany, NY: State University of New York Press.

Alliance for Excellent in Education (AEE). (2011). About the crisis. Retrieved from http://www.all4ed.org/about_the_crisis/promotingpower

Anderson, K., & Smith, G. (2005). Students' preconceptions of professors: Benefits and barriers according to ethnicity and gender. *Hispanic Journal of Behavioral Sciences,* 27(2), 184–201.

Anderson, L. (2011). Diversity: Numbers don't do it justice. *Blend.* Retrieved from http://www.missouristate.edu/assets/human/blend2ndedition2011.pdf

Annie E. Casey Foundation (AECF). (2011). Date across states. Retrieved from http://datacenter.kidscount.org/data/acrossstates/Rankings.aspx?ind=5199

Ansley, F. (1997). White supremacy (and what we should do about it). In R. Delgado and J. Stefancic (Eds.), *Critical white studies: Looking behind the mirror* (pp. 592–595). Philadelphia, PA: Temple University Press.

Antonio, A. (2002). Faculty of color reconsidered: Reassessing contributions to scholarship. *Journal of Higher Education, 73*(5), 582–602.

Antonio, A., Chang, M., Hakuta, K., Kenny, D., Levin, S., & Milem, J. (2004). Effects of racial diversity on complex thinking in college students. *Psychological Science, 15*(8), 507–510.

Anyon, J. (2005). *Radical possibilities: Education and a new social movement.* New York, NY: Routledge.

Anzaldúa, G. (1987). *Borderlands/la frontera: The new mestiza.* San Francisco, CA: Aunt Lute Books.

Apple, M. (2001). *Educating the "right" way: Markets, standards, God, and inequality.* New York, NY: Routledge.

Arnsdorf, I. (2011, August 18). Obama orders improved workforce diversity effort. *The Washington Post.* Retrieved from http://www.washingtonpost.com/local/dc-politics/executive-order-to-push-agencies-on-federal-workforce-diversity/2011/08/18/gIQAng5POJ_story.html

Association of American Colleges and Universities (AAC&U). (n.d.). Making excellence inclusive. Retrieved from http://www.aacu.org/compass/inclusive_excellence.cfm

Asukile, T. (2009). The Barack Obama new era: Race matters more than ever in America. *The Black Scholar, 38*(4), 41–43.

Bakhtin, M. (1981). *The Dialogic imagination: Four essays.* Austin, TX: University of Texas Press.

Banks, J. (2004). Remembering *Brown*: Silence, loss, rage, and hope. *Multicultural Perspectives, 6*(4), 6–8.

Bauman, G., Bustillos, L., Bensimon, E., Brown, C., & Bartee, R. (2005). *Achieving equitable educational outcomes with all students.* Washington, DC: Association of American Colleges and Universities (AAC&U).

Belenky, M., Clinchy, B., Goldberger, N., & Tarule, J. (1997). *Women's ways of knowing: The development of self, voice, and mind (10th anniversary edition).* New York, NY: Basic Books.

Bell, D. (2004). *Silent covenants: Brown v. Board of Education and the unfulfilled hopes for racial reform.* New York, NY: Oxford University Press.

Bell, D. (1995a). Racial realism—After we're gone: Prudent speculations on America in a post-racial epoch. In R. Delgado (Ed.), *Critical race theory: The cutting edge (first edition)* (pp. 25–32). Philadelphia, PA: Temple University Press.

Bell, D. (1995b). Racial realism. In K. Crenshaw, N. Gotanda, G. Peller, and K. Thomas (Eds.), *Critical race theory: The key writings that formed the movement* (pp. 302–314). New York, NY: The New Press.

Bell, D. (1995c). Brown vs. Board of Education: The interest convergence dilemma. In K. Crenshaw, N. Gotananda, G. Peller, and K. Thomas (Eds.), *Critical race theory:*

The key writings that formed a movement (pp. 20–29). New York, NY: The New Press.

Bell, D. (1992). *Faces at the bottom of the well: The permanence of racism.* New York, NY: Basic Books.

Bell, D. (1987). *And we are not saved: The elusive quest for racial justice.* New York, NY: Basic Books.

Bell, D. (1980). *Brown v. Board of Education* and the interest-convergence dilemma. *Harvard Law Review, 93*(3), 518–533.

Bell, D. (1976). Serving two masters: Integration ideals and client interests in school desegregation litigation. *The Yale Law Journal, 85*(4), 470–516.

Bennett, L. (1964). Tea and sympathy: Liberals and other white hopes. In L. Bennett (Ed.), *The Negro mood and other essays* (pp. 75–104). Chicago, IL: Johnson Publishing Company, Inc.

Bensimon, E. (2004). The diversity scorecard: A learning approach to institutional change. *Change 36*(1), 45–52.

Bentham, J. (1914). *Theory of legislation.* London, England: Oxford University Press.

Bergerson, A. (2003). Critical race theory and white racism: Is there room for white scholars in fighting racism in education? *Qualitative Studies in Education, 16*(1), 51–63.

Berlet, C. (2009). Race and the Right. In L. Burnham (Ed.), *Changing the race: Racial politics and the election of Barack Obama* (pp. 58–61). New York, NY: Applied Research Center.

Berlin, J. (1993). *Cultural studies in the English classroom.* New York, NY: Heinemann.

Berry, M. (1994). *Black resistance to white law: A history of constitutional racism in America.* New York, NY: Penguin Books.

Bhabha, H. (1990). *Nation narration.* New York, NY: Routledge.

Bhattacharya, K. (2009). Othering research, researching the other: De/colonizing approaches to qualitative inquiry. In J. Smart (Ed.), *Higher education: Handbook of theory and research* (pp. 105–150). Los Angeles, CA: Springer.

Birnbaum, R. (1992). *How academic leadership works.* San Francisco, CA: Jossey-Bass.

Blanchett, W. (2006). Disproportionate representation of African Americans in special education: Acknowledging the role of white privilege and racism. *Educational Researcher, 35*(6), 24–28.

Bloom, A. (1987). *The closing of the American mind: How higher education has failed democracy and impoverished the souls of today's students.* New York, NY: Simon & Schuster.

Board of Regents. (2011). Members. Retrieved from http://regents.louisiana.gov/index.cfm?md=pagebuilder&tmp=home&pid=253

Bolman, L., & Deal, T. (2003). *Reframing organizations: Artistry, choice, and leadership (third edition).* San Francisco, CA: Jossey-Bass.

Bonilla-Silva, E. (2009). *Racism without racists: Color-blind racism and the persistence of racial inequality in the United States (third edition).* Lanham, MD: Rowman & Littlefield.

Bonilla-Silva, E. (2006). *Racism without racists: Color-blind racism and the persistence of racial inequality in the United States (second edition).* Lanham, MD: Rowman & Littlefield.

Bonilla-Silva, E. (2003). New racism, color-blind racism, and the future of whiteness in America. In A. Doane and E. Bonilla-Silva (Eds.), *Whiteout: The continuing significance of racism* (pp. 271–284). New York, NY: Routledge.

Bonilla-Silva, E. (1997). Rethinking racism: Toward a structural interpretation. *American Sociological Review, 62*(3), 465–480.

Borg, E. (2003). Discourse community. *The ELT [English Language Teaching] Journal, 57*(4), 398–400.

Bork, R. (2003). *Slouching towards Gomorrah: Modern liberalism and American decline (rep sub edition)*. New York, NY: ReganBooks/HarperCollins.

Borman, K., Clarke, C., Cotner, B., & Lee, R. (2006). Cross-case analysis. In J. Green, G. Camili, and P. Elmore (Eds.), *Handbook of complementary methods in education research* (pp. 123–139). Mahwah, NJ: Lawrence Erlbaum Associates.

Bowen, W., & Bok, D. (1998). *The shape of the river: Long-term consequences of considering race in college and university admissions.* Princeton, NJ: Princeton University Press.

Bowers, M. (2006). *The sagebrush state: Nevada's history, government, and politics (third edition)*. Reno, NV: University of Nevada Press.

Bowman, N. (2010). Diversity experiences and cognitive development: A meta-analysis. *Review of Educational Research, 80*(1), 4–33.

Bredo, E. (2006). Philosophies of educational research. In J. Green, G. Camili, and P. Elmore (Eds.), *Handbook of complementary methods in education research* (pp. 3–31). Mahwah, NJ: Lawrence Erlbaum Associates.

Brenner, M. (2006). Interviewing in educational research. In J. Green, G. Camili, and P. Elmore (Eds.), *Handbook of complementary methods in education research* (pp. 357–370). Mahwah, NJ: Lawrence Erlbaum Associates.

Brook, T., Bourgon, J., & Blue, G. (2008). *Death by a thousand cuts.* Cambridge, MA: Harvard University Press.

Brooks, J., & Normore, A. (2010). Educational leadership and globalization: Literacy for a glocal perspective. *Educational Policy, 24*(1), 52–82.

Brown, A. (2009). Biracialism and the 2008 elections. In L. Burnham (Ed.), *Changing the race: Racial politics and the election of Barack Obama* (pp. 30–33). New York, NY: Applied Research Center.

Brown, D. (1971). *Bury my heart at Wounded Knee: An Indian history of the American west.* New York, NY: Holt, Rinehart, & Winston.

Brown v. Board of Education, 347 U.S. 483 (1954).

Bush v. Gore, 531 U.S. 98 (2000).

Campus Climate Subcommittee. (2008). *Campus climate subcommittee final report.* (Unpublished report). Knoxville, TN: University of Tennessee Strategic Planning Committee.

Campus Senate. (2010). University of ACME [sic] code on equity, diversity, and inclusion. Retrieved from http://www.president.umd.edu/policies/docs/VI-100B.pdf

Caplan, P., Nettles, M., Millett, C., Miller, S., DiCrecchio, N., & Chu, T. (2009). *The voices of diversity: What racial/ethnic minority students can tell us about advantages and disadvantages of attending predominantly white colleges.* Battlecreek, MI: W. K. Kellogg Foundation.

Carpenter, C., Durick, J., Grafman, M., Hardin, P., Harmon, N., Murray, G., Ramage, E., & Stallings, E. (1963, April 12). Statement by Alabama clergymen (also known as A call for unity). *The Birmingham News*. Retrieved from http://www.stanford.edu/group/King//frequentdocs/clergy.pdf

Carr, W., & Kemmis, S. (2005). Staying critical. *Educational Action Research, 13*(3), 347–358.

Carter, P. (2009). Equity and empathy: Toward racial and educational acievement in the Obama era. *Harvard Educational Review, 79*(2), 287–297.

Cave, D. (2008, November 7). Generation O gets its hopes up. *The New York Times*. Retrieved from http://www.nytimes.com/2008/11/09/fashion/09boomers .html?pagewanted=all

Chang, M., Denson, N., Saenz, V., & Misa, K. (2006). The educational benefits of sustaining cross-racial interaction among undergraduates. *Journal of Higher Education, 77*(3), 430–455.

Chang, M., Witt, D., Jones, J., & Hakuta, K. (Eds.). (2003). *Compelling interest: Examining the evidence on racial dynamics in colleges and universities*. Palo Alto, CA: Stanford Education.

Chapman, T. (2007). Interrogating classroom relationships and events: Using portraiture and critical race theory in education research. *Educational research, 36*(3), 156–162.

Chapman, T. (2006). Pedaling backward: Reflections of *Plessy* and *Brown* in Rockford Public Schools' desegregation efforts. In A. Dixson and C. Rousseau (Eds.), *Critical race theory in education: All God's children got a song* (pp. 67–89). New York, NY: Routledge.

Chomsky, N. (1997, November). Market democracy in a neoliberal order: Doctrines and reality. *Z Magazine Online*, Retrieved from http://www.chomsky.info/articles/199711--.htm

Clark, C. (2010). Just how important *is* diversity? *Diverse Issues in Higher Education, 26*(27), 21.

Clark, C. (2005). Timeline overview. Retrieved from http://www.ohrp.umd.edu/divtimeline/overview.html

Clark, C. (2003). Building authentic intergroup dialogue on campus: Living a commitment to shared governance and career path development through the full inclusion of *all* members of the university community. *Multicultural Education, 11*(2), 55–58.

Clark, C. (2002). Intergroup dialogue on campus. *Multicultural Education, 9*(4), 30–31.

Clark, C., & O'Donnell, J. (Eds.). (1999). *Becoming and unbecoming White: Owning and disowning a racial identity*. Westport, CT: Greenwood.

Clayton-Pederson, A., Parker, S., Smith, D., Moreno, J., & Teraguch, D. (2007). *Making a real difference with diversity*. Washington, DC: Association of American Colleges and Universities (AAC&U).

Cokorinos, L. (2003). *The assault on diversity: An organized challenge to racial and gender justice*. Lanham, MD: Rowman & Littlefield.

Cole, J. (2004). Black studies in liberal arts education. In J. Bobo, C. Hudley, and C. Michel (Eds.), *The Black studies reader* (pp. 21–34). New York, NY: Routledge.

Coles, G. (2001). Learning to read 'scientifically.' *Rethinking Schools, 15*(4). Retrieved from http://www.rethinkingschools.org/special_reports/bushplan/Read154.shtml

Collins, P. (1998). *Fighting words: Black women and the search for justice.* Minneapolis, MN: University of Minnesota Press.

Collins, P. (1990). *Black feminist thought: Knowledge, power and the politics of empowerment.* Boston, MA: Unwin Hyman.

Collins, P. (1986). Learning fron the outsider within: The sociological significance of black feminist thought. *Social Problems, 33*(6), S14–S32.

Commission for LGBT People. (2010). *And miles to go: The state of the campus from an LGBT [Lesbian, Gay, Bisexual, Transgender] perspective.* (Unpublished report). Knoxville, TN. University of Tennessee Commission for LGBT People.

Cone, J. (1986). *A black theology of liberation.* Maryknoll, NY: Orbis.

Conyers, J. (1997). African American Studies: Locating a niche in the public sphere of higher education. In J. Conyers (Ed.), *Africana studies: A disciplinary quest for both theory and method* (pp. 130–139). Jefferson, ME: McFarland.

Cooper, J., & Stevens, D. (Eds.). (2002). *Tenure in the sacred grove: Issues and strategies for women and minority faculty.* Albany, NY: State University of New York.

Crenshaw, K. (2011). Twenty years of critical race theory: Looking back to move forward. *Connecticut Law Review, 43*(5), 1253–1264.

Crenshaw, K. (1997). Color-blind dreams and racial nightmares: Reconfiguring racism in the post-civil rights era. In T. Morrison and C. Lacour (Eds.), *Birth of a nation'hood* (pp. 97–168). New York, NY: Pantheon Books.

Crenshaw, K. (1995). Race, reform, and retrenchment transformation and legitimating in anti-discrimination law. In K. Crenshaw, N. Gotanda, G. Peller, and K. Thomas (Eds.), *Critical race theory: The key writings that formed the movement* (pp. 103–126). New York, NY: The New Press.

Crenshaw, K. (1991a). Mapping the margins: Intersectionality, identity politics, and violence against women of color. *Stanford Law Review, 43*(6), 1241–1299.

Crenshaw, K. (1991b). Demarginalizing the intersection of race and sex: A Black feminist critique of antidiscrimination doctrine, feminist theory, and antiracist politics. In K. Bartlett and R. Kennedy (Eds.), *Feminist legal theory: Readings in law and gender* (pp. 57–80). Boulder, CO: Westview.

Crenshaw, K. (1988). Race, reform, and retrenchment: Transformation and legitimization in anti-discrimination law. *Harvard Law Review, 101*(7), 1331–1387.

Creswell, J. (2011). *Educational research: Planning, conducting, and evaluating quantitative and qualitative research (fourth edition).* Boston, MA: Pearson.

Creswell, J. (2009). *Research design: Qualitative, quantitative, and mixed methods approaches (third edition).* Thousand Oaks, CA: Sage.

Creswell, J. (2007). *Qualitative inquiry and research design: Choosing among five approaches (second edition).* Thousand Oaks, CA: Sage.

Darling-Hammond, L. (2009). President Obama and education: The possibility for dramatic improvements in teaching and learning. *Harvard Educational Review, 79*(2), 210–223.

Davis, P. (1989). Law as microaggression. *Yale Law Journal, 98*(8), 1559–1577.

Davis, T. (Director). (2010). *Jean-Michel Basquiat: Radiant child* [Documentary]. United States: Independent Lens.

DeCuir, J., & Dixson, A. (2004). 'So when it comes out, they aren't that surprised that it is there': Using critical race theory as a tool of analysis of race and racism in education. *Educational Researcher, 33*(5), 26–31.

Dei, G., Karumanchery, L., & Karumanchery-Luik, N. (2007). *Playing the race card: Exposing white power and privilege.* New York, NY: Peter Lang.

Delgado, R. (2000). Storytelling for oppositionists and other: A plea for narrative. In R. Delgado and J. Stefancic (Eds.), *Critical race theory: The cutting edge (second edition)* (pp. 2411–2441). Philadelphia, PA: Temple University Press.

Delgado, R. (1999). *When equality ends: Stories of race and resistance.* Boulder, CO: Westview.

Delgado, R. (Ed.). (1995a). *Critical race theory: The cutting edge.* Philadelphia, PA: Temple University Press.

Delgado, R. (1995b). *The Rodrigo chronicles: Conversations about America and race.* New York, NY: New York University Press.

Delgado, R. (1989). Storytelling for oppositionists and others: A plea for narrative. *Michigan Law Review, 87*(8), 2411–2441.

Delgado, R. (1984). The imperial scholar: Reflections on a review of civil rights literature. *University of Pennsylvania Law Review, 132*(3), 561–578.

Delgado R., & Stefancic, J. (Eds.). (2005). *The Latino/a condition: A critical reader (second edition).* New York, NY: New York University Press.

Delgado R., & Stefancic, J. (2001). *Critical race theory: An introduction.* New York, NY: New York University Press.

Delgado, R., & Stefancic, J. (Eds.). (2000). *Critical race theory: The cutting edge (second edition).* Philadelphia, PA: Temple University Press.

Delgado, R., & Stefancic, J. (Eds.). (1997a). *Critical white studies: Looking behind the mirror.* Philadelphia, PA: Temple University Press.

Delgado, R., & Stefancic, J. (1997b). Imposition. In R. Delgado and J. Stefancic (Eds.), *Critical white studies: Looking behind the mirror* (pp. 98–105). Philadelphia, PA: Temple University Press.

Delgado, R., & Stefancic, J. (1994). Imposition. *William and Mary Law Review, 35*(3), 1025–1059.

Delgado, R., & Stefancic, J. (1992). Images of the outsider in American law and culture: Can free expression remedy systemic social ills? *Cornell Law Review, 77*(6), 1258–1297.

Delgado Bernal, D. (2002). Critical race theory, LatCrit theory and critical raced-gendered epistemologies: Recognizing students of color as holders and creators of knowledge. *Qualitative Inquiry, 8*(1), 105–126.

Delgado Bernal, D., & Villalpando, O. (2002). An apartheid of knowledge in academia: The struggle over the 'legitimate' knowledge of faculty of color. *Equity and Excellence in Education, 35*(2), 169–180.

Delpit, L. (2006). *Other people's children: Cultural conflict in the classroom.* New York, NY: The New Press.

Democracy Now! (2010, November 10). Acclaimed Indian author Arundhati Roy on Obama's wars, poverty and India's Maoist rebels [Audio]. *DemocracyNow. org.* Retrieved from http://www.democracynow.org/2010/11/8/acclaimed_indian_ author_arundhati_roy_on

Denzin, N. (2007). The politics and ethic of performance pedagogy: Toward a pedagogy of hope. In P. McLaren and J. Kincheloe (Eds.), *Critical pedagogy: Where are we now* (pp. 127–142). New York, NY: Peter Lang.

Denzin, N. (1984). *The research act.* Englewood Cliffs, NJ: Prentice Hall.

DeVita, J. (2010). Gay male identity in the context of college: Implications for development, support, and campus climate. (Unpublished doctoral dissertation). University of Tennessee, Knoxville. DOI: http://trace.tennessee.edu/utk_graddiss/791/

Dewey, J. (1902). *The school and society and the child and the curriculum.* Chicago, IL: University of Chicago Press.

DiAngelo, R. (2011). White fragility. *International Journal of Critical Pedagogy, 3*(3), 53–71.

Dixson, A., & Dingus, J. (2007). Tyranny of the majority: Re-enfranchisement of African-American teacher educators teaching for democracy. *International Journal of Qualitative Studies in Education, 20*(6), 639–654.

Dixson, A., & Rousseau, C. (2006). *Critical race theory in education: All God's children got a song.* New York, NY: Routledge.

Dixson, A., & Rousseau, C. (2005). And we are still not saved: Critical race theory in education ten years later. *Race, Ethnicity, and Education, 8*(1), 7–27.

Doll, W. (1993). *A post-modern perspective on curriculum.* New York, NY: Teachers College Press.

Douglass, F. (1857). *Two speeches by Frederick Douglass.* Rochester, NY: Central Library of Rochester and Monroe County, Historic Monographs Collection. Retrieved from http://www.libraryweb.org/~digitized/books/Two_Speeches_by_ Frederick_Douglass.pdf

Driggs, D., & Goodall, L. (1996). *Nevada politics and government: Conservatism in an open society.* Lincoln, NE: University of Nebraska Press.

Drucker, J. (1994). *The visible word: Experimental typography and modern art, 1909– 1923.* Chicago, IL: The University of Chicago Press.

D'Souza, D. (1998). *Illiberal education: The politics of race and sex on campus.* New York, NY: The Free Press.

Dudziak, M. (1988). Desegregation as a cold war imperative. *Stanford Law Review, 41*(61), 61–121.

Duke, N., & Mallette, M. (2004). *Literacy research methodologies.* New York, NY: Guilford Press.

Dumville, M. (2007, November 8). Immediate reactions: Incident leads to campus controversy. *The Bullet.* Retrieved from http://umwbullet.com/2007/11/08/ immediate-reactions-incident-leads-to-campus-controversy/

Duncan, G. (2002). Beyond love: A critical race ethnography of the schooling of black males. *Equity and Excellence in Education, 35*(2), 131–143.

Duncan-Andrade, J., & Morrell, E. (2007). Critical pedagogy and popular culture in an urban secondary English classroom. In P. McLaren and J. Kincheloe (Eds.), *Critical pedagogy: Where are we now* (pp. 183–200). New York, NY: Peter Lang.

During, S. (2003). *The cultural studies reader (second edition)*. New York: Routledge.

Edgell, P., & Tranby, E. (2010). Shared visions? Diversity and cultural membership in American life. *Social Problems, 57*(2), 175–204.

Editorial (2011, August 19). Whites need not apply: Liberals don't want our government to mirror our society. *The Washington Times*. Retrieved from http://www .washingtontimes.com/news/2011/aug/19/obama-whites-need-not-apply/

Education Trust. (2010). *Opportunity adrift: Our flagship universities are straying from their public mission*. Washington, DC: Author.

Elementary and Secondary Education (ESEA) Act (1965). Pub. L. No. 89-10, § 79, Stat. 27.

Enck-Wanzer, D. (Ed.). (2010). *The Young Lords: A reader*. New York, NY: New York University Press.

Evans, N. (2002). The impact of an LGBT safe zone project on campus climate. *Journal of College Student Development, 43*(4), 522–539.

Exec. Order No. 13583 (2011). Retrieved from http://www.whitehouse.gov/the-press -office/2011/08/18/executive-order-establishing-coordinated-government-wide- initiative-prom

Exec. Order No. 10925 (1961). Retrieved from http://en.wikipedia.org/wiki/Executive_ Order_10925

Fasching-Varner, K. (2009). "No! The team ain't alright!" The institutional and individual problematics of race. *Social Identities, 15*(6), 811–829.

Fasching-Varner, K., & Dodo Seriki, V. (2012). "Just (don't) do it!" Tensions between articulated commitments and action at The ACME State University. In C. Clark, K. Fasching-Varner, and M. Brimhall-Vargas (Eds.), *Occupying the academy: Just how important is diversity work in higher education?* (pp. 140–152). Lanham, MD: Rowman & Littlefield.

Foucault, M (1986). *Disciplinary power and subjection*. New York, NY: New York University Press.

Foucault, M. (1980a). Truth and power. In C. Gordon (Ed.), *Power/knowledge: Selected interviews & other writings 1972–1977* (pp. 109–133). New York, NY: Pantheon Books.

Foucault, M. (1980b). Two lectures (C. Gordon, L. Marshall, J. Mepham & K. Soper, Trans.). In C. Gordon (Ed.), *Power/knowledge: Selected interviews & other writings 1972–1977* (pp. 78–108). New York, NY: Pantheon Books.

Fraser, G., & Hunt, D. (2011). Faculty diversity and search committee training: Learning from a critical incident. *Journal of Diversity in Higher Education, 4*(3), 185–98.

Freire, P. (2000). *Pedagogy of the oppressed (30th anniversary edition)*. New York, NY: Continuum.

Freire, P. (1970). *Pedagogy of the oppressed*. New York, NY: Seabury Press.

Frémaux, A. (2010, April 5). The educational crisis, symptom and crucible of societal crisis. *Truthout*. Retrieved from http://archive.truthout.org/the-educational-crisis- symptom-and-crucible-societal-crisis58505

Garcia, M., Hudgins, C., McTighe-Musil, C., Nettles, M., Sedlacek, W., & Smith, D. (2001). *Assessing campus diversity initiatives: A guide for campus practitioners*. Washington, DC: Association of American Colleges and Universities (AAC&U).

Gay, G. (2010). *Culturally responsive teaching: Theory, practice, & research (second edition)*. New York, NY: Teachers College Press.

Gay, G. (2000). *Culturally responsive teaching: Theory, research, & practice*. New York, NY: Teachers College Press.

Geertz, C. (1983). Local knowledge: Further essays in interpretive anthropology. In A. Swidler and J. Arditi (Eds.), *The new sociology of knowledge*. New York, NY: Basic Books.

Gillborn, D. (2005). Education policy as an act of white supremacy: Whiteness, critical race theory and education reform. *Journal of Education Policy, 20*(4), 485–505.

Gillborn, D., & Rollock, N. (2011). Critical race theory. *British Educational Research Association Online*. Retrieved from http://www.bera.ac.uk/files/2011/06/Critical-Race-Theory.pdf

Gioia, D., & Thomas, B. (1996). Identity, image and issue interpretation: Sense making during strategic change in academia. *Administrative Science Quarterly, 41*(3), 370–403.

Giroux, H. (2011a, April 5). Militarized conservatism and the end(s) of higher education. *Truthout*. Retrieved from http://truthout.org/militarized-conservatism-and-ends-higher-education

Giroux, H. (2011b, May 16). American democracy beyond casino capitalism and the torture state. *Truthout*. Retrieved from http://truthout.org/american-democracy-beyond-casino-capitalism-and-torture-state/1305143581

Giroux, H. (2010). Dumbing down teachers: Rethinking the crisis of public education and the demise of the social state. *Review of Education, Pedagogy, and Cultural Studies, 32*(4/5), 339–381.

Giroux, H. (1998). *Channel surfing: Racism, media and the destruction of today's youth*. New York, NY: St. Martin's Press.

Glazer, N. (1998). *We are all multiculturalists now*. Boston, MA: Harvard University Press.

Glesne, C. (2006). *Becoming qualitative researchers: An introduction (third edition)*. Boston, MA: Pearson Education, Inc.

Gose, B. (2006). The rise of the chief diversity officer. *The Chronicle of Higher Education*. Retrieved from http://www.thedivision.wsu.edu/Content/Documents/saed/rise%20of%20the%20cdo.pdf

Gramsci, A. (1971). *Selections from the prison notebooks*. New York, NY: International Publications.

Gratz v. Bollinger, 539 U.S. 244 (2003).

Greene, M. (2009). In search of a critical pedagogy. In A. Darder, M. Baltodano, and R. Torres (Eds.), *The critical pedagogy reader (second edition)* (pp. 84–96). New York, NY: Routledge.

Grey, B. (2008, April 3). High school drop-out rate in major U.S. cities at nearly 50 percent. *World Socialist Web Site (WSWS)*. Retrieved from http://www.wsws.org/articles/2008/apr2008/scho-a03.shtml

Griffith, B. (2007). *A philosophy of curriculum: The cautionary tale of simultaneous languages in a decentered world*. Rotterdam, NL: Sense Publishers.

Grutter v. Bollinger, 539 U.S. 306 (2003).

Guba, E., & Lincoln, Y. (1994). Competing paradigms in qualitative research. In N. Denzin and Y. Lincoln (Eds.), *Handbook of qualitative research* (pp. 105–117). Thousand Oaks, CA: Sage.

Guiner, L. (1994). *The tyranny of the majority: Fundamental fairness in representative democracy.* New York, NY: The Free Press.

Gurin, P., Dey, E., Hurtado, S., & Gurin, G. (2002). Diversity and higher education: Theory and impact on educational outcomes. *Harvard Educational Review, 72*(3), 330–366.

Gurin, P., Gurin, G., Dey, E., & Hurtado, S. (2004). The educational value of diversity. In P. Gurin, J. Lehman, and E. Lewis (with E. Dey, G. Gurin, & S. Hurtado) (Eds.), *Defending diversity: Affirmative Action at the University of Michigan* (pp. 97–188). Ann Arbor, MI: University of Michigan Press.

Gurin, P., Lehman, J., & Lewis, E. (with Dey, E., Gurin, G., & Hurtado, S.) (Eds.). (2007). *Defending diversity: Affirmative action at the University of Michigan (fourth edition).* Ann Arbor, MI: University of Michigan Press.

Hall, S. (1997). *Representation: Cultural representation and signifying practices.* Thousand Oaks, CA: Sage.

Hall, S. (1988). The toad in the garden: Thatcherism among the theorists. In C. Nelson and L. Grossberg (Eds.), *Marxism and the interpretation of culture* (pp. 35–74). Urbana, IL: University of Illinois Press.

Haney-López, I. (2006). *White by law: The legal construction of race (second edition).* New York, NY: New York University Press.

Harnden, T. (2009, August 3). Obama faces 30 death threats a day, stretching U.S. secret service. *The Telegraph.* Retrieved from http://www.telegraph.co.uk/news/worldnews/barackobama/5967942/Barack-Obama-faces-30-death-threats-a-day-stretching-US-Secret-Service.html

Harper, R., Patton, L., & Wooden, O. (2009). Access and equity for African American studies in higher education: A critical race historical analysis of policy efforts. *The Journal of Higher Education, 80*(4), 389–414.

Harper, S. (Ed.). (2008). *Creating inclusive campus environments for cross-cultural learning and strategic engagement.* Washington, DC: National Association of Student Personnel Administrators (NASPA).

Harris, C. (1995). Whiteness as property. In K. Crenshaw, N. Gotanda, G. Peller, and K. Thomas (Eds.), *Critical race theory: The key writings that formed the movement* (pp. 276–291). New York, NY: The New Press.

Harris, C. (1993). Whiteness as property. *Harvard Law Review, 106*(8), 1709–1791.

Hatch, J. (2002). *Doing qualitative research in education settings.* Albany, NY: State University of New York Press.

Henderson, L. (2011). Structuring to support the creation of a multicultural campus: A cross-case study at liberal arts colleges in upstate New York. (Unpublished doctoral dissertation). Capella University. ProQuest Dissertations No. 3460512.

Hinrichs, D., & Rosenberg, P. (2002). Attitudes toward gay, lesbian, and bisexual persons among heterosexual liberal arts college students. *Journal of Homosexuality, 43*(1), 61–84.

Hollins, E., & Guzman, M. (2005). Research on preparing teachers for diverse populations. In M. Cochran-Smith and K. Zeichner (Eds.), *Studying teacher education* (pp. 477–548). Mahwah, NJ: Lawrence Erlbaum Associates.

hooks, b. (2000). *Feminist theory: From margin to center.* Boston, MA: South End Press.

hooks, b. (1994). *Teaching to transgress: Education as the practice of freedom.* New York, NY: Routledge.

hooks, b. (1989). *Talking back: Thinking feminist, thinking black.* Boston, MA: South End Press.

Horkheimer, M. (1972 [1937]). *Critical theory* [based on the original essay, Traditional and critical theory]. New York, NY: Herder & Herder.

Howard, G. (2006). *We can't teach what we don't know: White teachers, multiracial schools.* New York, NY: Teachers College Press.

Howard, T. (2010). *Why race and culture matter in schools: Closing the achievement gap in America's classrooms.* New York, NY: Teachers College Press.

Hu, S., & Kuh, G. (2003). Diversity learning experiences and college student learning and development. *Journal of College Student Development, 44*(3), 320–334.

Hurtado, S. (2005). The next generation of diversity and intergroup relations research. *Journal of Social Issues, 61*(3), 595–610.

Hurtado, S. (2001). Linking diversity with educational purpose: How the diversity impacts the classroom environment and student development. In G. Orfield (Ed.), *Diversity challenged: Legal crisis and new evidence* (pp. 143–174). Cambridge, MA: Harvard Publishing Group.

Hurtado, S., Alvarez, C., Guillermo-Wann, C., Cuellar, M., & Arellano, L. (2012). A model for diverse learning environments: The scholarship on creating and assessing conditions for student success. In J. Smart and M. Paulsen (Eds.), *Higher education: Handbook of theory and research: Volume 27* (pp. 41–122). New York, NY: Springer Publishers.

Hurtado, S., Milem, J., Clayton-Pedersen, A., & Allen, W. (1999). *Improving the climate for racial/ethnic diversity in higher education: ASHE [Association for the Study of Higher Education]-ERIC [Education Resources Information Center] Report.* Washington, DC: George Washington University.

Hurtado, S., Milem, J., Clayton-Pederson, A., & Allen, W. (1998). Enacting campus climates for racial/ethnic diversity through educational policy and practice. *The Review of Higher Education. 21*(3), 278–297.

Institute for College Access & Success (ICAS). (2011). College InSight. Retrieved from http://www.college-insight.org

Jackson, B. (2006). Theory and practice of multicultural organization development. In B. Jones and M. Brazzel (Eds.), *The NTL [National Training Laboratories] handbook of organizational development and change* (pp. 139–154). San Francisco, CA: Pfeiffer.

Jackson, B., & Hardiman, R. (1994). Multicultural organization development. In E. Cross, J. Katz, F. Miller, and E. Seashore, (Eds.), *The promise of diversity: Over 40 voices discuss strategies for eliminating discrimination in organizations* (pp. 231–239). Burr Ridge, IL: Irwin.

Jackson, B., & Holvino, E. (1988). Developing multicultural organizations. *Journal of Religion and the Applied Behavioral Sciences, 9*(2), 14–19.

Jackson, J. (Ed.). (2007). *Strengthening the African American educational pipeline: Informing research, policy, and practice.* Albany, NY: State University of New York Press.

Jaschik, S. (2011, August 12). Change for chief diversity officers. *Inside Higher Ed.* Retrieved from http://www.insidehighered.com/news/2011/08/12/survey_provides_data_on_chief_diversity_officers

Jenkins, T. (2009). A seat at the table that I set: Beyond social justice allies. *About Campus, 14*(5), 27–29.

Jones, J. (2011). Who are we? Producing group identity through everyday practices of conflict and discourse. *Sociological Perspectives, 54*(2), 139–162.

Juárez, B., & Hayes, C. (2010). Social justice is not spoken here: Considering the nexus of knowledge, power, and the education of future teachers in the United States. *Power and Education, 2*(3), 233–252.

Karenga, M. (1993). *Introduction to black studies (second edition).* Los Angeles, CA: University of Sankore Press.

Karr, A. (1849, January). *Les Guêpes* [The Wasps].

Kendall, F. (2006). *Understanding white privilege: Creating pathways to authentic relationships across race.* New York, NY: Routledge.

Kennedy, D. (1990). A cultural pluralist case for affirmative action in legal academia. *Duke Law Journal, 1990*(4), 705–757.

Kezar, A. (Ed.). (2011). *Recognizing and serving low-income students in higher education: An examination of institutional policies, practices, and culture.* New York, NY: Routledge.

Kezar, A. (2001). *Understanding and facilitating organization change in the 21st century: Current research and conceptualizations (ASHE [Association for the Study of Higher Education]-ERIC [Education Resources Information Center] higher education report, volume 28, number 4).* New York, NY: John Wiley & Sons.

Kincheloe, J., & McLaren, P. (1994). Rethinking critical theory and qualitative research. In N. Denzin and Y. Lincoln (Eds.), *Handbook of qualitative research* (pp. 138–157). Newbury Park, CA: Sage.

Kincheloe, J., & Steinberg, S. (1997). *Changing multiculturalism.* Bristol, PA: Open University Press.

King, D., & Smith, R. (2011). *Still a house divided: Race and politics in Obama's America.* Princeton, NJ: Princeton University Press.

Kozol, J. (1991). *Savage inequalities: Children in America's schools.* New York, NY: HarperCollins.

Ladson-Billings, G. (2006). From the achievement gap to the education debt: Understanding achievement in U.S. schools. *Educational Researcher, 35*(7), 3–12.

Ladson-Billings, G. (2005a). The evolving role of critical race theory in educational scholarship. *Race, Ethnicity and Education, 8*(1), 115–119.

Ladson-Billings, G. (2005b). Is the team all right? Diversity and teacher education. *Journal of Teacher Education, 56*(2), 229–234.

Ladson-Billings, G. (2001). *Crossing over the Canaan.* New York, NY: Jossey-Bass.

Ladson-Billings, G. (1999). Just what is critical race theory and what's it doing in a *nice* field like education? In L. Parker, D. Deyhele, and S. Villenas (Eds.), *Race is . . . race isn't: Critical race theory and qualitative studies in education* (pp. 7–30). Boulder, CO: Westview.

Ladson-Billings, G. (1998). Just what is critical race theory and what's it doing in a nice field like education? *International Journal of Qualitative Studies in Education, 11*(1), 7–24.

Ladson-Billings, G. (1996). Silences as weapons: Challenges of a black professor teaching white students. *Theory into Practice, 35*(2), 79–85.

Ladson-Billings, G., & Tate, W. (1995). Toward a critical race theory of education. *Teachers College Record, 97*(1), 47–68.

Lankshear, C., Snyder, I., & Green, B. (2000). *Teachers and technoliteracy: Managing literacy, technology and learning in schools.* St. Leonards, Australia: Allen & Unwin.

Lawrence, C. (2005). Forbidden conversations: On race, privacy, and community (A continuing conversation with John Ely on racism and democracy), *The Yale Law Journal, 114*, 1353–1403.

Lawrence, C. (1995). The word and the river: Pedagogy as scholarship as struggle. In K. Crenshaw, N. Gotanda, G. Peller, and K. Thomas (Eds.), *Critical race theory: The key writings that formed the movement* (pp. 336–356). New York, NY: The New Press.

Lawrence, C. (1992). The word and the river: Pedagogy as scholarship as struggle. *Southern California Law Review, 65*(5), 2231–2298.

Lawrence, C., & Matsuda, M. (1997). *We won't go back: Making the case for affirmative action.* Boston, MA: Houghton Mifflin.

Lea, V. (2008). Environmental justice, race and education: Interrupting hegemony through culturally relevant educational projects. *Just Voices.* Retrieved from http://www.gettysburg.edu/about/offices/college_life/cps/just_voices_fall08.dot

Leonardo, Z. (2005). *Race, whiteness, and education.* New York, NY: Routledge.

Lewis, A. (2004). What group? Studying Whites and whiteness in the era of "color-blindness." *Sociological Theory, 22*(4), 624–646.

Lewis, A. (2001). There is no 'race' in the schoolyard: Color-blind ideology in an (almost) all white school. *American Educational Research Journal, 38*(4), 781–811.

Lilley, S. (2010, August 17). Grim graduation rates for black males highlight racial gap. *The Grio.* Retrieved from http://www.thegrio.com/specials/making-the-grade/grim-graduate-rates-for-black-males-highlight-racial-gap-in-schools.php

Lipsitz, G. (2006). *The possessive investment in whiteness: How white people profit from identity politics.* Philadelphia, PA: Temple University Press.

Lorde, A. (1984). The master's tools will never dismantle the master's house. In A. Lorde, *Sister outsider: Essays and speeches* (pp. 110–113). Berkeley, CA: Crossing Press.

Loveless, D. (2011). *From cyborg to cyberpunk: Teachers re/authoring identities.* (Unpublished doctoral dissertation). Texas A&M University, Corpus Christi. ProQuest Dissertations No. 3459440.

Luna, N. (2009). *Clark County dropout needs assessment report: Community readiness data collection process to address Latina/Latino school dropout.* Las Vegas, NV: University of Nevada Cooperative Extension.

Lynn, M., Yosso, T., Solórzano, D., & Parker, L. (2002). Critical race theory and education: Qualitative research in the new millennium. *Qualitative Inquiry, 8*(1), 3–6.

Madison, D. (2005). *Critical ethnography: Method, ethics, and performance.* London, England: Sage.

Maguire, P. (2007). A feminist participatory research framework. In Jaggar, A., *Just methods: An interdisciplinary feminist reader* (pp. 445–456). Boulder, CO: Paradigm Publishers.

Maher, F., & Tetrault, M. (2007). *Privilege and diversity in the academy.* New York, NY: Routledge.

March, J., & Olsen, J. (1976). *Ambiguity and choice in organizations.* Oslo, Norway: Universitetsforlaget.

Marquez, J. (2009). Diversity: The Obama effect. *Workforce Management, 88*(4), 1–21.

Martin, R. (1992). A model for studying the effects of social policy on education: Gauging the impact of race, sex, and class diversity. *Equity and Excellence, 25*(2–4), 53–56.

Matsuda, M., Lawrence, C., Delgado, R., & Crenshaw, K. (1993). *Words that wound: Critical race theory, assaultive speech, and the First Amendment.* Boulder, CO: Westview.

McKanders, K. (2010). Black and brown coalition building during the "post racial" Obama era. *St. Louis University Public Law Review, 29*(473), 473–499.

McLaren, P. (1999). Unthinking whiteness, rethinking democracy: Critical citizenship in Gringolandia. In C. Clark and J. O'Donnell (Eds.), *Becoming and unbecoming White: Owning and disowning a racial identity* (pp. 10–55). Westport, CT: Greenwood.

McLaren, P. (1997). *Revolutionary multiculturalism: Pedagogies of dissent for the new millennium.* Boulder, CO: Westview.

McLaren, P., & Kincheloe, J. (2007). *Critical pedagogy: Where are we now?* New York, NY: Peter Lang.

McPhail, M. (2003). Race and the (im)possibility of dialogue. In R. Anderson, L. Baxter, and K. Cisna, *Dialogue: Theorizing difference in communication studies* (pp. 209–224). Thousand Oaks, CA: Sage.

Melnick, S., & Zeichner, K. (1998). Teacher education's responsibility to address diversity issues: Enhancing institutional capacity. *Theory into Practice, 37*(2), 88–95.

Melnick, S., & Zeichner, K. (1997). Enhancing the capacity of teacher education institutions to address diversity issues. In J. King, E. Hollins, and W. Hayman (Eds.), *Preparing teachers for cultural diversity* (pp. 23–39). New York, NY: Teachers College Press.

Merriam, S. (1998). *Qualitative research and case study applications in education: Revised and expanded from case study research in education (second edition).* San Francisco, CA: Jossey-Bass.

Merryfield, M. (2000). Why aren't teachers being prepared to teach for diversity, equity, and global interconnectedness? A study of lived experiences in the making of multicultural and global educators. *Teaching and Teacher Education, 16*(4), 429–443.

Mettler, S. (2010). Reconstituting the submerged state: The challenges of social policy reform in the Obama era. *Perspectives on Politics, 8*(3), 803–824.

Milem, J., Chang, M., & Antonio, A. (2005). *Making diversity work on campus: A research-based perspective.* Washington, DC: Association of American Colleges and Universities (AAC&U).

Milem, J. & Hakuta, K. (2000). The benefits of racial and ethnic diversity in higher education. In D. Wilds (Ed.), *Minorities in higher education, 1999–2000: Seventeenth annual status Report* (pp. 39–67). Washington, DC: American Council on Education (ACE).

Milner, R. (2010). *Start where you are, but don't stay there: Understanding diversity, opportunity gaps, and teaching in today's classrooms.* Cambridge, MA: Harvard Education Press.

Moehring, E. (2007). *UNLV: The University of Nevada, Las Vegas: A history.* Reno, NV: University of Nevada Press.

Moerhing, E. (2000). *Resort city in the Sunbelt: Las Vegas, 1930–2000.* Reno, NV: University of Nevada Press.

Moehring, E., & Green, M. (2005). *Las Vegas: A centennial history.* Reno, NV: University of Nevada Press.

Montagu, A. (1997). *Man's most dangerous myth: The fallacy of race.* Walnut Creek, CA: AltaMira Press.

Moody, J. (2004). *Faculty diversity: Problems and solutions.* New York, NY: Routledge.

Morris, J. (2001). Forgotten voices of black education: Critical race perspectives on the implementation of a desegregation plan. *Educational Policy, 15*(4), 575–600.

Morrison, T. (1995). *Playing in the dark: Whiteness and literary imagination.* New York, NY: Vintage Books.

Mthethwa-Sommers, S. (2001). *Swimming against the tide: Narratives of social justice educators.* (Published doctoral dissertation). Toledo, OH: University of Toledo.

Muñoz, J., Ordoñez Jasis, R., Young, P., & McLaren, P. (2004). The hidden curriculum of domestication. *The Urban Review, 36*(3), 169–187.

Nagda, B., Gurin, P., & López, G. (2003). Transformative pedagogy for democracy and social justice. *Race, Ethnicity & Education, 6*(2), 165–191.

Nagda, B., & Zúñiga, X. (2003). Fostering meaningful racial engagement through intergroup dialogues. *Group Processes and Intergroup Relations, 6*(1), 111–128.

Nieto, S. (2000). Placing equity front and center: Some thoughts on transforming teacher education for a new century. *Journal of Teacher Education, 51*(3), 180–187.

Nieto, S. (1994). Affirmation, solidarity, and critique: Moving beyond tolerance in multicultural education. *Multicultural Education, 1*(4), 9–12, 35–38.

No Child Left Behind (NCLB) Act of 2001 (2002). Pub. L. No. 107-110, § 115, Stat. 1425.

Noor, K. (2008). Case study: A strategic methodology. *American Journal of Applied Science, 5*(11), 1602–1604.

Novkov, J. (2008). Rethinking race in American politics. *Political Research Quarterly, 61*(4), 649–659.

Obama, B. (2011, August 23). Miami Dade College commencement remarks. Retrieved from http://www.whitehouse.gov/the-press-office/2011/04/29/remarks-president-miami-dade-college-commencement

Obama, B. (2008a, March 18). Barack Obama's speech on race. *The New York Times.* Retrieved from http://www.nytimes.com/2008/03/18/us/politics/18text-obama .html?pagewanted=all

Obama, B. (2008b, November 4). 'This is your victory.' *CNN Politics.com.* Retrieved from edition.cnn.com/2008/POLITICS/11/04/obama.transcript/

Ogbu, J. (2008). *Minority status, oppositional culture, and schooling.* New York, NY: Routledge.

Oliver, M. (1992). Changing the social relations of research production. *Disability, handicap and society, 7*(2), 101–114.

Omi, M., & Winant, H. (1994). *Racial formation in the United States: From the 1960s to the 1990s.* New York, NY: Routledge.

Orfield, G. (Ed.). (2001). *Diversity challenged: Legal crisis and new evidence.* Cambridge, MA: Harvard Publishing Group.

Paglia, C. (1991). *Sexual personae: Art and decadence from Nefertiti to Emily Dickenson.* New York, NY: Vintage Books.

Parker, L., & Lynn, M. (2002). What's race got to do with it? Critical race theory's conflicts with and connections to qualitative research methodology and epistemology. *Qualitative Inquiry, 8*(1), 7–22.

Pascoe, C. (2007). *Dude, you're a fag: Masculinity and sexuality in high school.* Berkeley, CA: University of California Press.

Patterson, O. (2009, August 14). Race and diversity in the age of Obama. *The New York Times.* Retrieved from http://www.nytimes.com/2009/08/16/books/review/ Patterson-t.html

Pebley, A., & Sastry, N. (2004). Neighborhoods, poverty, and children's well-being. In K. Neckerman (Ed.), *Social inequality* (pp. 119–145). New York, NY: Russell Sage Foundation.

Percer, L. (2002). Going beyond the demonstrable range in educational scholarship: Exploring the intersections of poetry and research. *The Qualitative Report, 7*(2). Retrieved from http://www.nova.edu/ssss/QR/QR7-2/hayespercer.html

Perea, J., Delgado, R., Harris, A., & Wildman, S. (Eds.). (2007). *Race and races: Cases and resources for a diverse America (second edition).* Eagan, MN: Thompson West.

Perloff, M. (2010). *Unoriginal genius: Poetry by other means in the new century.* Chicago, IL: University of Chicago Press.

Peshkin, A. (1988). In search of subjectivity—One's own. *Educational Researcher, 17*(7), 17–22.

Pierce, C. (1974). Psychiatric problems of the Black minority. In. S. Arieti (Ed.), *American handbook of psychiatry* (pp. 512–23). New York, NY: Basic Books.

Pollard, L. (2004). Foundations for making racial diversity work. In F. Hale (Ed.), *What makes racial diversity work in higher education: Academic leaders present successful policies and strategies* (pp. 272–291). Sterling, VA: Stylus Publishing.

Popkewitz, T., & Fendler, L. (1999). *Critical theories in education: Changing terrains of knowledge and politics.* New York, NY: Routledge.

Pounder, C., Adelman, L., Herbes-Sommers, C., Strain, T., & Smith, L. (Producers). (2003). *Race: The power of an illusion* [DVD]. United States: California Newsreel.

Powers, W. (n.d.). Message from President Powers. Retrieved from http://www .utexas.edu/diversity/about/message_powers.php

Powers, W. (2006). President's inaugural address on the state of the university. Retrieved from http://www.utexas.edu/events/universityat123/address.html

Pratt, M. (1991). *Women, culture and politics in Latin America.* Berkeley, CA: University of California Press.

President's Commission for Diversity. (2006). Full final report. Retrieved from http://www.missouristate.edu/diversitycommission/10110.htm

Prestage, J., & Prestage, J. (1988). The consent decree as a tool for desegregation in higher education. *Urban League Review, 11*(1–2), 158–175.

Radin, M. (1982). Property and personhood. *Stanford Law Review, 34*(3), 957–1014.

Ravitch, D. (2010). *The death and life of the great American school system: How testing and choice are undermining education.* New York, NY: Perseus Books.

Renn, K. (2010). LGBT and queer research in higher education: The state and status of the field. *Educational Researcher, 39*(2), 132–141.

Rodriguez, D. (2011). Silence as speech: Meaning of silence for students of color in predominantly white classrooms. *International Review of Qualitative Research, 4*(1), 111–144.

Rojas, F. (forthcoming). Activism and the academy: Lessons from the evolution of ethnic studies. In N. Gross and S. Simmons (Eds.), *Liberal professors: The view from social science.* Baltimore, MD: The Johns Hopkins University Press.

Rojas, F. (2011). Institutions and disciplinary belief about Africana Studies. *The Western Journal of Black Studies, 35*(2), 92–105.

Rojas, F. (2007). *From black power to black studies: How a radical social movement became an academic discipline.* Baltimore, MD: Johns Hopkins University Press.

Rooks, N. (2006). *White money/Black power: The surprising history of African American studies and the crisis of race in higher education.* Boston, MA: Beacon Press.

Rose, S. (2007). *Social stratification in the United States: The American profile poster.* New York: The New Press.

Rose-Redwood, C. (2010). The challenge of fostering cross-cultural interactions: A case study of international graduate students' perceptions of diversity initiatives. *College Student Journal, 44*(2), 389–399.

Rothman, H. (2010). *The making of modern Nevada.* Reno, NV: University of Nevada Press.

Salmon, J. (2001). *The official Virginia Civil War battlefield guide.* Mechanicsburg, PA: Stackpole Books.

Schoem, D., & Hurtado, S. (Eds.). (2001). *Intergroup dialogue: Deliberative democracy in school, college, community, and workplace.* Ann Arbor, MI: University of Michigan Press.

Schoem, D., Hurtado, S., Sevig, T., Chesler, M., & Sumida, S. (Eds.). (2001). Intergroup dialogue: Democracy at work in theory and practice. In D. Schoem and S. Hurtado (Eds.), *Intergroup dialogue: Deliberative democracy in school, college, community, and workplace* (pp. 1–21). Ann Arbor, MI: University of Michigan Press.

Scott, W. (1998). *Organizations: Rational, natural and open systems.* Upper Saddle River, NJ: Prentice-Hall.

Scully, M., & Segal, A. (2002). Passion with an umbrella: Grassroots activists in the workplace. In M. Lounsbury and M. Ventresca (Eds.), *Research in the sociology of organizations, volume 19: Social structure and organizations revisited* (pp. 125–68). Greenwich, CT: JAI Press.

Sedlacek, W. (2004). *Beyond the big test: No cognitive assessment in higher education.* San Francisco, CA: Jossey-Bass.

Sleeter, C. (1996). *Multicultural education as social activism.* Albany, NY: State University of New York Press.

Sleeter, C., Torres, M., & Laughlin, P. (2004). Scaffolding conscientization through inquiry in teacher education. *Teacher Education Quarterly, 31*(1), 81–96.

Smircich, L., & Morgan, G. (1982). Leadership: The management of meaning. *The Journal of Applied Behavioral Science, 18*(3), 257–273.

Smith, D. (with Wolf, L., & Busenberg, B.). (1996). *Achieving faculty diversity: Debunking the myths.* Washington, DC: Association of American Colleges and Universities (AAC&U).

Smith, D., Gerbrick, G., Figueroa, M., Harris Watkins, G., Levitan, T., Cradoc Moore, L., Merchant, P., Dov Beliak, H., & Figueroa, B. (1997). *Diversity works: The emerging picture of how students benefit.* Washington, DC: Association of American Colleges and Universities (AAC&U).

Smith, D., Turner, C., Osei-Kofi, N., & Richards, S. (2004). Interrupting the usual: Successful strategies for hiring diverse faculty. *The Journal of Higher Education, 75*(2), 133–160.

Smith, D., Wolf, L., & Levitan, T. (Eds.). (1994). *Studying diversity in higher education: New directions for institutional research.* San Francisco, CA: Jossey-Bass.

Smith, W., Yosso, T., & Solórzano, D. (2006). Challenging racial battle fatigue on historically white campuses: A critical race examination of race-related stress. In C. Stanley (Ed.), *Faculty of color teaching in predominantly white colleges and universities* (pp. 299–327). Bolton, MA: Anker Books.

Solórzano, D. (1997). Images and words that wound: Critical race theory, racial stereotyping and teacher education. *Teacher Education Quarterly, 24*(3), 5–19.

Solórzano, D. (1998). Critical race theory, racial and gender microaggressions, and the experiences of Chicana and Chicano scholars. *International journal of qualitative studies in education,* 11(1), 121-36.

Solórzano, D., Ceja, M., & Yosso, T. (2000). Critical race theory, racial microaggressions and campus racial climate: The experiences of African American college students. *Journal of Negro Education, 69*(1), 60–73.

Solórzano, D., & Delgado Bernal, D. (2001). Examining transformational resistance through a critical race and LatCrit theory framework: Chicana and Chicano students in an urban context. *Urban education, 36*(3), 308–342.

Solórzano, D., & Yosso, T. (2002a). Critical race methodology: Counter-storytelling as an analytical framework for education research. *Qualitative Inquiry, 8*(1), 23–44.

Solórzano, D, & Yosso, T. (2002b). A critical race counter-story of race, racism, and affirmative action. *Equity and Excellence in Education, 35*(2), 155–168.

Stake, R. (2006). *Multiple case study analysis.* New York, NY: The Guilford Press.

Stake, R. (2005). Qualitative case studies. In N. Denzin and Y. Lincoln (Eds.), *The Sage handbook of qualitative research* (pp. 443–466). Thousand Oaks, CA: Sage.

Stake, R. (1995). *The art of case study research.* Thousand Oaks, CA: Sage.

Stanley, C. (2006a). Coloring the academic landscape: Faculty of color breaking the silence in predominantly white colleges and universities. *Educational Research Journal, 43*(4), 701–736.

Stanley, C. (2006b). *Faculty of color.* Bolton, MA: Anker Books.

State of ACME [sic]. (2011). Executive budget: 2009–2011 biennium. Retrieved from http://nsla.nevadaculture.org/statepubs/epubs/657473-2009-2011.pdf

Steele, C. (1997). A threat in the air: How stereotypes shape intellectual identity and performance. *American Psychologist, 52*(6), 613–629.

Stefancic, J., & Delgado, R. (1996). *No mercy: How conservative think tanks and foundations changed America's social agenda.* Philadelphia, PA: Temple University Press.

Steinberg, S. (2007). Where are we now? In P. McLaren and J. Kincheloe (Eds.), *Critical pedagogy: Where are we now* (pp. ix–x). New York, NY: Peter Lang.

Steinberg, S. (2001). *Multi/Intercultural conversations: A reader.* New York, NY: Peter Lang.

Stewart, A., Malley, J., & LaVaque-Manty, D. (Eds.). (2007). *Transforming science and engineering: Advancing academic women.* Ann Arbor, MI: University of Michigan Press.

St. Pierre, E. (2000). Post-structural feminism in education: An overview. *International Journal of Qualitative Studies in Education, 13*(5), 477–515.

Strayhorn, T., Blakewood, A., & DeVita, J. (2008). Factors affecting the college choice of African American gay male undergraduates: Implications for retention. *NASAP [National Association of Student Affairs Professionals] Journal, 11*(1), 88–108.

Suoranta, J., & Vadén, T. (2007). From social to socialist media: The critical potential of the wikiworld. In P. McLaren and J. Kincheloe's (Eds.), *Critical pedagogy: Where are we now* (pp. 143–162). New York, NY: Peter Lang.

Swindell, W. (1997). Notes on administration of Africana studies departments. In J. Conyers (Ed.), *Africana studies: A disciplinary quest for both theory and method* (pp. 16–28). Jefferson, ME: McFarland & Company.

Tannen, D. (1999). Fighting for our lives. In D. Tannen, *The argument culture: Stopping America's war of words* (pp. 3–26). New York: Random House Publishing Group.

Tapia, A. (2009). *The inclusion paradox: The Obama era and the transformation of global diversity.* Lincolnshire, IL: Hewitt Associates.

Tate, W. (1994). From inner city to ivory tower: Does my voice matter in the academy? *Urban Education, 29*(3), 245–269.

Tax, M. (2009). Barack, Hillary, and U.S. feminism. In L. Burnham (Ed.), *Changing the race: Racial politics and the election of Barack Obama* (pp. 62–66). New York, NY: Applied Research Center.

Taylor, E. (2009). The foundations of critical race theory in education: An introduction. In E. Taylor, D. Gillborn, and G. Ladson-Billings (Eds.), *Foundations of critical race theory in Education* (pp. 1–16). New York, NY: Routledge.

Taylor, E. (2000). Critical race theory and interest convergence in the backlash against affirmative action: Washington State and Initiative 200. *Teachers College Record 102*(3), 539–560.

Taylor, E. (1998). A primer on critical race theory. *Journal of Blacks in Higher Education, 19*(1), 122–124.

Taylor, E., Gillborn, D., & Ladson-Billings, G. (2009). *Foundations of critical race theory in education.* New York, NY: Routledge.

Tellis, W. (1997). Application of a case study methodology. *The qualitative report* [On-line serial], *3*(3), http://www.nova.edu/ssss/QR/QR3-3/tellis2.html

The Rachel Maddow Show (TRMS). (2011a). 'Occupy' is here to stay [Video]. *MSNBC.com*, November 15, 2011. Retrieved from http://video.msnbc.msn.com/the-rachel-maddow-show/45316180

The Rachel Maddow Show (TRMS). (2011b). First Amendment remedies: Occupy Wall Street library shows spine [Video]. *MSNBC.com*, November 15, 2011. Retrieved from http://video.msnbc.msn.com/the-rachel-maddow-show/45316274

Tierney, W. (1993). *Building communities of difference: Higher education in the 21st century.* Westport, CT: Bergin & Garvey.

Tierney, W. (1992). *Official encouragement, institutional discouragement: Minorities in academe—The Native American experience.* Norwood, NJ: Ablex Publishing Corporation.

Tough, P. (2008). *Whatever it takes: Geoffrey Canada's quest to change Harlem and America.* Austin, TX: Houghton Mifflin Harcourt.

Turner, C., González, J., & Wong Lau, K. (2011). Faculty women of color: The critical nexus of race and gender. *Journal of Diversity in Higher Education, 4*(4), 199–211.

Turner, C., Myers, S., & Creswell, J. (1999). Exploring underrepresentation: The case of faculty of color in the Midwest. *The Journal of Higher Education, 70*(1), 27–59.

Umbach, P. (2006). The contribution of faculty of color to undergraduate education. *Research in Higher Education, 47*(3), 317–345.

United States of America v. State of ACME [sic] (1987). Civil Action No. 87-025, Section I (6).

University of ACME (ACME) [sic]. (2011). About UMW: Fast facts. Retrieved from http://www.umw.edu/about/fast-facts/

University of ACME, Flagship (ACME) [sic]. (2011a). University of Maryland, College Park. Retrieved from en.wikipedia.org/wiki/University_of_Maryland,_College_Park

University of ACME, Flagship (ACME) [sic]. (2011b). College portrait. Retrieved from http://www.collegeportraits.org/MD/UMCP/characteristics

University of ACME, Flagship (ACME) [sic]. (2011c). Diversity timeline: 1907–1956. Retrieved from http://www.ohrp.umd.edu/divtimeline/1907_1956/1907_1956.html

University of ACME, Flagship (ACME) [sic]. (2010). Transforming Maryland: Expectations for excellence in diversity and inclusion. Retrieved from http://www.provost.umd.edu/Documents/Strategic_Plan_for_Diversity.pdf

University of ACME, Flagship (UA, Flagship) [sic]. (2011a). Campus profile. Retrieved from http://www.utexas.edu/about-ut/campus-profile

University of ACME, Flagship (UA, Flagship) [sic]. (2011b). 2010–2011 Impact report. Retrieved from http://www.utexas.edu/diversity/pdf/DDCE_ImpactReport.pdf

University of ACME, Flagship (UA, Flagship) [sic]. (2011c). About Gateway Scholars. Retrieved from http://www.utexas.edu/diversity/ddce/lcae/gateway.php

University of ACME, Flagship (UA, Flagship) [sic]. (2011d). Accountability report. Retrieved from http://www.txhighereddata.org/Interactive/Accountability/UNIV_Complete_PDF.cfm?FICE=003658

University of ACME, Flagship (UA, Flagship) [sic]. (2010). Class of first-time freshman not a white majority this fall semester at the University of Texas, Austin. Retrieved from http://www.utexas.edu/news/2010/09/14/student_enrollment2010/

University of ACME, Local Area (UALA) [sic]. (2011). About UNLV: Facts and stats. Retrieved from http://go.unlv.edu/about/glance/facts

University of ACME, Regional (UA, Regional) [sic]. (2011a). College portrait. Retrieved from http://www.collegeportraits.org/TX/UTSA

University of ACME, Regional (UA, Regional) [sic]. (2011b). Enrollment query. Enrollment Management System.

University of ACME System [sic]. (2009). *Plan 2008 and beyond: Reflections on the past, prospects for the future, toward inclusive excellence.* Adopted by the Board of Regents, University of Wisconsin System. Retrieved from http://www.wisconsin .edu/.../Plan2008InclusiveExcellence.pdf

University of ACME System [sic]. (1988). *Design for diversity.* Adopted by the Board of Regents, University of Wisconsin System. Retrieved from http://www.wisconsin .edu/edi/design/webd4d.pdf

University of ACME System Board of Regents [sic]. (1998). *Plan 2008: Educational quality through racial/ethnic diversity.* Adopted by the Board of Regents, University of Wisconsin System. Retrieved from http://www.wisconsin.edu/edi/plan/diversit .pdf

U.S. Census Bureau. (2011a). State and county quickfacts. Retrieved from http:// quickfacts.census.gov/qfd/states/32/3240000.html

U.S. Census Bureau. (2011b). State and county quickfacts. Retrieved from http:// quickfacts.census.gov/qfd/states/32000.html

U.S. Census Bureau. (2011c). State and county quickfacts. Retrieved from http:// quickfacts.census.gov/qfd/states/22000.html

U.S. Census Bureau. (2011d). State and county quickfacts. Retrieved from http:// quickfacts.census.gov/qfd/states/22/2205000.html

Valian, V. (2004). Beyond gender schemas: Improving the advancement of women in academia. *NWSA [National Women's Studies Association] Journal, 16*(1), 207–220.

Villegas, A., & Lucas, T. (2002). Preparing culturally responsive teachers: Rethinking the curriculum. *Journal of Teacher Education, 53*(1), 20–32.

Voting Rights Act (VRA) of 1965 (1965). Pub. L. No. 89-110, § 79, Stat. 437.

Wall, V., & Obear, K. (2008). Multicultural organizational development (MCOD): Exploring best practices to create socially just, inclusive campus communities. Retrieved from http://www.aacu.org/meetings/diversityandlearning/DL2008/ Resources/documents/AACUMCODhandouts2008-ObearandWall.pdf

Wall Street Journal (2008, November 5). President-Elect Obama: The voters rebuke Republicans for economic failure. *The Wall Street Journal.* Retrieved from http:// online.wsj.com/article/SB122586244657800863.html

Walters, R. (2007). Barack Obama and the politics of blackness. *Journal of Black Studies, 38*(1), 7–29.

Weick, K. (2006). Faith, evidence, and action: Better guesses in an unknowable world. *Organization Studies, 27*(11), 1723–1736.

Weick, K. (1983). Educational systems as loosely coupled systems. In J. Baldridge and T. Deal (Eds.), *The dynamics of organizational change.* Berkeley, CA: McCutchan Publishing.

Weiner, E. (2007). Critical pedagogy and the crisis of imagination. In P. McLaren and J. Kincheloe (Eds.), *Critical pedagogy: Where are we now* (pp. 57–78). New York, NY: Peter Lang.

West, C. (2011). Dr. King weeps from his grave: I had a dream, but. *The New York Times.* Retrieved November 13, 2011 from http://www.nytimes.com/2011/08/26/opinion/martin-luther-king-jr-would-want-a-revolution-not-a-memorial.html?_r=1

Wilds, D. (2000). *Minorities in higher education: Seventeenth annual status report.* Washington, DC: American Council on Education (ACE).

Will, G. (1992). Radical English. In P. Berman (Ed.), *Debating P.C.: The controversy over political correctness on college campuses* (pp. 134–147). New York, NY: Dell.

Williams, D., Berger, J., & McClendon, S. (2005). *Toward a model of inclusive excellence and change in postsecondary institutions.* Washington, DC: Association of American Colleges and Universities (AAC&U).

Williams, D., & Wade-Golden, K. (2012a). *Strategic diversity leadership: Inspiring change and transformation in higher education.* Fairfax, VA: Stylus Publishing Press.

Williams, D., & Wade-Golden, K. (2012b). *The chief diversity officer: Strategy, structure, and change management.* Fairfax, VA: Stylus Publishing Press.

Williams, D., & Wade-Golden, K. (2011). *The chief diversity officer: Strategy, structure, and change management.* Sterling, VA: Stylus Publishing.

Williams, D., & Wade-Golden, K. (2008a). *The chief diversity officer: A primer for college and university presidents.* Washington, DC: American Council on Education (ACE).

Williams, D., & Wade-Golden, K. (2008b). The chief diversity officer. *CUPA-HR [College and University Professional Association for Human Resources] Journal, 58*(1), 38–47.

Williams, D., & Wade-Golden, K. (2007). The chief diversity officer. *College and University Professional Association for Human Resources Journal, 58*(1), 38–47.

Williams, R. (1995). Foreword. In R. Delgado, *The Rodrigo chronicles: Conversations about America and race* (pp. xi–xvi). New York, NY: New York University Press.

Williams, R. (1977). *Marxism and literature.* Oxford, England: Oxford University Press.

Wilson, W. (1987). *The truly disadvantaged: The inner city, the underclass, and public policy.* Chicago, IL: The University of Chicago Press.

Winant, H. (2000). Race and race theory. *Annual Review of Sociology, 26*(1), 169–185.

Wing, B. (2009). Race: The changing electorate and the electoral college. In L. Burnham (Ed.), *Changing the race: Racial politics and the election of Barack Obama* (pp. 34–39). New York, NY: Applied Research Center.

Women's Studies Consortium (WSC). (1999). *Tranforming women's education: The history of women's studies in the University of Wisconsin System.* Madison, WI: Office of University Publications.

Wright, R. (1945). *Black boy.* New York, NY: Harpers & Brothers.

Yin, R. (2009). *Case study research: Design and methods (fourth edition).* Thousand Oaks, CA: Sage.

Yin, R. (2003). *Case study research: Design and methods (third edition).* Thousand Oaks, CA: Sage.

Yin, R. (1994). *Case study research: Design and methods (second edition).* Thousand Oaks, CA: Sage.

Yin, R. (1993). *Application of case study research.* Thousand Oaks, CA: Sage.

Yosso, T. (2005). Whose culture has capital? A CRT discussion of community cultural wealth. *Race Ethnicity and Education, 8*(1), 69–91.

Zamani-Gallaher, E., O'Neil Green, D., Brown, C., & Stovall, D. (2009). *The case for affirmative action on campus: Concepts of equity, considerations for practice.* Fairfax, VA: Stylus Publishing Press.

Zamudio, M., Russell, C., Rios, F., & Bridgeman, J. (2011). *Critical race theory matters: Education and ideology.* New York, NY: Routledge.

Zuckerbrod, N. (2007). 1 out of 10 schools are "dropout factories." *USA Today.* Retrieved from http://www.usatoday.com/news/education/2007-10-30-dropout -factories_N.htm?csp=34

Index

Bury My Heart at Wounded Knee: An Indian History of the American West (Brown), 195

Caplan, Paula J., 56
Carey, Roderick L., 17, 174–82, 200
Carr, Wilfred, 37
casino capitalism, 160, 199
CDO (Chief Diversity Officer), 2, 13–16, 21–22, 63
Chávez, Cesar, 68
Chomsky, Noam, 53
Chu, Tony, 56
Clark, Christine, xvii–xix, xxi–xxiii, 1–19, 23–37, 199, 203–10
Clinton, Bill, 120–22
CMCST (Critical Multicultural and Cultural Studies Theory), 96–97, 102
code switching, 111
coherence and conformance, 113–14
Cole, Johnnetta B., 134
Collins, Patricia Hill, 42
colorblindness and objectivity, 16, 44–45, 52–57, 155–62, 164, 172, 192
Cone, James A., 29
conservative politics, 2–3, 46, 76–77, 86, 100, 204–5, 208–9
counterstories, 5–6, 42, 53, 128, 154–55, 163–66, 199
Cox, Leah K., 16, 115–25, 199
Crenshaw, Kimberlé Williams, 26, 71–72, 78, 147, 160
Creswell, John W., 6
Critical Action Research, 37
Criticalist research, 116
critical pedagogy, 108
CRT (Critical Race Theory), 4–6, 25–26, 50, 87–88, 133, 154, 194–95, *196*; African American studies, 134–35; centrality of experiential knowledge, 177; covert discourses, 184; demonization or marginalization, 52; embedded power relations, 116; Obama era as postracial, 44–45;

permanence of race, 176. *See also* counterstories
CS (Cultural Studies), 96
CSM (Case Study Method), 6–7, 22, 24–25, 41, 51–52, 62, 108–14, 185
CT (Critical Theory), 4, 88, 96, 108–14
CWS (Critical Whiteness Studies), 42–43, 46–47. *See also* Whiteness; White supremacy

DCEP (Diversity and Community Engagement Portfolio), 61–70
The Declining Significance of Race (Wilson), 170
Delgado, Richard, 42–43, 89, 163, 166, 204, 208
desegregation, 15–16, 66–67, 69–70, 98, 174; resistance and resegregation, 38–39, 117, 172, 203, 208
DeVita, James M., 16, 71–81, 200
Dewey, John, 107
dialogue, 17–18
DiAngelo, Robin, 158, 204, 208
DiCrecchio, Nicole, 56
Dingus, Jeannine E., 178
Diversity and Civic Engagement Organizational and Structural Model, 39–41
diversity and equity work, xiii–xv, 17, 28, 37, 84, 152, 200–201; community engagement, 64–67; data presentation, 55–56; proposals for future, 204–5, 208–13; psychological or symbolic aspects, 67–68; structural change, 59–60, 85–95, 105; as struggle, 19, 103–5, *197*, 197–99
diversity and equity workers, xix, xxii, 12–13, 152; challenges and rewards, 9–11, 28–29, 79–80, 94, 213; support from colleagues and leaders, 160–62, 172–73
Dixson, Adrienne, 178
Dodo Seriki, Vanessa, 16, 140–52, 198
Don't Ask, Don't Tell policy, 203, 207
Douglass, Frederick, xv

emancipatory research paradigm, 117
Executive Order 13583 (2011), 2–3
explanation building, 24–25, 41

Faces at the Bottom of the Well (Bell),
    xviii, xxiii, 194
faculty diversity, 16–17, 68, 137–39,
    160–61, 163–65, 172, 175–76
false generosity of oppressed, 28–29
Fasching-Varner, Kenneth J., xvii–xix,
    xxi–xxiii, 1–19, 140–52, 198, 203–10
Ferguson, S. Kiersten, 16, 61–70, 200
financial pressures and strategies, 31,
    36–37, 40–41, 46–49, 86, 100–103,
    204, 208. *See also* market-based
    values and decisions
Food Safety Modernization Act (2011),
    203, 207
Ford Foundation, 129
Foucault, Michel, 85, 88
Freedom Rides (1961), 122–25
Freire, Paulo, xiv, 28, 112
Frémaux, Anne, 160
Fujimoto, Eugene Oropeza, 17, 163–73,
    198

Geertz, Clifford, 88
gender. *See* LGBT and LGBTQ (lesbian,
    gay, bisexual, transgender or queer);
    women
General Motors takeover (2009), 203,
    207
geography, xiii–xiv, 23–24, 97–98
GI Bill, 203, 207
Gillborn, David, 116
Giroux, Henry A., 160, 199
Gold, Shaunna Payne, 16, 115–25, 199
goodness problem, 17, 183–84, 193, 200
Gratz v. Bollinger (2003), 2
Griffith, Bryant, 16, 106–14, 198
Grutter v. Bollinger (2003), 2

Hale, Frank, Jr., 213
Hall, Stuart, 95
Harper, Shaun R., 42

Harris, Cheryl I., 25, 32–33, 143, 145
hate speech and violence, xiv
Hayes, Cleveland, 17, 183–93, 200
healthcare reform, 203, 207
hegemonic thinking and structures, 53,
    57–59, 101–2, 104–5, 198
Holvino, Evangelina, 26
hooks, bell, 154
Horkheimer, Max, 4
Hurtado, Sylvia, 66

ideological becoming, 113
imperial scholarship concept, 89, 204,
    208
inclusion and Inclusive Excellence,
    99–100, 107–15
interest convergence, 6, 25–29, 42, 47,
    66, 92–93, 157, 169–70
intersectionality of identity, 16, 71–72,
    74, 76, 78, 80–81, 200
investigator triangulation, 25
IOD (Imperial Organizational
    Development), 89

Jackson, Bailey W., 21–22, 26, 84–85,
    118, 138–39
Jaschik, Scott, 40
Jefferson, Thomas, 189
Jenkins, Toby, 124
Jennings, Michael E., 16, 126–35, 201
Jones, Glenda, 16, 96–105, 198
Jordan, Barbara, 68
Juárez, Brenda G., 17, 183–93, 200

Karr, Alphonse, 194
Kemmis, Stephen deCamois, 37
Kendall, Frances E., 53, 57
Kennedy, Duncan, 68
Kincheloe, Joe, 107, 113
King, Martin Luther, Jr., 68, 183
Kozol, Jonathan, 177

Ladson-Billings, Gloria, 146, 194–95
Lawrence, Charles R., III, 88, 152
Lea, Virginia, 16, 96–105, 198

About the Editors and Contributors

Editors

Christine Clark is professor and senior scholar for multicultural education, and Founding Vice President for Diversity and Inclusion at the University of Nevada, Las Vegas. Clark was a Fulbright Senior Scholar in México and Guatemala, where she conducted research on school and community violence. Clark serves on the editorial board for *Multicultural Perspectives*, the journal of the National Association for Multicultural Education (NAME), and is the associate editor for the Higher Education section of *Multicultural Education*. In 2010, Clark was appointed to the National Advisory Committee of the National Conference on Race and Ethnicity (NCORE), and in 2011 she was appointed to the STEM Academic Advisory Commission (SAAC), a joint initiative of the Academic Network, Inc., and the National Institutes of Health (NIH) Office of Equal Opportunity and Diversity Management (OEODM). Clark's research focuses on White antiracist identity development, dismantling the school-to-prison pipeline, sociopolitically located multicultural education, and multicultural organization development.

Kenneth J. Fasching-Varner is the Shirley B. Barton Professor in Elementary Education at Louisiana State University. His areas of expertise include educational foundations, preservice teacher development, reflective practice, literacy, second-language development, Critical Race Theory, culturally relevant pedagogy, and multicultural education. Previously Fasching-Varner was an assistant professor of literacy and bilingual education at Edgewood College in Madison, Wisconsin, and assistant professor of literacy at St. John Fisher College in Rochester, New York. Fasching-Varner has a multifaceted research agenda, centered in Critical Race Theory, which examines White racial identity development as it relates to educator identity, culturally relevant engagement, and the development of legal literacy in judicial and educational contexts.

Mark Brimhall-Vargas is associate director of the Office of Diversity Education and Compliance (ODEC), an arm of the Office of the President, and a visiting scholar for Multicultural Education and Organizational Development in the Center for Leadership and Organizational Change (CLOC), both at the University of Maryland, College Park. He has a PhD in educational policy and leadership from the University of Maryland, College Park with areas of expertise in religious identity development and its impact on dialogue experiences, dialogic pedagogy, and postmodern social theory. Brimhall-Vargas also has an MPP from Harvard University, with areas of specialization in equity- and diversity-related policy research, development, assessment, and advocacy; budget planning and analysis; and consensus process and decision making.

Contributors

Katrice A. Albert is vice provost for equity, diversity, and community outreach at Louisiana State University. In this post she is the chief diversity officer and is responsible for developing and implementing strategic initiatives and policies aimed at cultivating a campus environment that embraces individual difference, sustains inclusion, and enhances institutional access and equity. Albert also teaches in the university's Department of Educational Theory, Policy and Practice. Additionally, she writes, speaks, and consults on issues of cultural competence, corporate social responsibility, educational and workforce diversity, gender and dynamics of power, the complexities of diverse populations, the application of psychological knowledge to ethnic minorities and other underrepresented populations, and community-university partnerships.

Allison Daniel Anders is assistant professor of cultural studies at the University of Tennessee, Knoxville. She earned her doctorate in education from the University of North Carolina, Chapel Hill with minors in cultural studies, political science, and women's studies. She currently cochairs the Safe Zone initiative at the university. Anders has presented at numerous conferences, including the American Educational Studies Association (AESA) and International Congress on Qualitative Inquiry (ICQI). Her recent publications include book chapters on postcritical pedagogy and ethics in cultural studies, and a research article in the *Journal of Correctional Education.*

A. Leslie Anderson is a certified diversity professional and counselor educator. She conducts antiracism trainings and acts as a consultant for universities and business customers. Anderson also participates in her local community as a lecturer and social-justice advocate. Her research examines the impact of diversity training on the attitudes of counselor-trainees, and the application of Critical Race Theory to higher education.

Marco J. Barker is assistant to the vice provost and director of educational equity in the Office of Equity, Diversity, and Community Outreach at Louisiana State University. His professional expertise includes developing special and innovative initiatives aimed at enhancing diversity recruitment and retention, and promoting equity among students, staff, and faculty. His scholarship examines administrative leadership, service learning, and the role of racial and cultural differences in developmental relationships, with a focus on doctoral advising.

Roderick L. Carey is a doctoral student in the Department of Teaching, Learning, Policy and Leadership at the University of Maryland College Park, where he specializes in minority and urban education. Carey spent four years as a high-school English teacher, coach, and instructional leader in urban Washington, DC, charter schools. Carey has a Bachelor of Arts degree in English and secondary education from Boston College, and a Master of Education degree from the Harvard University Graduate School of Education. Carey teaches undergraduate- and masters-level courses on diversity and equity for current and future classroom teachers. His research interests include the school, community, and societal factors influencing high-achieving Black and Latino adolescents, the historical and sociological implications of Black and Latino education in the United States, and teacher education for diversity and equity.

Leah K. Cox is currently the special assistant to the president for diversity and inclusion and director of the James Farmer Scholars Program at the University of Mary Washington (UMW). Previously Cox served as assistant dean of academic services and director of the Student Transition Program. Prior to her tenure at UMW, Cox served as a program information specialist for George Mason University, a student services specialist for Northern Virginia Community College, a prevention and education specialist for the United States Marine Corps, project coordinator for the Maryland State Department of Education, and placement services coordinator and minority student specialist for Gallaudet University. Cox received a bachelor's degree in education from Western Maryland College, a master's degree in counseling from the University of Arizona, and a PhD in counseling personnel services from the University of Maryland, College Park.

James M. DeVita is assistant professor of counselor education-college student affairs at the University of West Georgia. James earned his doctorate in higher education administration from the University of Tennessee, Knoxville, where his dissertation included three research projects on the experiences and development of gay male college students. He currently serves as a cochair on the program committee for the Association for the Study of Higher Education (ASHE), and on the editorial board of the *Journal of Student Affairs and Research and Practice.* DeVita has presented at various national and international conferences, including the American Educational Research Association (AERA) and the American College Personnel Association (ACPA). He has also published several book chapters and research articles in journals such as the *Journal of African American Studies* and *NASAP Journal.* His current projects examine the experiences of targeted populations in higher education, particularly LGBT and racial/ethnic minorities.

Vanessa Dodo Seriki is assistant professor of science education at the University of Houston, Clear Lake. As a graduate of an urban PK–12 school, Dodo Seriki has dedicated her professional work life to empowering the often voiceless, urban students who yearn to engage in science learning. Before earning a doctorate, Dodo Seriki worked as a secondary science teacher in two urban school districts, Portsmouth, Virginia, and Baltimore, Maryland. Addressing issues of diversity substantively is at the center of her work, thus her work critiques diversity "lip service" within PK–12 and higher education settings. Dodo Seriki is a passionate advocate on behalf of diverse populations at all levels of education. She is also passionate about helping educational institutions live their commitment to diversity.

S. Kiersten Ferguson is a postdoctoral fellow with Campus Diversity and Strategic Initiatives in the Division of Diversity and Community Engagement (DDCE) at the University of Texas, Austin. She also teaches as an adjunct lecturer in the Department of Education Policy and Leadership within the Annette Caldwell Simmons School of Education and Human Development at Southern Methodist University. Ferguson received her PhD in educational administration with a doctoral portfolio in women's and gender studies, and her master's degree in curriculum and instruction from The University of Texas, Austin. She received her bachelor's degree in government/international relations and cultural anthropology from the University of Notre Dame.

Eugene Oropeza Fujimoto is assistant professor in the Department of Educational Leadership at California State University, Fullerton. His research includes critical analysis of leadership in higher education, efforts to close racial achievement gaps, and the hiring of diverse faculty. For over 20 years Fujimoto has worked in equity, diversity, and affirmative action in higher education. He has taught in ethnic studies, organizational and instructional leadership, and organizational theory. He most recently presented his work at the Association for the Study of Higher Education Conference, the Critical Race Studies in Education Conference, and the National Conference on Race and Ethnicity in Higher Education (NCORE). His diversity work is motivated by the sacrifices of his Issei and Nisei ancestors, his wife Maria, and his daughter, Yoshie, and son, Isamu, who embody hope for the future.

Shaunna Payne Gold serves as the associate director of assessment programs and student development at the University of Maryland, College Park, an adjunct professorial lecturer in educational leadership at The George Washington University, and the owner and founder of Gold Doctoral Consulting. Gold received a bachelor's degree in business administration from James Madison University, a master's of divinity from Eastern Mennonite University, and a doctor of education in higher education administration from the George Washington University.

Bryant Griffith is professor at Texas A&M University, Corpus Christi, and director of the Curriculum and Instruction Doctoral Program. Previously, Griffith was professor and director of the School of Education at Acadia University, Canada's first "lap top" university, and professor and associate dean at the University of Calgary. He writes and researches in the area of epistemological issues in education.

Cleveland Hayes is associate professor of education in the Education and Teacher Development Department at the University of La Verne. At La Verne, Hayes teaches methods courses to elementary and secondary teacher candidates, as well as beginning research methods. Hayes' research interest includes Critical Race Theory, historical and contemporary issues in Black education, Latino student experience, and pedagogical practices of Latino teachers.

Bailey W. Jackson is Professor Emeritus of Education at the University of Massachusetts, Amherst. During his tenure in the university's School of Education he has held a number of administrative positions, including as dean for 11 years. Jackson was instrumental in the establishment of the school's master's- and doctoral-level Social Justice Education Program. This program is unique in its focus on the study of social oppression and liberation in education. Jackson is recognized nationally and internationally as one of the pioneering and leading theorists in the area of Black Identity Development, and has recently coedited and authored chapters in *New Perspectives on Racial Identity Development: Integrating Emerging Frameworks* (second edition, 2012, with Charmaine Wijeyesinghe). He is also one of the primary architects of Multicultural Organization Development (MCOD). His recent work in MCOD provides a framework for internal and external change agents working to advance the development of multicultural systems.

Michael E. Jennings serves as associate dean in the College of Education and Human Development (COEHD) and is also an associate professor in the Department of Educational Leadership and Policy Studies at the University of Texas, San Antonio. Jennings' primary field of focus is the social foundations of education. His graduate training was completed at the University of North Carolina at Chapel Hill where he received an MA in political science (focusing on political theory) and a PhD in the social foundations of education. His research focuses on: (a) cultural and racial diversity, (b) Critical Race Theory, and (c) educational biography/autoethnography.

Glenda Jones is associate professor in the Department of English and Philosophy and the director of the Women and Gender Studies Program at the University of Wisconsin, Stout. She was a teacher for many years in the public-school system in Utah and New Mexico, and an instructor at Malcolm X College in Chicago. Jones currently works on issues of diversity and inclusive excellence. She is an active researcher in the area of composition theory and practice, high impact practices and minority retention, and representations of motherhood in academia.

Brenda G. Juárez is assistant professor in the Social Justice Education Program in the School of Education at the University of Massachusetts, Amherst. Her current research focuses on understanding the role that culture plays in the effective teaching practices and perspectives of exemplary African American teachers of Black and other students of color. Juárez's research has appeared in publications such as *Democracy and Education, Journal of Black Studies, Race Ethnicity and Education, Power and Education,* and *International Journal of Qualitative Studies in Education.* She is coauthor of the book *White Parents, Black Children: Understanding Adoption and Race,* published by Rowman & Littlefield.

Virginia Lea is associate professor of critical multiculturalism at the University of Wisconsin, Stout. Her previous publications include two coedited volumes, published by Peter Lang, on transforming hegemony as Whiteness in the classroom. Lea tries to live a commitment to socioeconomic, sociopolitical, and socioeducational caring; to equity; and to justice through social and edu-cultural activism, research, and teaching.

Douglas J. Loveless is assistant professor in the Department of Early, Elementary and Reading Education at James Madison University. Previously, Loveless worked in dual-language schools, college-readiness programs, and supplementary literacy programs for students of all ages. He writes and researches in the area of literacy issues in education.

Shirley Mthethwa-Sommers is assistant professor in the Department of Social and Psychological Foundations of Education, and director of the Frontier Center for Urban Education at Nazareth College of Rochester, New York. She teaches and researches about social justice education in K–12 and higher education.

Sonia Nieto, Professor Emerita of Language, Literacy, and Culture, School of Education, University of Massachusetts, Amherst, has taught students from elementary school through doctoral studies. Her research focuses on multicultural education, teacher education, and the education of Latinos, immigrants, and other students of culturally and linguistically diverse backgrounds. Nieto has written many journal articles and book chapters and several books on these topics, including her most recently published *Affirming Diversity: The Sociopolitical Context of Multicultural Education* (sixth edition, 2012, with Patty Bode), *The Light in Their Eyes: Creating Multicultural Learning Communities* (second edition, 2010), and *Language, Culture, and Teaching: Critical Perspectives* (second edition, 2010). She serves on several regional and national advisory boards that focus on educational equity and social justice, and she has received many academic and community awards for her scholarship, teaching, and advocacy, including four honorary doctorates. In 2011, Nieto was selected as a Fellow of the American Educational Research Association (AERA) and as a Laureate for Kappa Delta Pi.

Steven Thurston Oliver serves as assistant vice president for institutional diversity at the University of Kentucky. Oliver's career is dedicated to diversity issues in higher education; he seeks to increase access to, and inclusiveness at, every institutional level to generate meaningful engagement of differences across campus. Oliver's current research interests include exploring the experiences of Black males attending predominantly White institutions, and LGBT issues in higher education. Oliver earned his doctorate in the sociology of education from New York University's Steinhardt School for Culture, Education, and Human Development. He earned a master's degree in educational leadership and policy studies from the University of Washington, and his Bachelor of Arts degree in international studies from Antioch College, in Yellow Springs, Ohio.

Sherri L. Sanders serves as associate vice president for campus diversity and strategic initiatives within the Division of Diversity and Community Engagement (DDCE) at the University of Texas, Austin. In this role, she leads the development and implementation of the division-wide strategic planning process and the institution's diversity plan. Prior to joining DDCE in 2007, Sanders served as associate dean of students where she oversaw academic enrichment services, student judicial services, services for students with disabilities, and student emergency services. In 2004, Sanders was a Fulbright Scholar to Germany as part of the International Education Administrators Program. She is a clinical associate professor within the Department of Educational Administration at the university. Sanders received her PhD in higher education administration from the University of Texas, Austin, an MA in college student personnel administration from Bowling Green State University, and a BS in psychology from Louisiana State University.

Margaret-Mary Sulentic Dowell is assistant professor of reading/literacy at Louisiana State University. Previously, Sulentic Dowell was assistant superintendent in East Baton Rouge Parish, where she supervised 64 elementary sites. She was also a public-school teacher for 20 years. Additionally, Sulentic Dowell is a National Board Certified Teacher in the area of early adolescence/English language arts. In 2007, she was awarded the Kenneth S. Goodman in Defense of Good Teaching Award, and she is the current editor of *Literacy & Social Responsibility eJournal*. Sulentic Dowell's research agenda is focused on literacy in urban settings and includes three strands: (1) the complexities of literacy leadership, (2) providing access to literature, and (3) service-learning as a pathway to prepare preservice teachers to teach reading authentically in urban environs.

Hollace Anne Teuber is associate professor of speech communication at the University of Wisconsin, Stout. Her research interests include intercultural communication, diversity in action, and preservation of living native cultures. A Native Hawaiian and first generation college graduate, Teuber works to promote equity and social justice for ethnic minorities and minority groups in higher education by teaching acceptance and inclusion as a basic human right. Her dedication to breaking down barriers for majority and minority people to create an inclusive environment has been her life's mission and goal.

Gregory J. Vincent was named vice president for diversity and community engagement at the University of Texas, Austin, in 2006. Vincent's portfolio is one of the most comprehensive of its kind. Encompassing more than 50 units and initiatives, this portfolio serves as a model for other institutions across the nation. Vincent is a professor in the School of Law and the Department of Higher Education and holds the W. K. Kellogg Professorship in Community College Leadership. He was recently honored with the Dewitty/Overton Award from the NAACP, the Marks of Excellence Award from the National Forum of Black Public Administrators, and the Prairie View Interscholastic League Lifetime Achievement Award. A native of New York City, Vincent earned his Bachelor of Arts degree from Hobart and William Smith Colleges, his law degree from the Ohio State University Moritz College of Law, and his doctorate from the University of Pennsylvania.

Damon A. Williams is vice provost for strategic diversity initiatives, and associate vice chancellor for diversity, equity, and educational achievement at the University of Wisconsin-Madison. He also serves as chief diversity officer, and is a clinical faculty member in the Department of Educational Leadership and Policy Analysis (ELPA) in the School of Education. As scholar, administrator, and educator, Williams has worked with over 200 institutions and has authored numerous publications in the area of strategic planning for diversity, organizational change in higher education, and the role of the chief diversity officer across all sectors of organizational life.

Susan Wolfgram is associate professor in the Department of Human Development and Family Studies at the University of Wisconsin, Stout. Inclusive education and social justice are central to her research and pedagogy. Wolfgram has presented work nationally and internationally on the inclusion of students in social-justice work outside of the classroom, and on increasing all students' access to high-impact teaching practices.

Laura S. Yee is a doctoral student in the Department of Teaching, Learning, Policy and Leadership at the University of Maryland, College Park where she specializes in minority and urban education. Yee spent seven years teaching in urban and suburban settings in the Washington, DC, metro area. Yee has a Bachelor of Arts in theatre and art history from Middlebury College, a master's in teaching from the American University, and a Master's of Education in special education from the Curry School at the University of Virginia. Yee is working on several research studies, teaches undergraduate- and masters-level courses for teacher candidates, and has expertise in teacher professional development for diversity and equity.